VICTORIAN SHIPS

JOHN WARD'S MARINE MANUAL

Gordon Bell & Arthur Credland

To Alex Wood

Arthur Credland 2010

BLACKTHORN PRESS

Blackthorn Press, Blackthorn House
Middleton Rd, Pickering YO18 8AL
United Kingdom

ISBN 978 1 906259 14 3

www.blackthornpress.com

Printed and bound in Great Britain by CPI Antony Rowe, Chippenham and Eastbourne

CONTENTS

INTRODUCTION

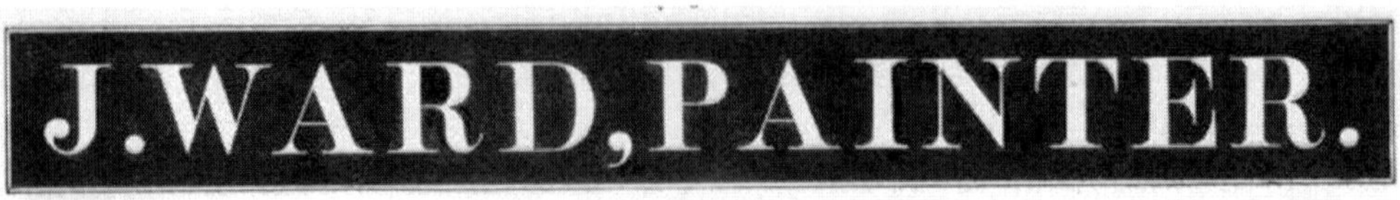

Within the space of seven and a half hours, one of England's finest marine painters succumbed to cholera in an epidemic that swept through Hull in 1849. John Ward was one of two thousand of his fellow citizens who were victims of the disease in the summer of that year. Many bodies were consigned to common graves, diggers worked night and day, and the burial ground took on the appearance of a ploughed field. His own committal took place the next day in the Castle Street Cemetery next to the Railway Dock. It is a mark of his standing that a century later his headstone found protection with the guardians of the safety and welfare of mariners at Hull Trinity House.

John Ward was in his fifty-first year and intent on compiling a landmark *"Guide to Drawing and for the purposes of Painting and the Marine Profession generally"*. In a series of exquisitely detailed prints, he planned to record the principal merchant and naval vessels of Victorian Britain. Whilst similar schemes had appeared in earlier times, none had the scope or distinctiveness of his vision.

In the archives of Hull Maritime Museum is what remains of his project. These few boxes of images are but a fraction of the hundreds of prints and drawings sold from his studio after his death. The challenge of this book has been not only to assemble them in a sequence that echoes his intentions but also to offer a reminder of his original endeavour to inspire followers of the art and craft of marine painting.

His vocation involved a life-long engagement with both aspects of this challenge. He constantly sought to obtain the most up to date details of the vessels of his era and to acquire the skills that would enable him to portray their features. In this way, his career embraced a remarkable transition from the crafts of painting to the art of the painter. His passage from artisan to artist was to be an essential celebration of these twin aspects, defining his originality and marking him out as a luminary influence.

John Ward's apprenticeship to a house painter and decorator in a major port offered him opportunities for work in a variety of buildings and vessels of all types. His desire to extend his skills to picture making most probably arose from the basic disciplines derived from his Master, Thomas Meggitt and the example of his fellow apprentices who were themselves producing occasional marine pictures. In this way, Meggitt's Workshop was more than a place of work; it assumed the character of a School of Art, an institution that Hull would finally acquire several decades later.

However, whilst the techniques needed for the craft of painting could be mastered through repetition, tuition, and the pressures of practicalities, the art of painting was to do with the realms of imagination that lay well beyond the confines of his apprenticeship. The portals of this wider world were opened through a newly formed library and an institute that assisted workers to improve their skills through low cost part time study. More directly, it

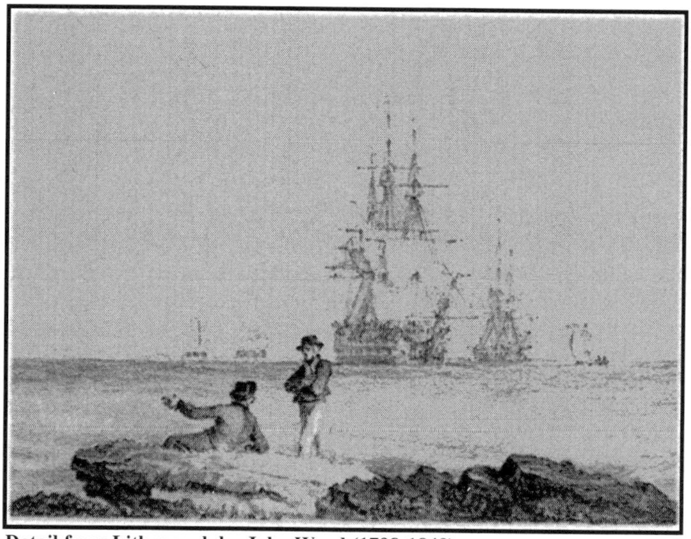

Detail from Lithograph by John Ward (1798-1849)

was Hull's "Promotion of the Fine Arts" and "The First Exhibition of Pictures" that enabled aspiring painters to experience the world of the artist at first hand.

The year was 1827 and John Ward was twenty-nine. He was now married, established in business on his own account, and shortly to be honoured as the Installed Master of Humber Lodge No. 57 of Freemasons. By 1831, he had exhibited his first oil painting at the Royal Academy.

In the years that followed, he combined his practice as a local painter with his ambitions of becoming an artist, studying the works of other marine artists, and being encouraged through an increasing number of commissions and patrons. Exhibiting in Hull and London led to a level of success and recognition that eventually enabled him to take on an apprentice. This most significant development enabled Ward to focus his energies, expand his teaching activities and experiment with printmaking. He acquired a press for making lithographic prints and set about gathering material at major shipyards and working towards publishing a Marine Manual as a guide for others with similar ambitions.

A revealing aspect of his ability to bridge both the arts and crafts of painting is contained within his little handbook for sign writers, published in the final years of his life. Here, he acknowledges in the introduction that he was 'upwards of thirty years as House and Sign Pinter' (sic). Within its covers, he included a number of merchant shipping prints providing both a useful reference for painting different kinds of letters and securing a means of advertising his 'Marine Studies' in order to bring them to a wider audience. Unwittingly perhaps, this modest handbook continued a tradition of demonstrating the drawing of letters celebrated by Renaissance masters, most notably the great German painter, Albrecht Dürer.

John Ward's premature death prevented the attainment of his goal. Chapter Three of this book seeks to redress this situation by offering an insight into how Ward's Manual might have looked. Chapter One outlines the background against which Ward, as a tradesman in a provincial port, found the inspiration and opportunity to rise to eminence as an artist. Chapter Two offers an account of his sources of support and influence and the details of his crucial exploration of printmaking. The final chapter reflects on the personality of a man who was able to overcome the limitations of his upbringing by taking advantage of its best features and creating a means for us to enter into his world through the outstanding quality of the images he created.

Acknowledgements

We would particularly like to thank Alan Avery, Blackthorn Press; André Brannan, local historian, for details of Ward's rescue of a young boy from Hull Docks; Robin Diaper, Hull Museums for access to the Ward collection; Encore Editions; the Peabody Essex Museum Salem, and N R Omell Gallery for permission to use their illustrations; the staff of the Ferens Gallery; Emma Floyd, Paul Mellon Centre for Studies in British Art; Alan and Edna Hinton; Dr B Hovell and the Secretary of Humber Lodge No.57, and the local studies staff of Newcastle City Library.

All the prints, unless otherwise stated are in the Hull Maritime Museum which contains the largest collection of Ward lithographs. This publication has only been possible thanks to the generosity of Hull Museums in enabling us to reproduce this remarkable series of images and we gratefully acknowledge the support and help of Simon Green, Head of Culture and Life Style.

Gordon Bell and Arthur Credland, April 2010.

Chapter 1

John Ward of Hull: Ship Painter and Painter of Ships

As a young apprentice, John Ward would typically have applied paint mops to the timbers of ships in the dockyards of Hull. By the time he was thirty-three, this 'artisan painter' was exhibiting marine paintings at the Royal Academy.

Those early years from his birth in 1798 to the coronation of Queen Victoria in 1838, ushered in far reaching changes in politics, society and the arts. Sometimes referred to as "the long eighteenth century", Britain had been at war with France and America, the Prince of Wales had ruled as Regent during the illness of his father George III, and a "United Kingdom" of England, Ireland, Scotland and Wales had been formed. A uniquely British Empire was rapidly developing to become the largest Empire in history with over two hundred parts of the world colonised or administered at some time. Industrialisation was sweeping across the country, criss-crossed by canals, railways and ever more durable roads. Coal and steam provided power for increasing numbers of mills, furnaces, locomotives and sea-going vessels. Iron forging and bridge building expanded dramatically. Factories employing mass labour created new towns, cities, and urbanised landscapes with streets lit by gas. The entire system of government was reformed with votes for Catholics, the creation of political parties, and elections to Parliament and Local Councils. The Bank of England was developed as a key financial institution, an official census introduced, income tax levied, and the registration of births marriages and deaths required by law. Not least through these radical years, the local Hull MP, William Wilberforce, pioneered the abolition of trading in slaves.

In the visual arts, a new movement in watercolour painting had found increasing favour and the Royal Academy, founded by King George III in 1768, had moved to the east wing of the newly built National Gallery. In the provinces, art galleries and societies of artists were slowly establishing themselves as economic growth improved living conditions. Lithography, introduced from the continent and promoted by Rudolf Ackermann (1764-1834) from his influential shop and gallery in the Strand, London, enabled artists to replicate their work as highly saleable prints. John Ward was to make good use of this new technology for his bold project for a "Marine Manual".

Little is known about his childhood as the son of Abraham Ward, a master mariner from Derby. As a youth, he was apprenticed to Thomas Meggitt (1772-1851), a house and ship painter of 10 George Yard, Hull. Meggitt had succeeded his master, William Benison, in the business of house, ship and sign painting in 1800. The range of the services he offered was extensive as may be seen from the reverse of his trade card. (see Figs 1 and 2). Meggitt's workshop proved to be the nursery that produced some of the best marine painters in Hull at the beginning of the nineteenth century.[1]

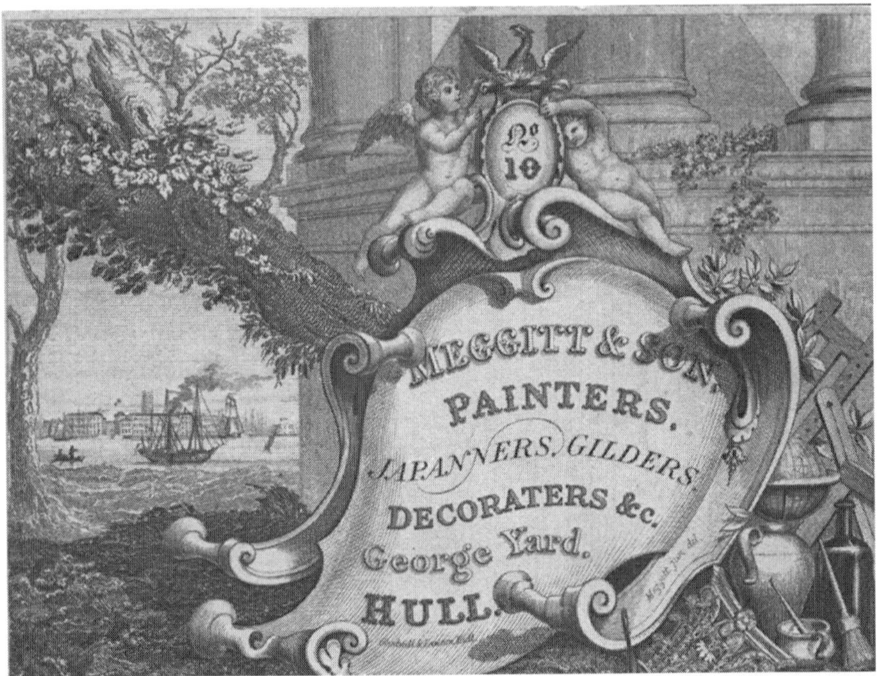

Fig. 1 Meggitt trade card; designed by Thomas Smith Meggitt, (engraved by Goodwill and Lawson, fl. 1831-1867). Hull Maritime Museum.

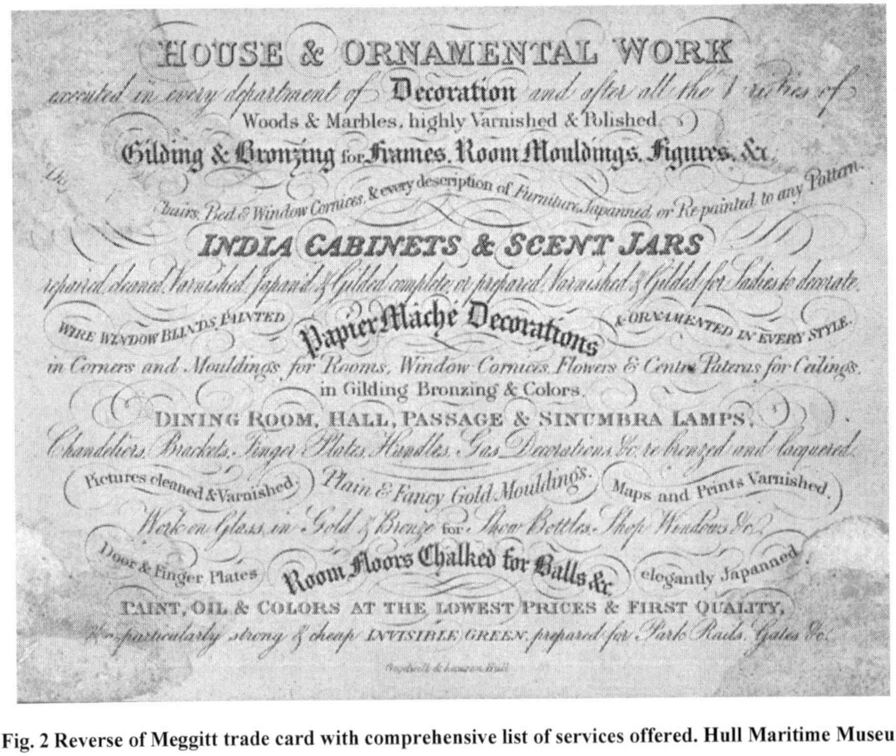

HOUSE & ORNAMENTAL WORK
executed in every department of Decoration and after all the Varieties of
Woods & Marbles, highly Varnished & Polished.
Gilding & Bronzing for Frames, Room Mouldings, Figures, &c.
Chairs, Bed & Window Cornices, & every description of Furniture, Japanned or Re-painted to any Pattern.
INDIA CABINETS & SCENT JARS
repaired, cleaned, Varnished, Japan'd & Gilded complete, or prepared Varnished & Gilded for Ladies to decorate.
WIRE WINDOW BLINDS PAINTED & ORNAMENTED IN EVERY STYLE.
Papier Maché Decorations
in Corners and Mouldings for Rooms, Window Cornices, Flowers & Centre Pateras for Ceilings,
in Gilding Bronzing & Colors.
DINING ROOM, HALL, PASSAGE & SINUMBRA LAMPS,
Chandeliers, Brackets, Finger Plates, Handles, Gas Decorations &c. re-bronzed and lacquered.
Pictures cleaned & Varnished. Plain & Fancy Gold Mouldings. Maps and Prints Varnished.
Work on Glass, in Gold & Bronze for Show Bottles, Shop Windows &c.
Door & Finger Plates Room Floors Chalked for Balls &c. elegantly Japanned.
PAINT, OIL & COLORS AT THE LOWEST PRICES & FIRST QUALITY,
particularly strong & cheap INVISIBLE GREEN, prepared for Park Rails, Gates &c.
Goodwill & Lawson, Hull.

Fig. 2 Reverse of Meggitt trade card with comprehensive list of services offered. Hull Maritime Museum.

Marine Painting in Hull c.1800

Becoming an artist in the provinces at the beginning of the nineteenth century was a chancy business. A variety of jobbing painters, many of dubious quality and competence, moved from town to town making a modest living,. Their clients were frequently those of lesser means and discrimination. Wealthier merchants and gentry could afford to commission painters of a much higher calibre such as Sir George Chalmers (1720-1791) and John Russell (1745-1806), both able portrait painters who found patronage in Hull.

The local artists, like so many throughout the land, were essentially artisan painters who learned the basic skills of mixing and handling paints while apprenticed to house and ship painters. For those who had ambitions beyond sign painting and decorating, there was no opportunity to develop their skills in an art school nor could they easily find a showcase for their work in established exhibition venues.

The town of Hull was still quite small but as the population doubled in size from around 22,000 in 1800 to an estimated 40,000 thirty years later, it was both vigorous and cosmopolitan. William Cobbett (1763-1835) the radical reformer visited in 1830;

> At Hull I "lectured" (I laugh at the word) to about seven hundred persons,..... We had what they call the summer theatre, which was crowded in every part except on the stage; and the next evening, the stage was crowded too'.
>
> 'It is a little city of London: streets, shops everything like it; clean as the best parts of London and the people are bustling and attentive. The town of Hull is surrounded with commodious docks for shipping. These docks are separated in three or four places by drawbridges so that as you walk round the town you walk by the side of the dock and the ships ......I hate commercial towns in general; there is generally something loathsome in the look and so stern and unfeeling in the manners of sea-faring people that I have always, from my very youth disliked sea-ports but really the sight of this nice town, the manners of the people, the civil and kind and cordial reception that I met with, and the clean streets, and especially the pretty gardens in every direction as you walk into the country have made Hull though a seaport a place that I shall always look back to with delight.

However, his comments about emigration from Hull give some indication of social conditions at the time;

> Ten large ships have gone this spring, laden with these fugitives, from the fangs of taxation; some bound direct to the ports of the United States; others, like those at Yarmouth, for Quebec. Those that have most money, go direct to the United States. The single men, who are taken for a mere trifle in the Canada ships, go that way, have nothing but their carcasses to carry over the rocks and swamps, and through the myriads of place-men and pensioners in that miserable region; there are about fifteen more ships going from this one port this spring.[2]

Between 1778 and 1829, a series of interconnected docks had been completed, extending from the River Hull to the Humber following the line of the mediaeval walls which had been demolished in the process. In effect the mediaeval town had become an island with the Georgian new town spreading outwards beyond the encircling docks.

The Aire and Calder Navigation, Don Navigation, Leeds and Liverpool Canal and the Trent waterway systems brought cheaper and quicker transport than by the old overland routes from the industrial towns of the North and Midlands. By 1840, Hull was also linked

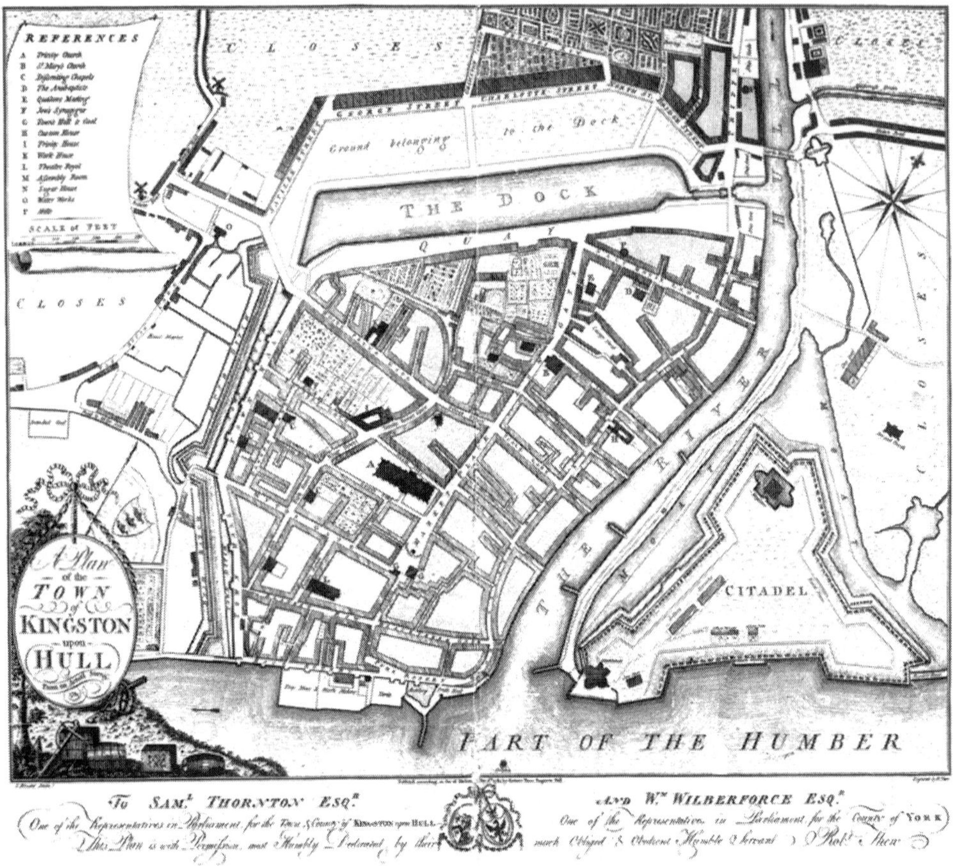

Fig. 3 Robert Thew's plan of Hull in 1784, dedicated to Samuel Thornton and William Wilberforce, M.P.s for Hull.

to the growing network of railways. Woollens, manufactured goods, metal work, lead, and cottons from Manchester came into the docks for export while timber, flax, hemp, tar pitch, linseed and iron were imported from the Baltic and Scandinavia.

Hull had recovered quickly from the effects of the French wars which ceased at last with the British victory at Waterloo in 1815. In the 1820s, the Arctic whaling trade reached its peak with fifty to sixty vessels heading north each spring in search of the Greenland whale; a favourite subject for some of Ward's most accomplished works. Baltic trade had dominated the town's mercantile shipping since the Middle Ages and despite overall prosperity, the icing up of the Baltic ports for four or five months in the winter was the cause of seasonal unemployment. As the century progressed the resulting hardship was eased by the expansion of Mediterranean trade and the development of the North Sea fishery.

There were 'artistic' contacts with the continent too. We know that William Barton (d.1814) sometime resident of Hull and occasional marine painter but living in Austria as a painter and presenter of panoramas, was sending interior designs to Thomas Meggitt who advertised that;

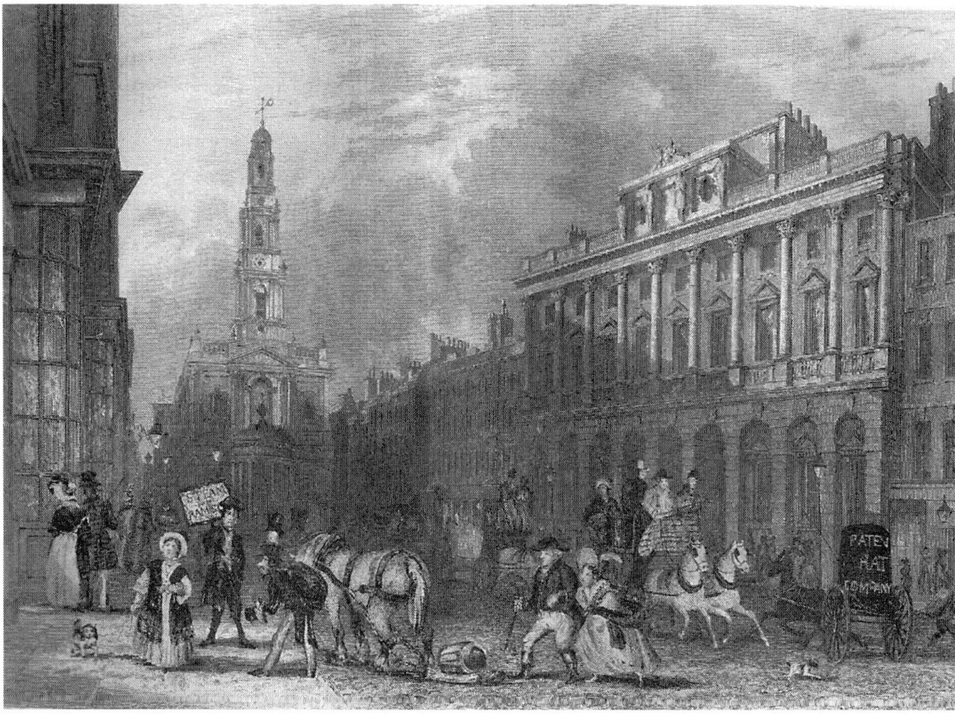

Fig. 4 Somerset House, home of the Royal Academy until c.1837, now occupied by the Courtauld Institute of Art.

> he stains and paints rooms, in the German fashion now so prevalent in London; and is in possession of patterns printed in Vienna to various designs for ceilings and walls together with a room furnished in his house done under the inspection of Mr. Barton of Vienna.

Thomas Fletcher (1759-1823) is the earliest identifiable marine artist in the town whose canvas of the Hull whale ships *Molly* and *Friends* was painted about 1802. He was presumably apprenticed to his father (or grandfather?), John Fletcher, another Hull house and ship painter.

Amongst John Fletcher's notable apprentices was Julius Caesar Ibbetson (1759-1817) who was destined to become one of the founders of the English landscape-painting tradition. Ibbetson's frustrations as an enterprising young man are recorded by Joseph Farington (1747-1821), one of the first students at the Royal Academy and later, highly influential in its affairs. He was elected as an Academician in 1785 and his diary, written between 1793 and 1821, provides an invaluable insight into the art world at the turn of the eighteenth century. Farington was deeply involved in many of the changes that took place at that time and liaised with government officials on many of the Academy's projects. Of Ibbetson, he writes;

> ...his occupation was only ... painting from daylight to night the inside and outside of ships in the port of that town. His remonstrances were ridiculed by his master and he could only practise drawing and other painting at stolen hours. He did notwithstanding, so far advance in the art to paint several signs which were much admired.[3]

Sign painting gave would-be artists the opportunity of working on a scale more familiar to the painter in his studio with his panel or canvas. Ward had a particular interest in the art of lettering and later in life wrote a manual on this subject for young painters (see Fig 27).

Given the skills acquired by Ward and his fellow artists, they must have received some special instruction in realising a convincing image of a ship or have had some appreciation of the tradition of marine painting of their times. Such knowledge and understanding was unlikely to have been derived solely from routine training in mixing and preparing pigments or from practising the techniques necessary for painting and varnishing.

Assuming Ward began his own apprenticeship in 1812 at the age of fourteen, he would then have spent the next seven years not only learning the basic skills of house, ship and sign painting but also developing his abilities as a marine painter. In this regard, he was progressively well served in Hull by the steady growth of institutions and organisations concerned with improving education and providing support for the arts, most notably at the newly formed Mechanics' Institute and from the encouragement of merchants, ship owners and ship masters.

It may be recalled that at the turn of the century, there were no art institutions outside of London and Dublin. However, in 1803, the Norwich Society of Artists was established and held its first exhibition two years later. In 1808, the Edinburgh Academy was formed and the Northern Society at Leeds was founded in the following year. Liverpool followed suit in 1810 and within the next twenty years there was a flood of provincial societies including Birmingham, Bradford, Hull, Manchester, and Newcastle. Though these societies promoted the arts to a growing audience and provided opportunities for artists to exhibit their work, teaching was seldom a major consideration in those early days.[4]

In the Metropolis, the would-be artist might obtain an apprenticeship in the studio of an established painter. Here, 'he' (for the world of nineteenth century painters was overwhelmingly male) would be employed mixing paints and preparing canvases in return for occasional instruction from the master. However, much was learned simply by having the opportunity of seeing the master in action. In the provinces, the surest way of acquiring the basic skills was as an artisan painter. Possibly the young tyro might be able to afford a few lessons with a local drawing master, but generally such men made their living by teaching the accomplishments of drawing and painting to the wives, sons, and daughters of the local gentry, merchants, and wealthier tradesmen.

Ward benefitted through the enterprise of Dr John Alderson (1785-1829). He was senior physician at the Hull General Infirmary and the major force in promoting 'the polite arts'. He was active in the Hull Subscription Library and the prime mover in establishing both the Hull Literary and Philosophical Society in 1822 and the Hull Mechanics' Institute in 1825. Born at Lowestoft, the son of a dissenting minister, he settled in Hull in 1787 and acquired through marriage interesting links to important artistic figures. His niece Amelia Alderson (1769-1853), poet and novelist, became the second wife of the portrait and history painter, John Opie (1761-1807). Another niece, Eliza Alderson, married Henry Perronet Briggs RA (1792-1844) whose career began as a history painter and later turned to portraiture. It was Briggs who was commissioned by his cousin, the barrister John Vincent Thompson (1785-1856) and son-in-law of Dr John Alderson, to paint a large canvas; *The Romans Teaching the Mechanical Arts to the Ancient Britons*. This was presented to the Hull Mechanics' Institute in 1832 and is now in the Ferens Gallery, Hull.

As early as 1804, Dr Alderson encouraged the Hull Subscription Library (founded in 1775 by Thomas Lee, a local soap maker) to vote £50 for a lecture course on scientific and commercial subjects. In 1805, George Birkbeck (1776-1841), the originator of the highly successful Mechanics' Institutes that aimed to provide education for the working-man, gave a series of lectures on Mechanical Philosophy. He clearly made a considerable impact amongst local men of influence and a portrait of Birkbeck was bequeathed to the library by John Russell RA. (qv) who made a lengthy visit to Hull and died in the town in 1806.

Another contributor to the regular Institute lecture series was Benjamin Robert Haydon (1786-1846), exhibitor at the Royal Academy, historical painter, essayist, and outspoken critic of the tastes of the times. He embarked on a popular national lecture tour, mainly to Mechanics' Institutes. He also took the opportunity of viewing historical paintings in the chief buildings of Britain whilst on tour including Edinburgh, Manchester, Liverpool, Leeds, Leicester, and Newcastle. His diary records his impression of Hull;

> May 3rd 1839
>
> I never witnessed more enthusiasm anywhere than at Hull, the last night. The people are slow, but feel deeply. A School of Design was begun, and I do not doubt its complete establishment.[5]

Like most others throughout the country, Hull Mechanics' Institute offered drawing classes. Their main aim was to improve the graphic skills of the artisan and thereby ultimately advance the quality of British design and manufacture. It was a propitious time for this reaching out by the privileged classes to the working-man, and indeed to women who increasingly joined courses for drawing, typically during daytime hours.[6] In some cases, schools of art blossomed within the Mechanics' Institutes while others were independent. In fact, most of the Institutes carried on with their drawing classes, even if they were not recognised as a school of design, concentrating their efforts on architectural and mechanical drawing for men and free-hand drawing and painting from plants for women.

The Hull Mechanic's Institute was a significant resource for the less privileged. We know from the autobiography of Thomas Wilkinson Wallis (1821-1903), apprenticed as a woodcarver in 1835, that in the same year that he joined the Mechanics' Institute, he had ...'an abundance of books, and a drawing class of which I availed myself as much as possible' and also recorded the existence of a collection of plaster casts providing models for drawing. He attended the Annual General Meeting in 1838 when the total membership was 794 with an income of £354.15s.7d;

> The library contained about 2,230 volumes, the circulation being about 17,000 volumes annually. In addition to the library and classes provided by the institution, the committee arranged for a winter's weekly course of lectures free to the members, extending over nearly six months. They were prepared and delivered in most cases by members of the Institution.

John Ward was a subscribing member of the Mechanics' Institute. It seems highly likely that he not only gained instruction from its classes and library in developing his skills but that later in his career he also shared his knowledge of marine painting with others.[7] The Literary and Philosophical Society, like the Subscription Library, tended to restrict membership to the mercantile and professional men of Hull although it did support a regular series of lectures open to the public. The Mechanics' Institute had a wider constituency, appealing both to artists and artisans seeking to improve their circumstances by increasing their skills and to townsfolk endeavouring to broaden their horizons.

Promoting the Fine Arts in Hull

Dr John Alderson was also involved in the formation of the 'Hull and East Riding Institute for the Promotion of the Fine Arts' which initially had no permanent existence or established home despite its grand title. Founded in 1827, the 'Hull and East Riding Institute' held its inaugural exhibition in the same year. (Fig. 8) There were four 'judges' whom, we assume, formed a selection panel since there is no evidence that prizes were awarded to the contributing artists who were mostly offering work for sale. Dr Alderson was one of the judges, as was his eldest son, Dr Christopher Richard Alderson. Joseph Farington's Diary tells us that in 1804;

> Dr Alderson is in great practise in Hull and makes, it is supposed, £3000 a year ... Dr Alderson's eldest son has a passion for drawing. He is 17 years old & wishes to be a painter. His father encourages him to draw, but fears it for a Profession.

The 1827 show included works by both old masters and leading contemporary artists in oils and watercolours. It took place at the 'Public Rooms' in North Street, close to where Ward later lived. A celebratory dinner was held on the 20 July. Tickets were priced at ten shillings to include a bottle of wine. Some idea of the comparative cost today may be gathered from recalling that an agricultural worker would be paid around twelve shillings a week, a skilled craftsman around four shillings a day, and a shipbuilder around twenty five shillings a week. On another measure of comparative worth, the dinner ticket would have cost the equivalent of £35 today. Three days after the celebratory dinner, the inaugural exhibition opened to the public.

The introduction to the exhibition catalogue expressed…'hope, that a building may be erected, suitable among other purposes, to that of an Exhibition Room, and worthy of the opulence and importance of the town of Hull'. These ambitions were later to be handsomely realised by the new Public Rooms, completed in 1834. In the following year they provided an impressive venue for an "Exhibition of the Fine Arts" where John Ward showed nine oils including several views on the Humber (see Fig. 5).

The artisan painters with a lesser talent than Ward may well have felt marginalised from the activities of the Hull and East Riding Institution for the Promotion of the Fine Arts as they were organised mainly by the professional men and merchants of the Hull Literary and Philosophical Society. Seeking an opportunity to exhibit their own skills, they banded together to create a panorama. More than two years in the making, mostly executed by members of the Mechanics Institute, it had evidently been planned when the Hull and East Riding Institution held its first exhibition.

Entitled the *Grand Moving Peristrephic Panorama of the Siege of Hull in 1643*, it depicted in eight views, three thousand square feet of canvas and two hundred figures, scenes from the Civil War with the first section depicting the waterfront of contemporary Hull from the citadel to the Humber Dock basin. Opened at the Olympic Circus, Hull from March to May 1829 and two months later at Leeds, the aim was to raise money for the Mechanics' Institute. Its design and purpose provides an insight into the vigorous pursuit of the visual arts in Ward's Hull and the relations of 'high art' to popular culture.

Panoramas became a fashionable feature of late eighteenth and nineteenth century entertainment.[8] Frequently presented in a round building, the spectators would typically mount a platform in the middle and view the scenes arranged around the walls, as in the remarkable example of the Regents Park Colosseum that opened in the same year as the Hull Panorama (see Fig 6).

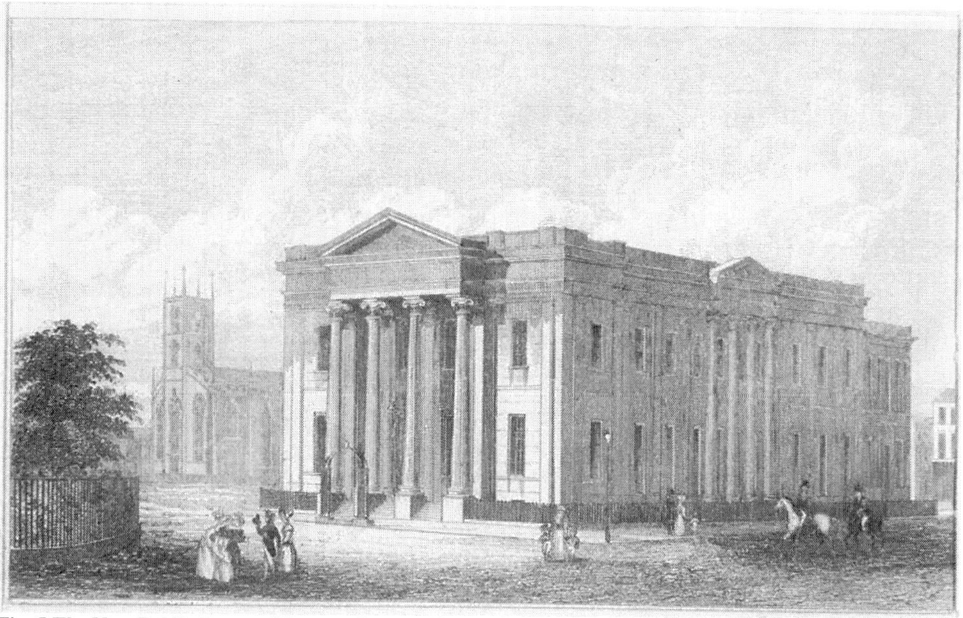

Fig. 5 The New Public Rooms, Kingston Square, Jarratt Street, Hull, home of the Literary and Philosophical Society until 1854 and the Hull School of Art till 1861. Converted in 1939 to become Hull's 'New Theatre', it still retains its original associations with the arts.

Modelled on the Pantheon in Rome, with echoes of the vast building in Paris erected in honour of the future King Louis XVI, featuring hydraulics, pyrotechnics, galleries, prize exhibitions of paintings, and shops, the Regent's Park Colosseum comprised an immense domed, sixteen sided building and portico designed by Decimus Burton (1800-1881). The main attraction was a panoramic painting of over 40,000 square feet of London as viewed from the ball and cross surmounting the dome of St. Paul's. The original drawings (2,000 of them) were executed by Thomas Hornor (1785-1844), country estate surveyor, cartographer, landscape gardener and watercolourist who was born in Hull of a family of Quaker grocers.

It was through Hornor's exceptional skills and entrepreneurial flair that the entire Colosseum project was created. A novel feature for the intrepid visitor was to enter one of the first passenger lifts in London, replete with Elizabethan décor, designed to take up to twelve people;

> By the aid of machinery that carries a moveable room through the centre of the building, the visitor is raised to a level with the summit of the panorama and thus spared the trouble of mounting a staircase.[9]....The machinery, by which this elevation is accomplished, is both simple and effective. The power employed is that of water, so contrived as to proportion its strength to the number of persons it has to raise;.......At a given signal the apartment then rises: the panorama being all the while invisible to the spectator; until at length, arriving at the first platform, he stands on what appears to be the portion of the cathedral that is called the iron gallery; ..... the whole of the metropolis of London, with its various great features...spreading on all sides, and in every direction around him.[10]

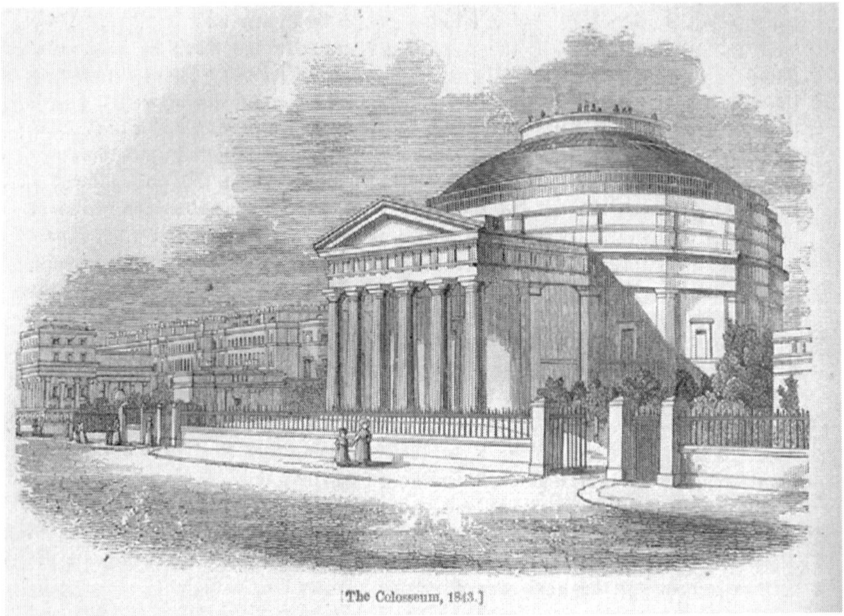

Fig. 6 The Regent's Park Colosseum.

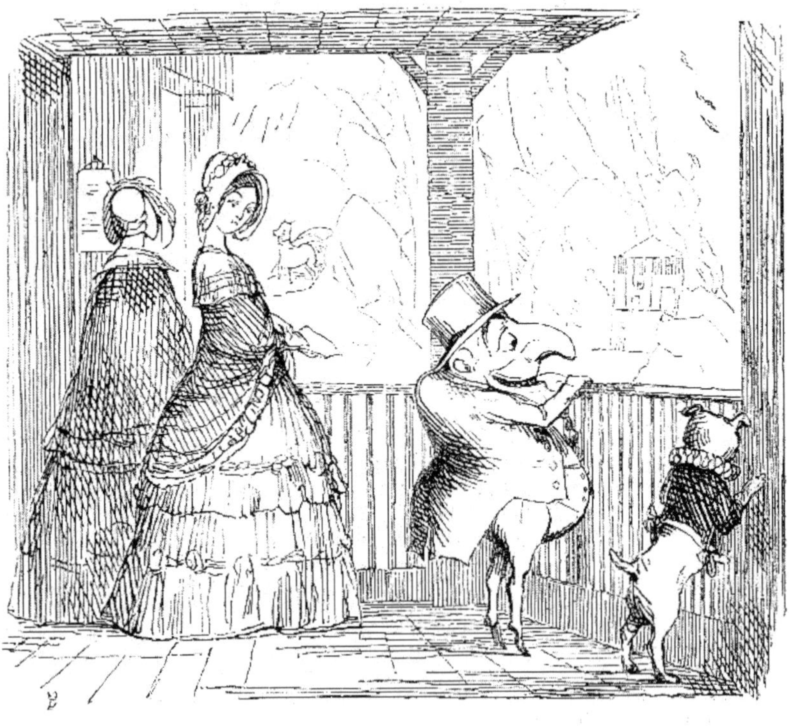

Fig. 7 Mr Punch enjoys the view in the Colosseum.

The Colosseum attracted over one million visitors; a worthy Victorian precursor to the "London Eye". After sixteen years, it was remodelled and refurbished and visited by the incorrigible "Mr Punch";

> On entering the portico, and turning left, we get into a corridor, which may, if we like, fancy is the entrance to the Vatican. Having dropped a tear over the fate of the six unfortunate popes, we rush forward into the refreshment-room, and seek consolation in Bath-buns and cherry-brandy. We next find ourselves in the glyptotheca, or Museum of Sculpture, formerly called the Saloon of Art.....(it)...used to be pitch dark, and was well supplied with old newspapers, which, as it was impossible to read them, were as good as new......in place of the old original temporary booth of pink cotton, we have now a magnificent circular saloon, fitted with works of sculpture from the studios of some of the most eminent sculptors. But while the mind may feast, our physical refreshment has not been neglected, for there peeps from beneath the tapestry – nestling under tasteful hangings of silk – a snug little stall, where the joyous Banbury, and the cheerful jam-puff may be had for the asking – and paying for.
>
> *Punch*, July-Dec. 1845

The Hull Panorama, whilst seeking to satisfy the prevailing tastes for patriotism, amusement, and learning, chose a type of Panorama more suitable for touring. This depended for its effects on the painted canvas being carried on spools and ropes in order to create movement. It was typically viewed through a proscenium arch and slowly revealed to the audience. This spectacle was sometimes accompanied by a commentary delivered by a "Delineator" or "Professor" who would regale the spectators with tales of the scenes displayed. A contemporary example was presented in London by the Marshall Brothers, chief exponents of this type of Panorama;

> Marshall's Peristrephic Panorama of the Battles of Ligny, Les Quatre Bras, and Waterloo, accompanied by a full Military Band is open every day – and in the evening by gas-light, 5 Spring Gardens.[11]

London, with its many theatres, nurtured the talents of scene painters who were ideally suited to the devices necessary for creating successful panoramas. Several such painters eventually became celebrated marine artists including Philippe Jacques de Loutherbourg (1740-1812) who exhibited battle canvases in Hull in 1800, Clarkson Stanfield (1793-1867) who began his artistic career as a scene painter, and the Whitby-born George Chambers (1803-1840), the latter two artists formerly serving at sea and well acquainted with the marine environment.

The case of George Chambers is of particular interest because of his close connections with Hull, especially at the time of the first fine arts exhibition and the project for a panorama. As a boy, he went to sea in a Humber keel owned by his uncle and by the age of thirteen served on a vessel trading along the north east coast from Whitby to London. As a consequence, he knew Hull very well. By 1827 he had completed sketches from various viewpoints in the Humber Estuary and been commissioned to paint a Whitby-built vessel on canvas entitled *View of the Port of Hull with the Spartan*. In the same year, he was employed by Thomas Hornor to complete the vast panorama of London.[12] It is tempting to speculate that George Chambers was in some way associated with the Hull Panorama project.

Similarly, John Ward, as a contributor to the Fine Arts Institution exhibitions, a subscriber to the Mechanics Institute, the leading light of Hull marine painting and himself risen from the ranks of house decorators and painters, may well have felt obliged to support his lowlier brethren. The composition of *The Buoy Yacht 'Zephyr'* depicted with a view of Hull's waterfront has more than a hint of being influenced by a panorama design, suggesting he may have been involved in the composition of the contemporary section. It is also tempting to speculate that the only surviving watercolour study of the Hull waterfront by Ward may also derive from this project (see Fig 24).

Other marine artists exhibiting in Hull at this time, some four years before Ward's successful submission to the Royal Academy, included a fellow apprentice at Meggit's yard, Thomas Binks (1799-1852). We know from surviving paintings that Binks was depicting marine subjects at approximately the same time as Ward's first works, e.g the *East Indiaman 'East Indian'* (1819) and the *Paddle Steamer Kingston* (1824). Binks showed two works at the Hull 1827 exhibition; *Marine View on the Humber from the Jetty at South End* and *Sea piece off Dover*. Ward exhibited three paintings based on works by William Anderson (1757-1837); *Northfleet, copied from Anderson*; *Limehouse Reach, from Anderson* and *Sailing Match, from Anderson.*

A keynote quotation from the President of the Royal Academy, Sir Martin Shee (1769 – 1850), 'Rhymes on Art' sets the tone for an inaugural provincial exhibition;

> Prize not the skill of foreign realms alone,
> Nor deem it Taste to stigmatize your own.

A glance at other artists exhibiting at the 1827 exhibition gives some indication of the range of styles and media on view during Ward's formative years. These included the watercolourists G F Robson (1790-1833) – a former President of the Old Watercolour Society and several works by Henry Gastineau (1791-1876), just two of the twenty-six artists who were resident in London. Provincial artists such as George Arnald (painter to the Duke of Gloucester), C H Schwanfelder of Leeds, and William Etty of York (an apprentice in the printing office of the Hull Packet for seven and a half years) submitted works that were displayed amongst the two hundred and eighty five items on view. One of the most prolific entrants was the animal and portrait painter, Thomas Fairbairn Wilson (fl. 1808-1846). Although resident in Hull between 1823 and 1846, he appears to have hailed from the north east where he was active from the beginning of the century.

The works of local drawing masters, Phineas Lowther (d.1856 aged 76), his son Michaelangelo Lowther, and Mr Bregazzi, featured in the exhibition. Another local drawing master, Frederick Lowther (brother of Phineas) had studied under John Varley (1778-1842), a notable figure in the then newly resurgent tradition of watercolour painting in Britain. In total, fourteen coastal and marine subjects were shown at the 1827 exhibition in rooms hung with scarlet cloth attracting 1,327 visitors at one shilling each.

The next exhibition came two years later in 1829. The opening address of the catalogue proclaims its aims as 'fostering genius and correcting taste':

> THE HULL AND EAST RIDING INSTITUTION FOR THE PROMOTION OF THE FINE ARTS, was founded in February 1827. The First Exhibition was opened to the Public in the July following; when several Pictures were sold, and the receipts at the door fully met the expenses of an unavoidably expensive year.
> The Committee conceive it cannot be necessary to enlarge upon the advantages afforded, both to the Artist and the Public, by Exhibitions of this sort: whilst the genius of the former is fostered and his talents improved, the taste of the latter is corrected, and its judgment matured.

THE

HULL AND EAST-RIDING

INSTITUTION

FOR THE

PROMOTION OF THE FINE ARTS.

FOUNDED FEBRUARY 21, 1827.

FIRST EXHIBITION OF PICTURES,

OPENED JULY 23, 1827.

"Prize not the skill of foreign realms alone,
Nor deem it Taste to stigmatize your own."
M. A. Shee, R. A.

"Painting raises the mind, by accommodating the images of things to our desires."
Lord Bacon.

"Art itself is Nature."
Shakspeare.

HULL:

PRINTED BY THOMAS TOPPING, LOWGATE.

PRICE SIXPENCE.

Fig. 8 Catalogue for the 'First Exhibition of Pictures', July 23rd 1827.

Henry Gastineau (qv) is again well represented. Both Samuel Prout (1783-1852) – *Cottage in Cornwall* and A V Copley Fielding (1787-1855) - *Blenheim*, appear for the first time together with J M W Turner RA (1775-1851) - *Crypt of Kirkstall Abbey*. Unlike the catalogue of the 1835 exhibition which lists exhibits by medium and room, it is difficult to judge whether such works were originals or prints. For example, Prout published several series of etchings of cottages e.g. *Picturesque Studies of Cottages* (Rudolf Ackermann 1816) and Turner published a mezzotint of the crypt of Kirkstall Abbey in his *Liber Studiorum* (1812). Thomas Binks submitted *Sea View, with schooner 'Guard'*, whilst Ward exhibited six works: *Marine View*; *A Calm*; *View on the Humber Bank, taken from Mr. English's Jetty*; *Vessels becalmed*; *Dead Calm*; and *Northfleet on the Thames*.

It seems evident that these exhibitions provided an opportunity for established local artists such as Ward and Binks who were regarded as a cut above the generality of artisan painters, to show their work alongside other artists. In this way, they were able to compare their work with artists from elsewhere in the provinces and from artists in London with reputations extending beyond their place of residence.

From Artisan to Artist: A Brief Outline of Ward's Career.

The earliest work we can assign to Ward is a rendering in oils of *The Wreck of the Troopship 'Thomas' on the Stony Binks off Spurnhead* in 1821. He would have been twenty-three at the time and although two years out of his apprenticeship, may still have been working for Meggitt. This work is not signed, but the attribution to Ward is an old one and there is no reason to reject it. The composition is good and there is evidence of painstaking effort to make an accurate record of an historic event.

His imagination was no doubt fired, not only by this event, but the prevailing mood of the times and its focus on momentous maritime events. Echoes of this legacy can be found in contemporary accounts recorded by the son of the Plymouth born painter Benjamin Haydon (qv);

> I have often heard him describe his recollections of those days, after the war had begun, how the Sound was filled with fighting-fleets preparing for sea, or triumphantly returning, battered and blackened, with shattered spars and torn sails, but with the captured ships of the enemy in tow; and how gallant frigates, amidst the cheers of thousands of people, were to be seen rounding the point into the inner harbour, with the Union Jack floating proudly above the Tricolour or the Spanish flag, while the guns of the batteries thundered out salutes in honour of the victors. . . . Men and women talked of nothing else but battles and sieges, and actions by sea or land, of Nelson, of Marat, Robespierre, Tom Paine, and, in time, Napoleon. Their children were even taken on board the captured ships to examine the effects of action, and habitually played with bone guillotines, cutting off the King of France's head, and toys put together and sold by French prisoners. . .[13]

Ten years after the end of the Napoleonic wars, at the age of twenty seven, John Ward married Esther Leonard on 18 April, 1825 at Holy Trinity Church, Hull. She was the daughter of a butcher and cow keeper, and they subsequently had four daughters. It seems that Ward's business premises were at 103 High Street from 1826 (if not before) and by 1832, the family was living at 23 North Street.

Acceptance of Ward's first picture by the Royal Academy in 1831 was a landmark in his career. It is a small panel (now in a private collection) showing a coastal scene with sailing vessels on calm water with fishermen hauling nets in the foreground. It is typical of the genre of marine painting introduced to Britain two centuries previously by the Van de Veldes, the foremost family of 17th century Dutch marine painters, and confirms the considerable influence of the Scottish-born marine artist, William Anderson (1757-1837), (see Fig 10).

There was a gap of nine years before Ward next exhibited in London at the Academy. This break is probably indicative of a busy and successful career. With so many commissions, he would frequently have been unable to find time to work on special exhibition pieces. Meanwhile, Ward showed nine pictures at the Hull Exhibition of Fine Arts in 1835, including several *Views on the Humber*, *Stoneferry*, *View of Mr Gleadows Warehouse on Fire taken from the Garrison Jetty*, and *Storm after Charles Martin Powell.* A copy of a painting by Charles Martin Powell (1775-1824) of *Calais Pier* was displayed in the Hull 1827 exhibition, submitted by "W. Coates, Marine Painter of Hull". William Coates painted works on panel that have similarities to that of Thomas Binks (qv) and William Griffin (1800-1883). They were painted in a style reminiscent of the former artist's well-crafted seas and Griffin's use of a heavy glaze. Both Binks and Griffin were fellow apprentices of Ward at Meggit's yard. Coates appears only once in the trade directories in 1823 described as a marine painter at 2, North Street. This was the address that Ward occupied at the end of his life, but in 1823 was residing at 161 High Street. Thereafter, Coates is listed as a publican, victualler, and marine store dealer at 40, then 41 High Street.[14]

The demand for ship portraits evidently grew as the century progressed and both George Chambers in 1827, and J W Carmichael two years later, received commissions to paint in Hull. This patronage no doubt acted as a spur to the local artists who were establishing themselves at the time.

The 1830s were years of intense activity for Ward when he produced a quantity of small panel paintings depicting the entrance to the old harbour and variations on the theme of ships on the Humber. They were on a small scale with figures of mariners and fisher folk introduced to great effect to lend colour, perspective, and scale. Generalised pictures of ships are usually included with the sea treated in a manner derived from Anderson (qv) but with a bright atmosphere and figures that have the appearance of real individuals, not just roughly sketched in to fill the composition.

These panels were probably reasonably inexpensive and were offered for general sale rather than being specific commissions. They evidently satisfied a local demand for small-scale images of ships, often with some indication of the local topography. Ward's main preoccupation was, however, meeting the demands of shipbuilders, ship owners, and ship's masters interested in the accurate delineation of specific vessels, typically shown in two or three views to record the maximum amount of detail.

He regularly managed to create a satisfying portrayal with varying degrees of scenic interest and was usually hugely superior in this respect to most of his contemporaries. This is particularly true of his whaling pictures which contain a wealth of interesting detail. For example, *The William Lee* in the Arctic, was painted about 1831 for Captain Richard Hill whose name appears inscribed on the whaleboat in the foreground. It shows on the one canvas the entire sequence of the whaling operation, from harpooning to flensing and the vessel itself in three views. This painting and Ward's other whaling scenes of the period are the more impressive for the magnificent treatment of the icebergs and floes and the accurate rendition of their features. These achievements were unparalleled by any of his local contemporaries and seems to indicate that he paid at least one visit to the northern seas in order to sketch the Arctic topography. The ships themselves were usually drawn whilst in dock, aided perhaps by a builder's draught.

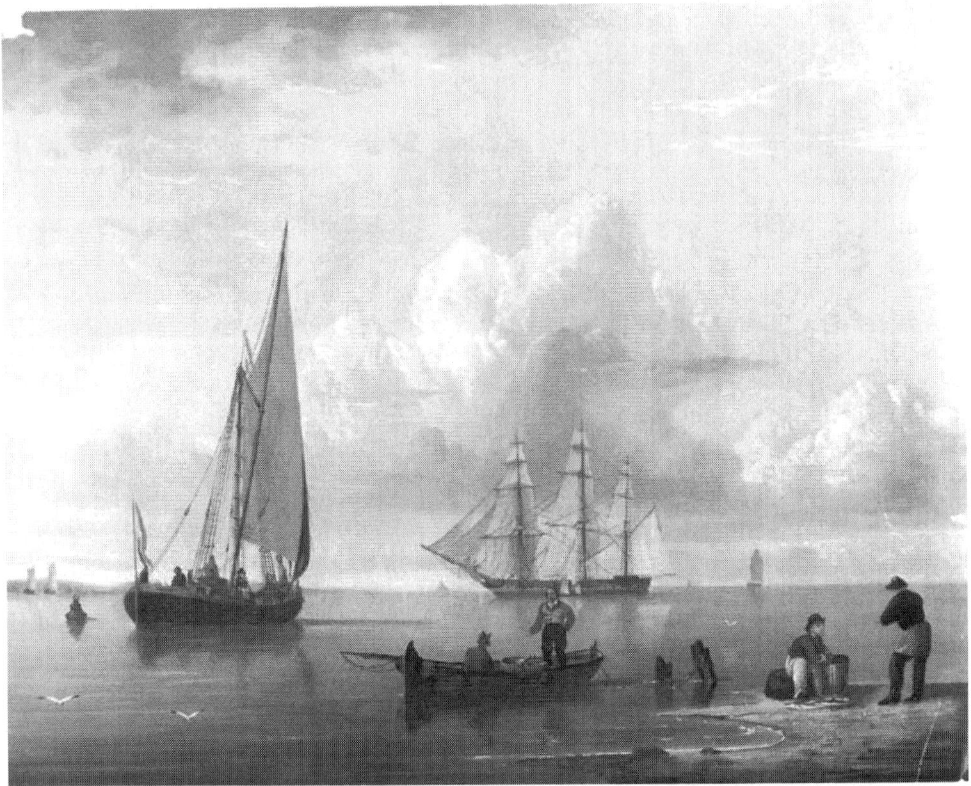

Fig. 9 John Ward (1798-1849) *Sea Piece*, exhibited at the Royal Academy, 1831, oil on panel, 10 in. x 13½ in. Private collection.

Other compositions are considerably enhanced by the inclusion of Hull's waterfront in close up, as in the case of the *Buoy Yacht 'Zephyr'* (c.1835), or pictured from a distance giving an even more extensive view of the town, as in the canvas of *PS Forfarshire* (1836 or 1838).

The impact of William Anderson on John Ward's small-scale seascapes is obvious. However, the other influences that helped towards establishing Ward's individual style are not at all clear. We know he copied a picture by Powell and owned another by Ovenden, two near contemporaries. We also know that George Chambers and J W Carmichael visited Hull in 1827 and 1829 respectively, during Ward's formative years. Chambers handsome canvas showing the *Spartan* off the Hull waterfront, now in the Ferens Gallery, could well have formed a model for some of Ward's paintings in the following decade. However, Ward had little to learn from Carmichael in terms of composition and knowledge of ship construction and the only direct link we can find between the two artists is a watercolour copy Carmichael made of Ward's lithograph of the *Dandie Dinmont* in 1848 (see Fig 12). Most probably Carmichael's main interest was the knowledge that it had been built in South Shields, a locality that was very familiar to him.

The keen rivalry between the local steam packet companies, particularly in the Hull-London cargo and passenger trade, resulted in commissions to portray these prestigious paddle steamers. These were aquatinted by Richard Gilson Reeve (1803-1889) and published as prints with the *Victoria* published for the Hull Steam Packet Co. in 1838 and

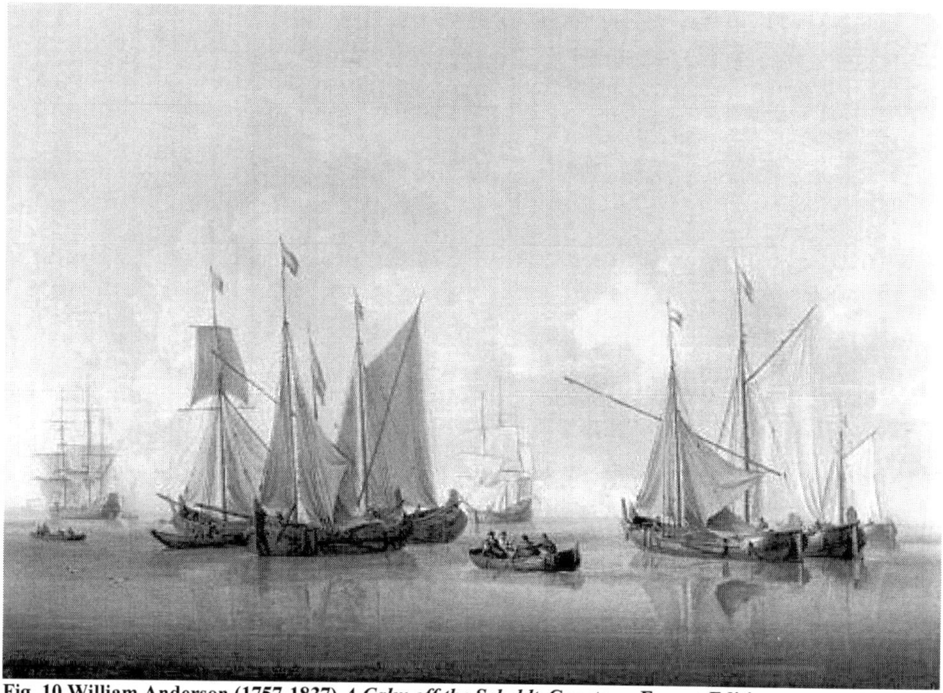

Fig. 10 William Anderson (1757-1837) *A Calm off the Scheldt*. Courtesy: Encore Editions.

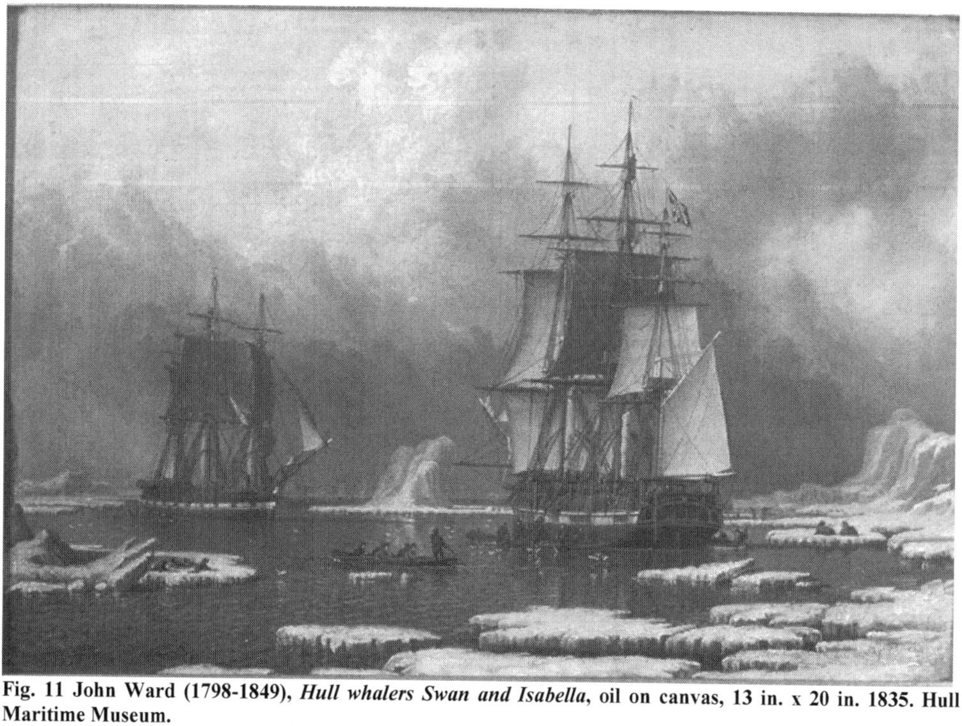

Fig. 11 John Ward (1798-1849), *Hull whalers Swan and Isabella*, oil on canvas, 13 in. x 20 in. 1835. Hull Maritime Museum.

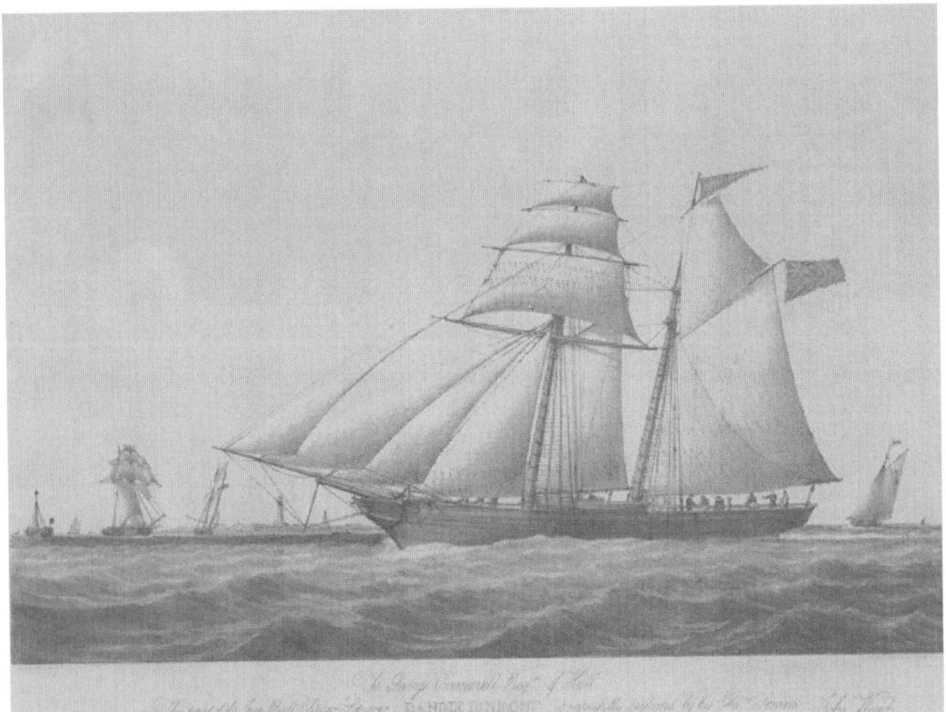

Fig. 12 John Ward (1798-1849) *Dandie Dinmont*, lithograph, iron hulled schooner dedicated to owner, George Cammell of Hull, 1848. Hull Maritime Museum.

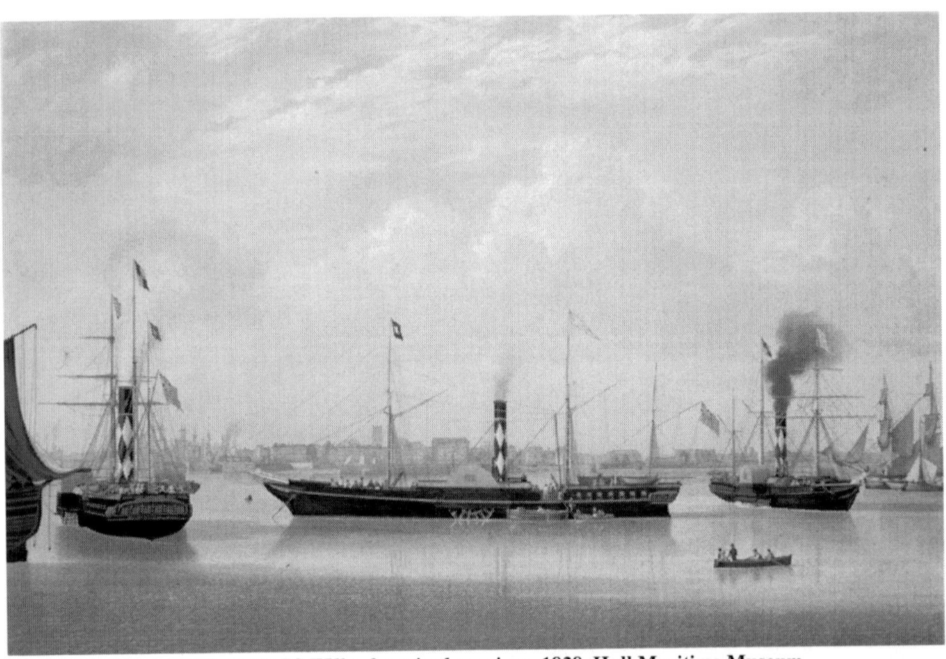

Fig. 13 John Ward (1798-1849) *PS Wilberforce in three views*. 1838. Hull Maritime Museum.

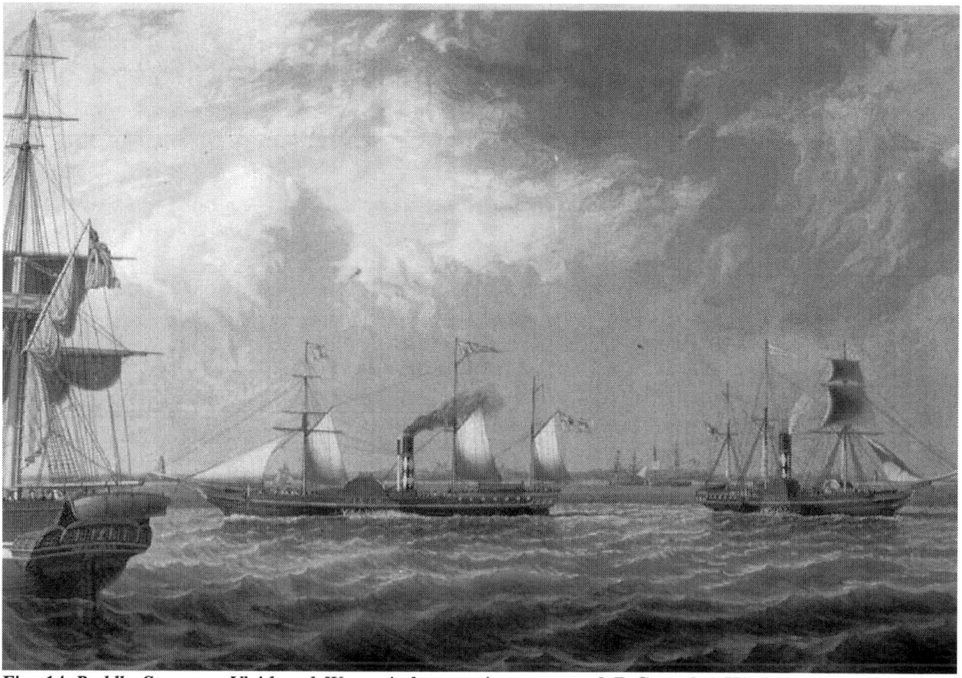

Fig. 14 ***Paddle Steamers Vivid and Waterwitch*****, aquatint, engraved R.G. and A.W. Reeve, Humber Steam Packet Co., 1839; on sale "1 guinea plain and £1 11s. 6d. coloured". Hull Maritime Museum.**

the equally splendid *Wilberforce, in three views* was produced in the same year for their rivals, the Humber Union Steam Packet Co. (see Fig. 13). The *Vivid* and *Waterwitch*, for the same company, by R.G. and A.W. Reeve, followed in 1839 (see Fig. 14).

Hull's waterfront appears as a very attractive background to all of these paintings and prints. The magnificent original oil painting of the *Victoria* hangs in the Hull Trinity House and the river, sparkling in the sun, is captured in a manner worthy of the French impressionists.

In 1839, Ward was commissioned to paint the *Return of the 'William Lee'*, a vessel which then belonged jointly to Thomas Thompson, George Liddell, and its manager, Joseph Gee. Once a whaler and already recorded on canvas by Ward in this role, she is depicted coming into the Humber Dock basin after re-establishing Hull's direct trade with Calcutta. Now in the Ferens Gallery, it is an outstanding piece of work. It shows the artist at the peak of his powers, capturing a bright, calm, January day with a wonderful play of light and shade in a composition which is without doubt one of the finest marine paintings by any artist of the nineteenth century.

The *Chase and Dagger* was executed in 1839 for Joseph Gee when he was the port's leading ship owner. This scene, of two handsome Baltic brigs sailing in a heavy swell, is untypical of Ward who is more usually a master of vessels in calm waters. The *Chase*, leaning at a rakish angle to the wind, handsomely displays the crest of Gee of Bishop Burton carved on the stern and depicted on the flag at the foremast. At this same period, William Griffin painted a great many of the Gee paddle-steamers, but Ward's lively rendition of the latter's *Queen of Scotland*, *Rob Roy*, and *Helen McGregor* (1843) - now in the Peabody Essex Museum, Salem, Mass, outshines them all.

Fine canvases were also produced by Ward for smaller firms; *The barque Edward* and *The snow William* were painted around 1830 for the owners and masters William and Bartholomew Fowler-Sutton; and the *Ruby, Wanderer and Garnet* were painted for Priest and Son about 1844. The latter concern was not a big Company in numbers of vessels, but was extremely enterprising and in 1845 sent the first vessel direct from Hull to China.

On 3 February 1843, Ward placed the following announcement in the Hull Advertiser newspaper;

> J Ward, 23 North Street, Charlotte Street, having arranged his draughts and drawings of ships is desirous of giving instruction in marine drawing as applicable to marine painting, and feels confident from his experience as a marine draughtsman to impart such information as will ensure him the support of those anxious to obtain a knowledge thereof. Terms known on application, where specimens can be seen. Portraits of vessels accurately drawn and painted.

His advertisement also clearly indicates that he had continued in the trade of house and ship painter. Given the time and attention his pictures must have demanded, he presumably had given this part of the business over to a business associate. This is apparently the son of John Willoughby, portrait and landscape painter. Willoughby Jr. appears in the trade directories for 1846 as a painter and gilder living at 23 North Street with a workshop at 68 Osborne Street. This indicates that he was living in Ward's house whilst working on his own account; although Ward himself had moved to 2 North Street at about this time, indicating that he probably vacated 23 North street in favour of Willoughby.

It would appear that Ward, at the age of forty-five and at the height of his powers, was probably comfortably situated and confident of a bright future.

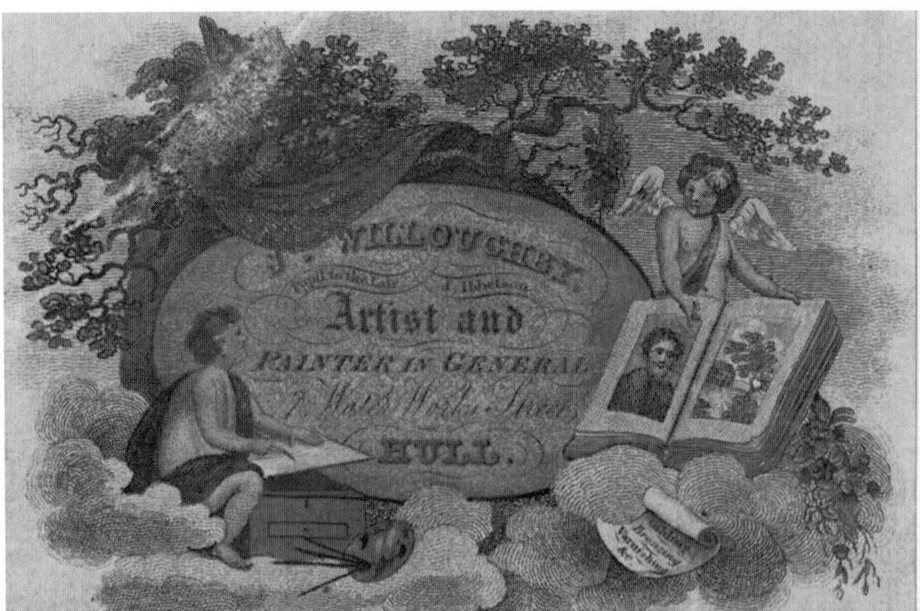

Fig. 15 Trade card of John Willoughby, 7, Waterworks Street, Hull; 'pupil to late J. Ibbetson', engraved Consitt and Goodwill, fl. 1817-30. Hull Maritime Museum.

Ward's Drawings and Watercolours.

Ward was never a topographical painter but there are important topographical elements, especially of the Hull waterfront in some of his oil paintings. The few surviving drawings and watercolours are studies for his oils and for his series of lithographs produced in the 1840s for his projected manual of marine painting. For example, the pen drawing of the brig *Dagger* in the National Maritime Museum no doubt relates to the painting of the *Chase and Dagger* in the Ferens Art Gallery. The latter vessel was built in 1839 for Joseph Gee, merchant and ship owner, and George Liddell, banker, and is depicted in profile as in the drawing, but reversed left to right, heeling over towards the viewer rather than strictly upright.

Another drawing in the Peabody Essex Museum, Salem, is a squared-up pen sketch by Ward that is reproduced exactly in a small oil painting on a panel acquired for the Hull Maritime Museum in 1980 (see Fig 16). This is the paddle steamer launched in 1836 in the yard of Curling Young on the Thames. A vessel in the Hull - London coasting trade, it more than once attracted the attention of marine artists.

Two large-scale pen and ink sketches of a vessel of war by Ward are also in the collections of the Hull Maritime Museum (see Fig.20). Both are accurately drawn but with a free-flowing line and an open manner that successfully characterise the vessel without the image being at all congested or over-stuffed with detail. In a similar vein is a drawing of a sloop (see Fig.21).

A starboard profile of a thirty-six gun frigate is the main subject of the lithographed print version but Ward had clearly worked hard to enrich the watercolour composition without detracting from the central image (Fig.18 shows one example of these watercolour studies). A barge has been added in the left foreground with vessels on the distant horizon while on the right, a cutter is heading towards the viewer with a headland and lighthouse beyond, reminiscent of Flamborough Head. A buoy appears in both watercolours, but one study has only a single, tiny vessel, near the horizon, in an otherwise empty sea. The second study includes the headland and lighthouse and a more prominent fishing boat while the frigate itself is substantially the same in both watercolours and print. There is, however, one noticeable difference between these watercolours. This is the way the main courses are furled and hung from the yards, a detail that is slightly different, yet again, in the lithograph.

Both watercolours are fully coloured and are executed in a painterly fashion with no visible pen or pencil outlines. Since the orientation of the composition is the same in all three works, this suggests a tracing made on transfer paper and then reversed onto the lithographic stone for the print version. The prepared surface would take up the impression from the paper, reversed back to its original orientation.

Two small pencil drawings of a topsail schooner; a three-quarter stern view and a three-quarter bow view (see Fig.22) are clearly preliminary outlines for Ward's projected series of lithographed ship types. Both are drawn on white card (5½" x 7½") with the bow view marked up in one-inch squares.

A pen and wash sketch of the same grouping of vessels as found in the lithograph entitled "Merchant Vessels" (see Chapter 3) is not executed in a manner similar to any of the drawings and watercolours already described. Rather than being a study for the print, it

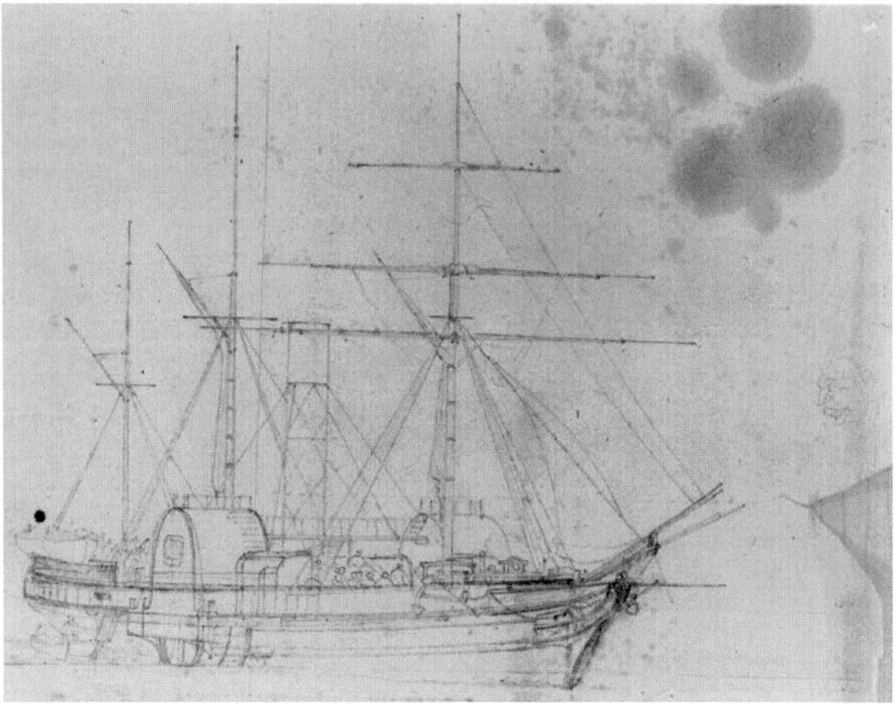

Fig. 16 John Ward (1798-1849) *P.S. Waterwitch*, pencil, 8¾ in. x 6 in.
Courtesy: Peabody Essex Museum, Salem, Mass.

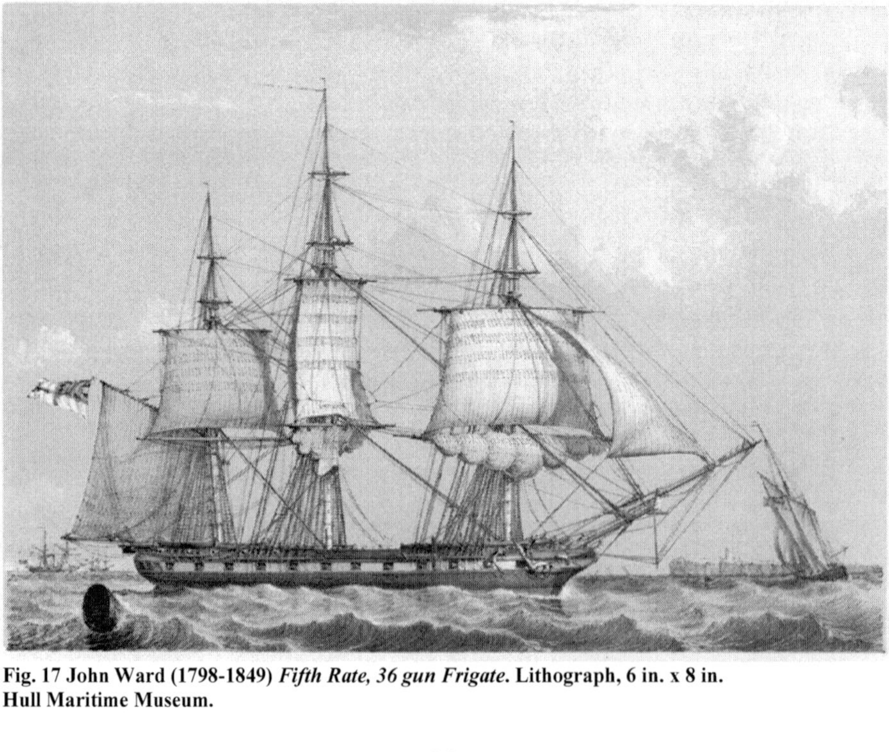

Fig. 17 John Ward (1798-1849) *Fifth Rate, 36 gun Frigate*. Lithograph, 6 in. x 8 in.
Hull Maritime Museum.

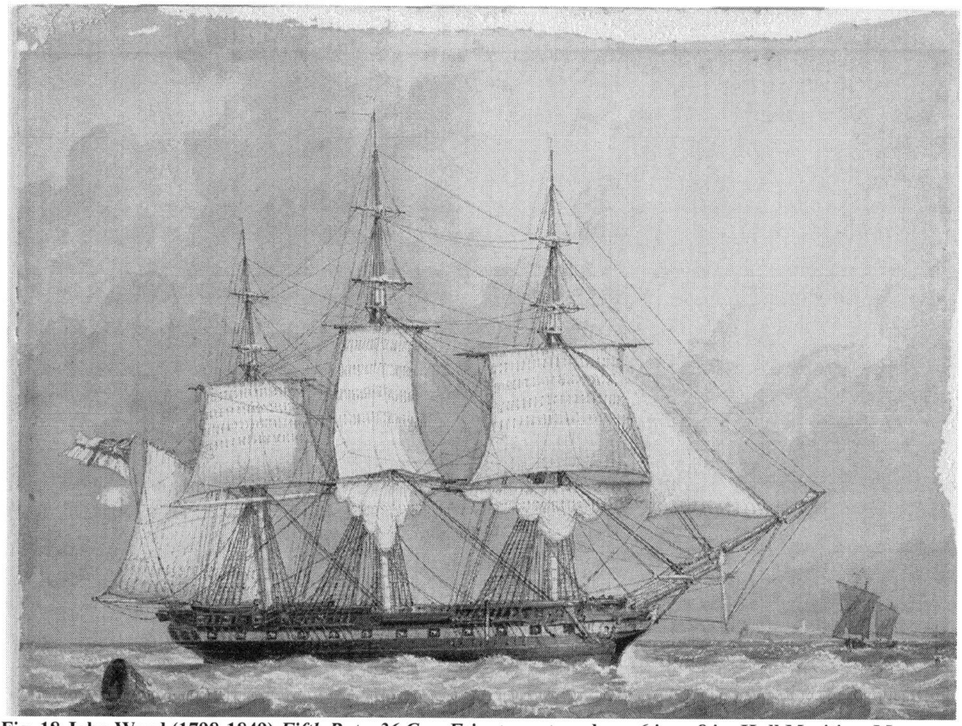

Fig. 18 John Ward (1798-1849) ***Fifth Rate, 36 Gun Frigate*****, watercolour, 6 in. x 8 in. Hull Maritime Museum.**

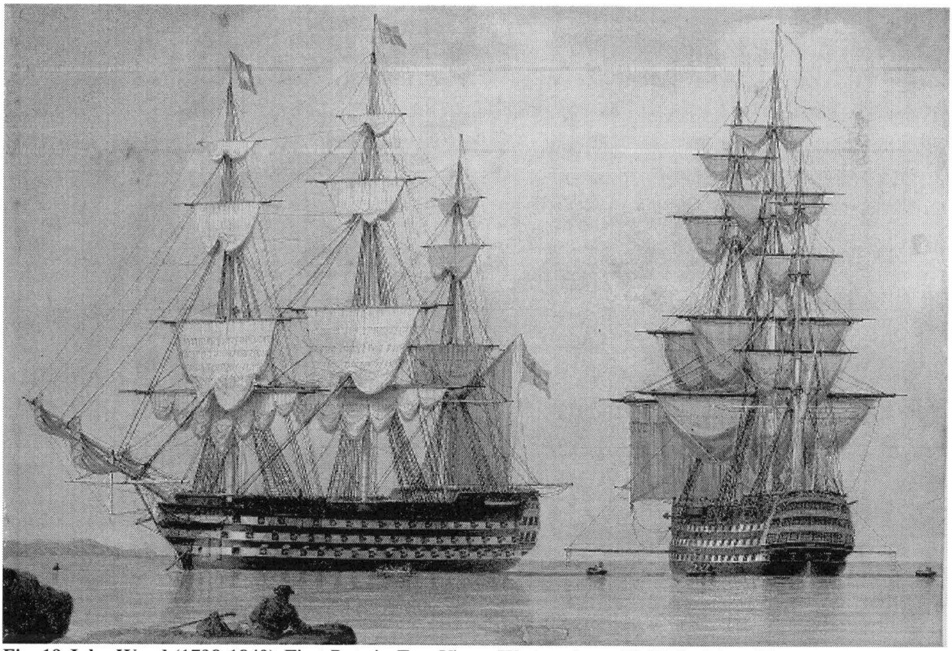

Fig. 19 John Ward (1798-1849) ***First Rate in Two Views*****. Watercolour. Hull Maritime Museum.**

is likely to have been copied from it by Ward's pupil and assistant, W F Settle (1821-1897). This same composition is also used in a small panel painting by Ward. The scene is slightly extended to the left with the addition of a mooring dolphin and a small vessel in the distance. The principal craft can be identified as the brig *Maese* built for W & C L Ringrose in 1841, the *Amazon* built in 1811 and owned by John Brodrick (a squared-up pen sketch by Ward of the *Amazon*, drawn in profile, is in the Peabody Essex Museum, Salem) and the schooner *Dandie Dinmont* built in 1848 for George Cammell of Hull. The latter indicates that this must have one of the last oils executed by Ward before his premature death in 1849.

Although it is clear that Ward could not be considered a topographical artist, a single watercolour study survives of a primarily topographical subject. This is a view of the Hull at the South End, looking across the River Hull to the South blockhouse. The scene is enlivened by a horse and cart, a woman with children with other sundry figures, and the Duke of Clarence public house to the left of the picture. No finished work of this subject in any medium has been discovered (see Fig.24).

John Ward's relative (cousin or nephew) William Frederick Settle (qv) joined Ward's studio after having been made a gift of his indentures by John Craggs, a printer and stationer. Settle's parents had originally discouraged him from taking up art as a profession. Instead, he was apprenticed to Craggs, a well-known local printer, binder and publisher who, among other things, published a guide to Hull. Settle had moved in with Ward's family early in 1841 and continued to live in his house for some time after Ward's death. It is likely that he retained as a source of working material, examples of the prints and drawings that were otherwise dispersed in Ward's studio sale in 1853.

For a time, Settle was regarded as the official artist to the Royal Yorkshire Yacht Club, a 'post' to which Ward had probably been appointed previously. Certainly, Ward produced the fine commemorative print for the first regatta in 1847 and Settle produced a similar lithograph of the 1851 regatta (see Fig.26).

Even at this time in Ward's life, when his reputation as a marine artist was fully established, he was not too proud to acknowledge his humble origins as a house and ship painter. In 1848, Ward published a small booklet entitled *The English Alphabet arranged for the use of House and sign Painters, writers etc* which explains, with examples, how to construct various kinds of letters in due proportion (see Fig.27). Neatly lithographed, each page of letters is faced with a page of descriptive text, whilst on the reverse is one of his studies of ship types.

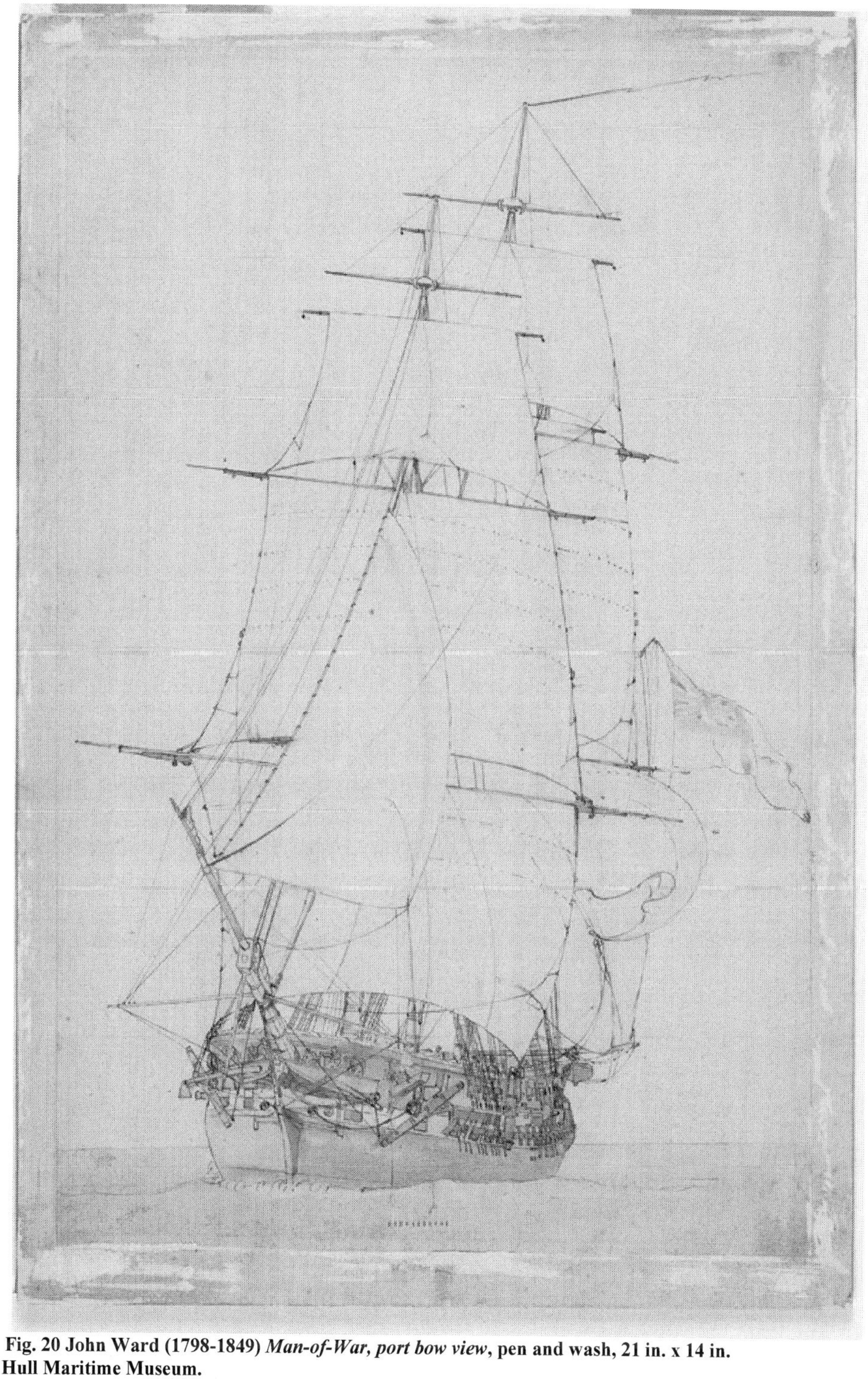

Fig. 20 John Ward (1798-1849) ***Man-of-War, port bow view*****, pen and wash, 21 in. x 14 in. Hull Maritime Museum.**

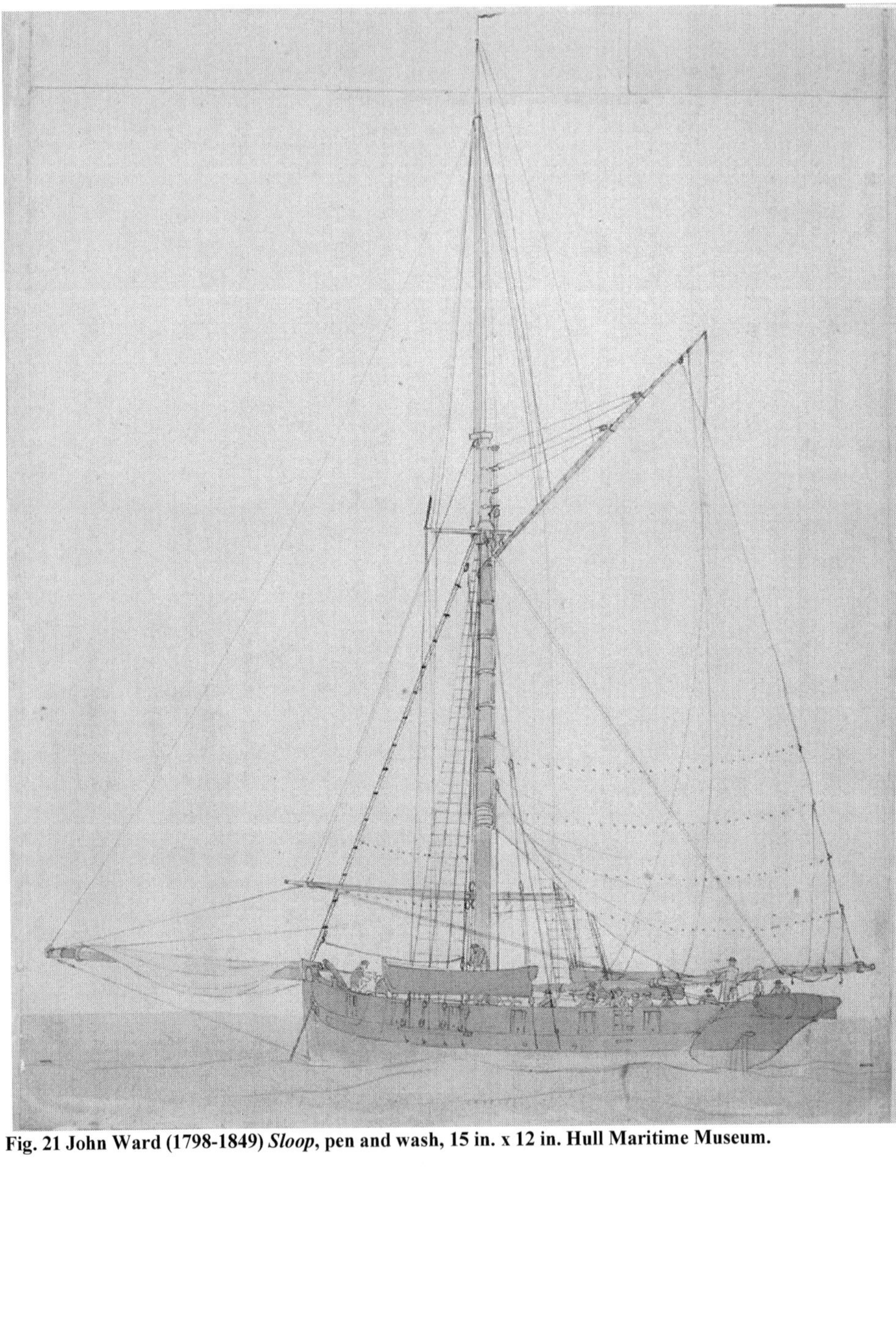

Fig. 21 John Ward (1798-1849) *Sloop*, pen and wash, 15 in. x 12 in. Hull Maritime Museum.

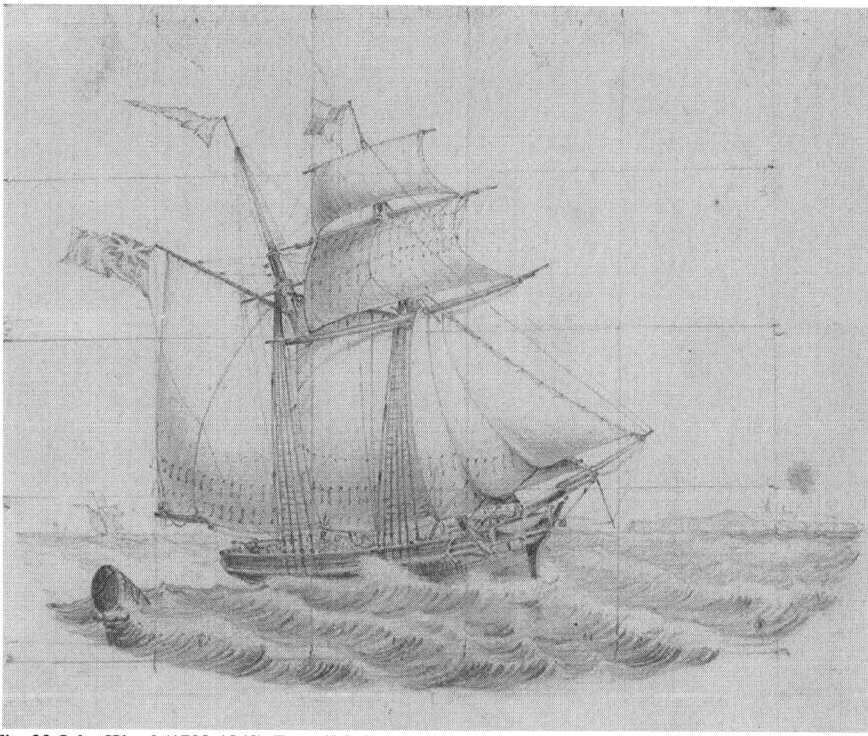

Fig. 22 John Ward (1798-1848) *Topsail Schooner*, pencil, 5 ½ in. x 7 in. Hull Maritime Museum.

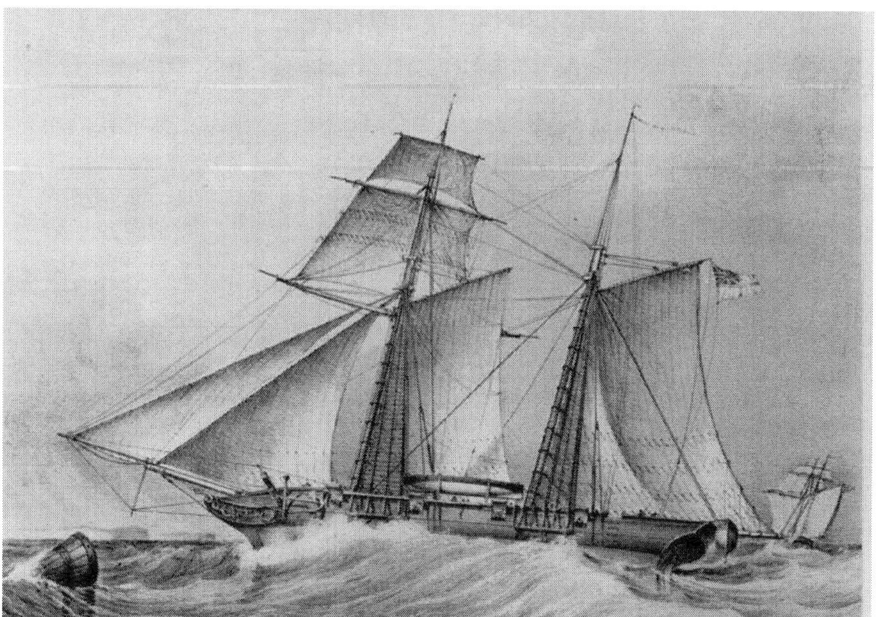

Fig. 23 John Ward (1798-1849) ***The Armed Schooner Wanderer Larboard tack, broadside view, blowing fresh***. Lithograph. Hull Maritime Museum.

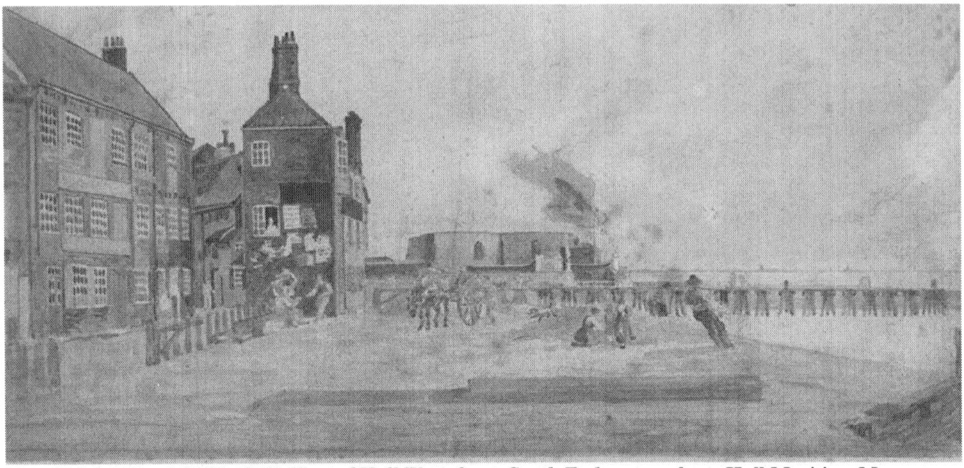

Fig. 24 John Ward (1798-1849) ***View of Hull Waterfront, South End*****, watercolour. Hull Maritime Museum.**

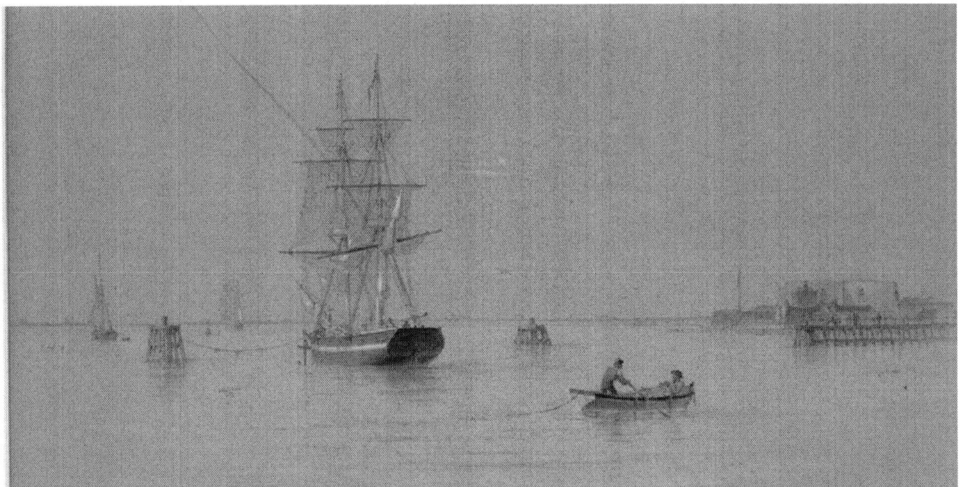

Fig. 25 William Frederick Settle (1821-1897) ***Vessel Moored off the South Blockhouse*****, signed 'W Fred Settle', pencil and watercolour, 7 ¾ in. x 13 ¼. Hull Maritime Museum.**

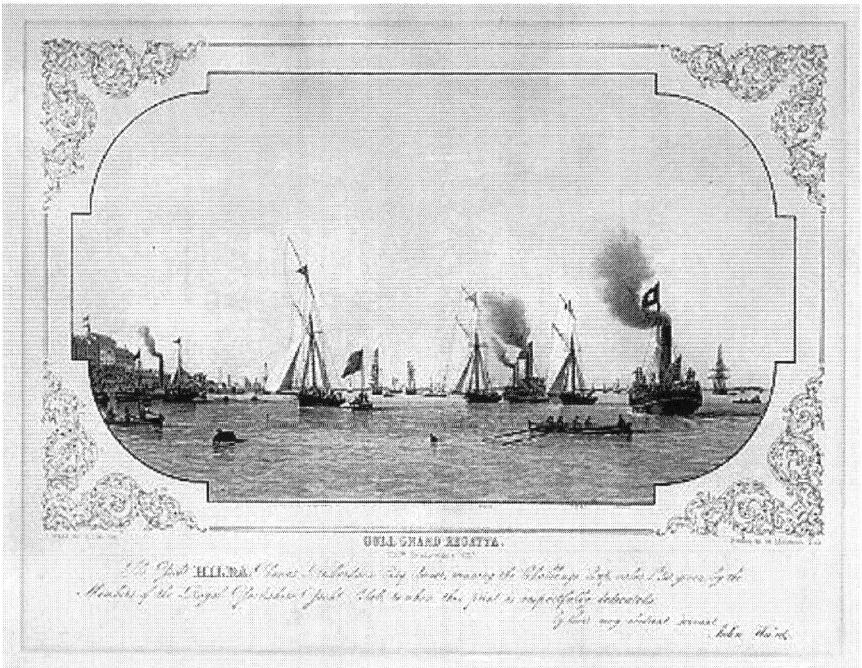

Fig. 26 John Ward (1798-1849) *Royal Yorkshire Yacht Club, Hull Grand Regatta*, 29th September 1847. Lithograph. Hull Maritime Museum

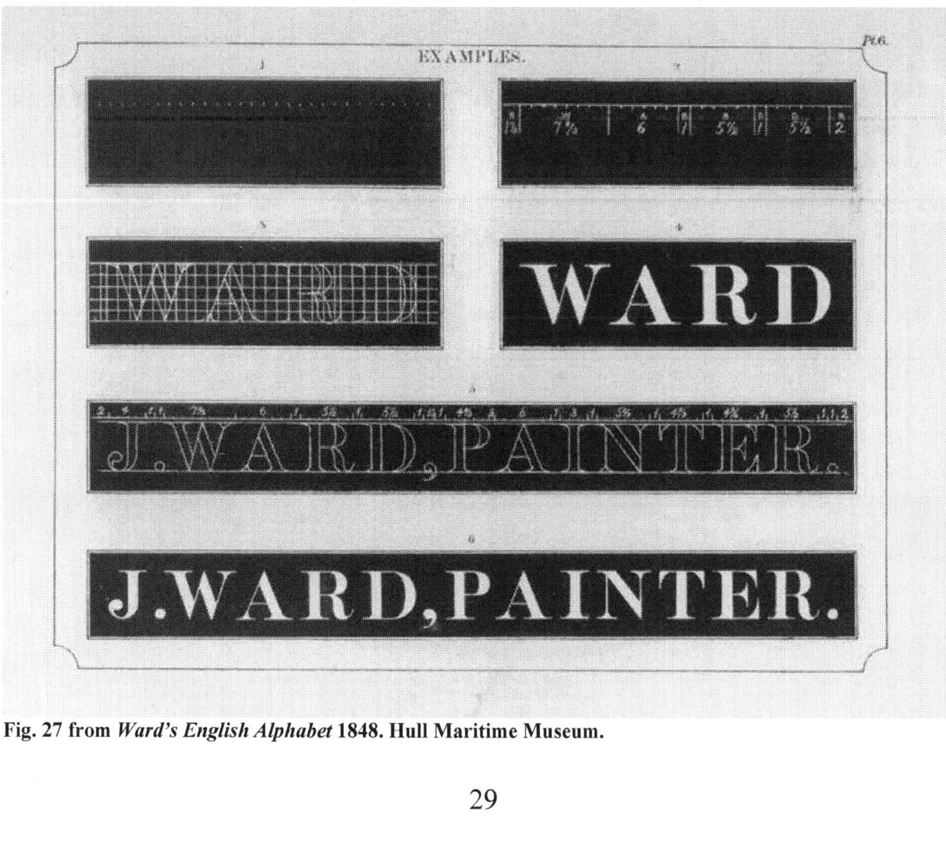

Fig. 27 from *Ward's English Alphabet* 1848. Hull Maritime Museum.

Chapter 2

Marine Painters and Printmaking in Britain: 1800 - 1850

John Ward progressed from the everyday business of painting the timbers of ships to making meticulous images of them in created seascapes. This remarkable transition from an artisan painter to one of the finest marine artists of his generation was achieved without the benefit of living in London, as many of his contemporaries thought necessary. His eventual success was doubtless due to the example of his peers and opportunities in the cultural life of Hull as this blossomed in the first half of the nineteenth century. At Ward's birth, the population of Hull was around 22,000. By the end of the nineteenth century it had increased tenfold; theatres, docks, hospitals, civic buildings, galleries, parks, roads, railways, shops, services, schools and housing were built at an astonishing rate. Ward was transformed as Hull was transformed. But how was this transformation achieved? Who were the main sources of influence and what inspiration and lessons might he have gained from the emerging tradition of marine painting in Britain at this time?

Chief among his personal influences was very probably that of his father, Captain Abraham Ward (c1761-1835). He sailed out of Hull as master of various vessels trading to Spain and Russia between c. 1794 and 1807 and served with the Southern Convoy during the wars with France.[1] This richly varied seafaring background would have made its mark during his son's formative years though the attribution to Abraham Ward of an oil painting of the whaler 'Swan', (active 1815-1840) to Abraham Ward is dubious. Another more distant influence may have been the Hull painter, William Ward (1781-1802), possibly a relative – an uncle perhaps, although such a connection has not been established from the local archive (see Fig 28).

More directly, it was to be William Anderson (1757-1837) who exercised a profound influence on the young apprentice at Meggit's Yard. We know from the inventory of the works sold from Ward's studio that he had at some stage acquired several of Anderson's paintings. These included two versions of "Shipping off Northfleet" and a "View of the Thames at Greenwich". We also know that he submitted three works "After Anderson" to the Hull Inaugural Fine Arts Exhibition in 1827. Marine subjects had become very popular and were purchased by many collectors.

Anderson's reputed background as a shipwright would have greatly helped towards a sympathetic understanding of the artistic ambitions of manual workers in the maritime trades. Anderson, aged fifty-five in 1812, was a regular exhibitor at the Royal Academy from 1787 and the British Institution from 1810, exhibiting over sixty works at London venues in his lifetime. His eldest son, William Guido Anderson was a promising young marine artist who also exhibited at the Royal Academy in 1799 before serving as a midshipman on the 74-gun HMS *Bellona* where, two years later, he was fatally wounded at the Battle of Copenhagen.[2] His father's portrayal of this vessel (or similar) is shown in Fig.29.

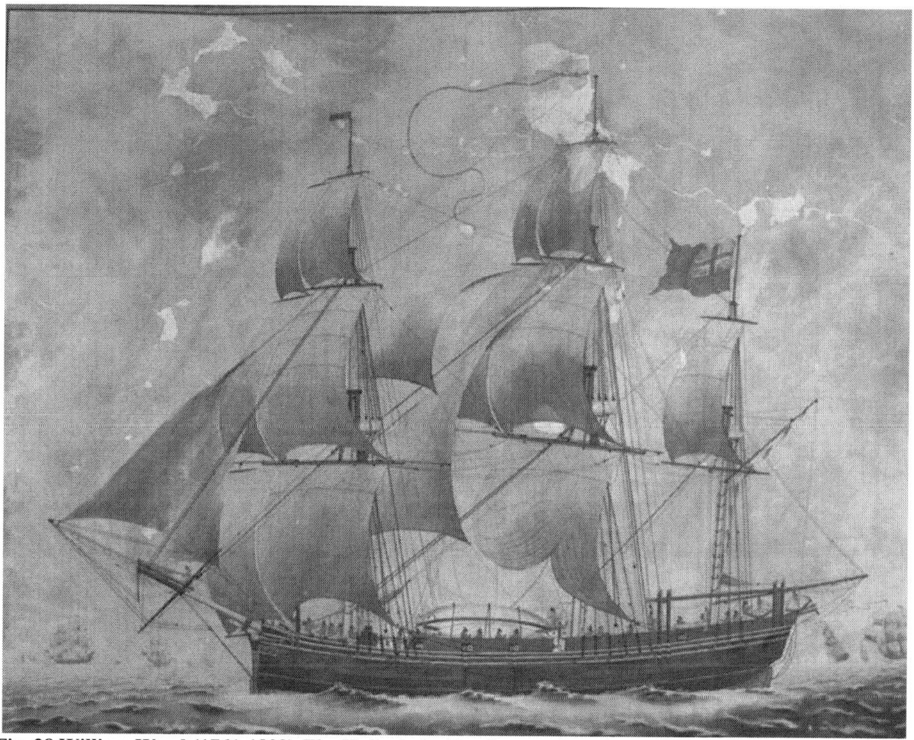

Fig. 28 William Ward (1761-1802) ***The Hull whaler Truelove,*** **watercolour, 1801. Hull Maritime Museum.**

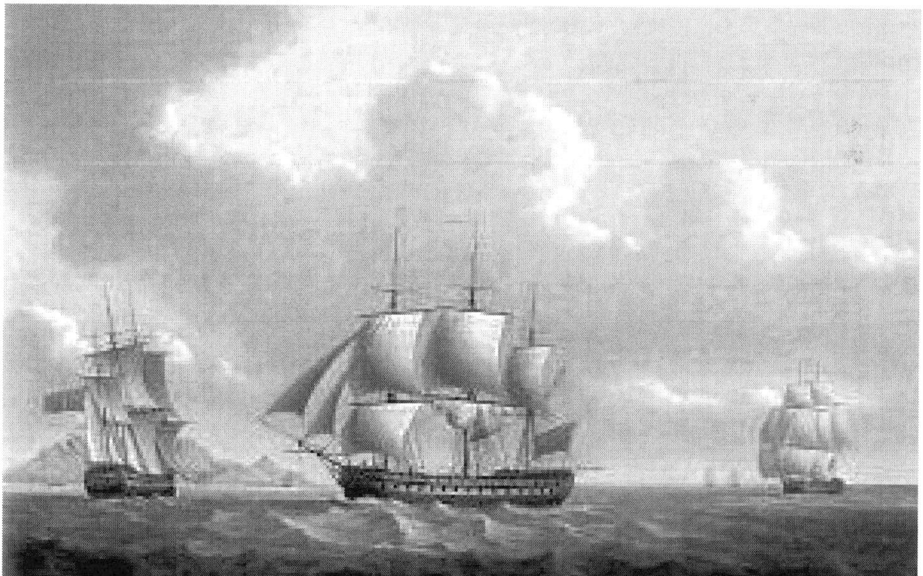

Fig. 29 William Anderson (1757-1837) ***A 74-Gun Third Rate in three positions off Table Bay, Cape of Good Hope, with Table Mountain in the distance.*** **Signed and dated 1790. Courtesy: Encore Editions.**

William Anderson (Sr) was living in London and at the height of his powers when Ward began his apprenticeship c.1812. Anderson's connections with Hull may well have developed through commissions from patrons in Hull and the north, although there is no evidence of personal contacts with Ward. However, it is tempting to speculate that it may have been a teenage encounter with the huge Anderson canvas depicting the Battle of the Nile (1798), presented to Hull Trinity House in 1813, that triggered or entrenched his passion for marine painting. It is, however, uncertain as to whether he would have gained access as a young man unless by special favour of one of the brethren.

Anderson's painting of the Battle of the Nile commemorates a British fleet of fifteen ships under Nelson's command that took by surprise and largely destroyed a French fleet in Aboukir Bay, thus cutting off supplies to Napoleon's army in Egypt. It was a well noted and momentous victory at the time demonstrating the tactical ability of the British Navy. Anderson's patrons included serving naval officers whose insistence on accuracy of detail was well served by his commitment to draughtsmanship and close attention to the topography and dynamics of vessels at sea.

A link with Hull may have arisen through Anderson's connections with Julius Caesar Ibbetson (1759-1817). Ibbetson was born in Leeds and apprenticed for five years from 1772 to the Fletcher family of house and ship painters in Hull. It is to this family that the earliest ship portrait from the hand of a Hull artist can be attributed - a canvas of the whale ships *Molly* and *Friends* by Thomas Fletcher c1796-1802. However, Ibbetson's apprenticeship with Fletcher was not altogether suited to his ambitions, although the reception he enjoyed at Hull and York theatres for his scene painting was a distinct encouragement to a seventeen year old apprentice.

By 1777 Ibbetson was 'safely moored in a picture dealer's garret' in London, receiving 'very inadequate prices' and experiencing 'the tricks of the picture-dealing trade'.[3] Farington (qv) quotes a letter from Ibbetson complaining that; 'He had been for four years in the hands of those Harpies [4] the Picture Dealers, and described their frauds with humour and acrimony'. Being driven to doubtful practices was a common fate awaiting the early marine painters, especially amongst those with artisan backgrounds and without sponsorship. Ward circumvented such indignities by staying in Hull and dividing his time between the commonplace business of trade painting and taking commissions from known clients for specific pictures.

Ibbetson was a neighbour of Anderson in London and became a family friend, returning briefly to Hull in 1800. Three years later, Ibbetson published a manual of painting; *An Accidence, or Gamut, of Painting in Oil and Watercolour*. Quite possibly, this found its way into the hands of some of the more literate apprentices, particularly as they shared the same background and inclinations as the author. His publication was largely confined to the technicalities of media and colours with examples but with occasional illustrations etched by him. Its contents also contained further dire warnings for artists to avoid the 'Humbuggologia' of picture dealers, considering them to be 'serpents' and to living artists as 'hawks to singing birds'.

J. C. Ibbetson's final move to Yorkshire around this time may have encouraged Anderson to visit the north. However, the only available clues are Anderson's views of Berwick and Tynemouth exhibited at the Royal Academy in 1824. Three years later, ten Anderson works appeared in the Hull exhibition, no less than six belonging to John Day, an attorney. However, we have no way of knowing whether Day or any of the other lenders purchased directly from the artist whether in London or Hull. In the same 1827 exhibition, Ibbetsons's posthumous reputation was recognised at this exhibition by three of his paintings being shown in the section devoted to "Deceased Masters".

Two years before Anderson's death, Ward submitted nine works to the Hull Exhibition in 1835 including a storm piece "after Powell" - another artist who clearly had a direct influence on Ward's own development. Charles Martin Powell was listed as a "Deceased Master" in the 1827 exhibition and was represented by two "Sea Views" He is little known and his identifiable pictures are now scarce. He commenced life as a sailor and though self taught, exhibited forty paintings at the Royal Academy and British Institution between 1807 and 1821. He painted numerous other works during his career, influenced by the seventeenth century Dutch painter Ludolf Bakhuizen (1631-1708). However, Powell's wife and eight children were left in poverty after his death. His paintings are characterised by clarity of drawing of the vessels and well realised figures, both striking attributes of the work of Ward.

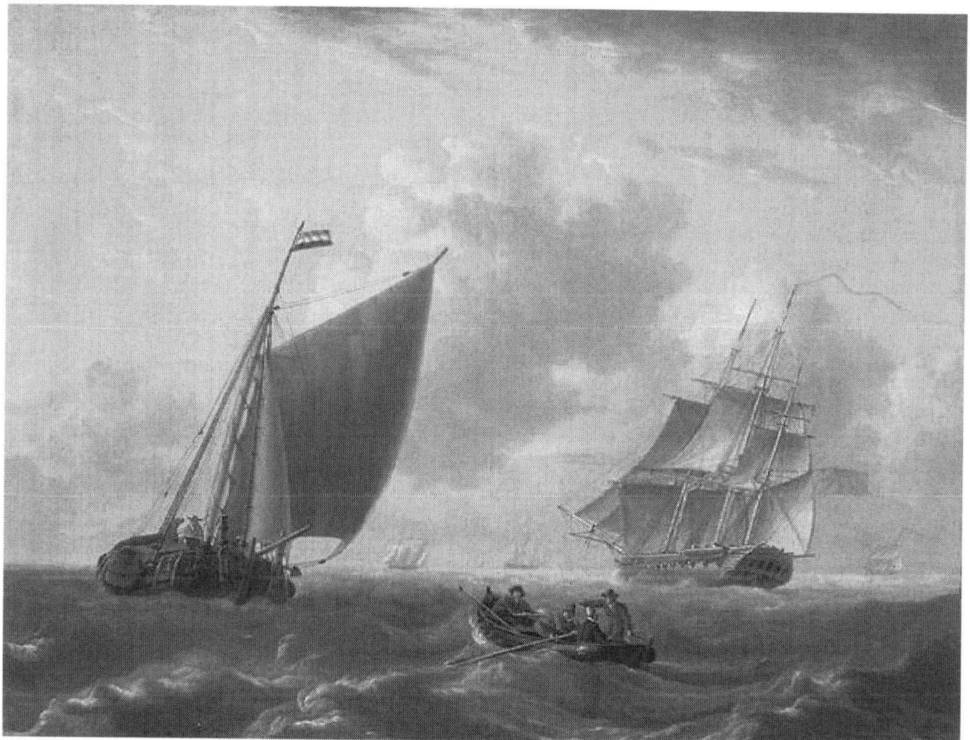

Fig. 30 Charles Martin Powell (1775-1824) ***An English Frigate with Dutch Shipping***
Courtesy: N R Omell Gallery

In addition to paintings by Anderson, works by three other artists were owned by Ward; Ovenden, Peeters, and Whitcombe. A painting by the first of these artists, recorded by surname only, was loaned by Ward to the 1842 exhibition at the Mechanic's Institute. 'Ovenden' may refer to an obscure artist residing at addresses in the Strand and Islington who exhibited a series of paintings of freshwater fish at the Royal Academy between 1817 and 1832, or perhaps more likely, to a F.W. Ovenden (fl.1834-1843) who exhibited a "Shore Scene" there in 1836. Six other marine landscapes by the latter artist were also shown at various exhibitions of the Society of British Artists, his last piece being a "Shore Scene, Staiths (sic), Yorkshire" in 1843. The Society, founded in 1823, provided five spacious exhibition rooms in elegant premises designed for the purpose by John Nash

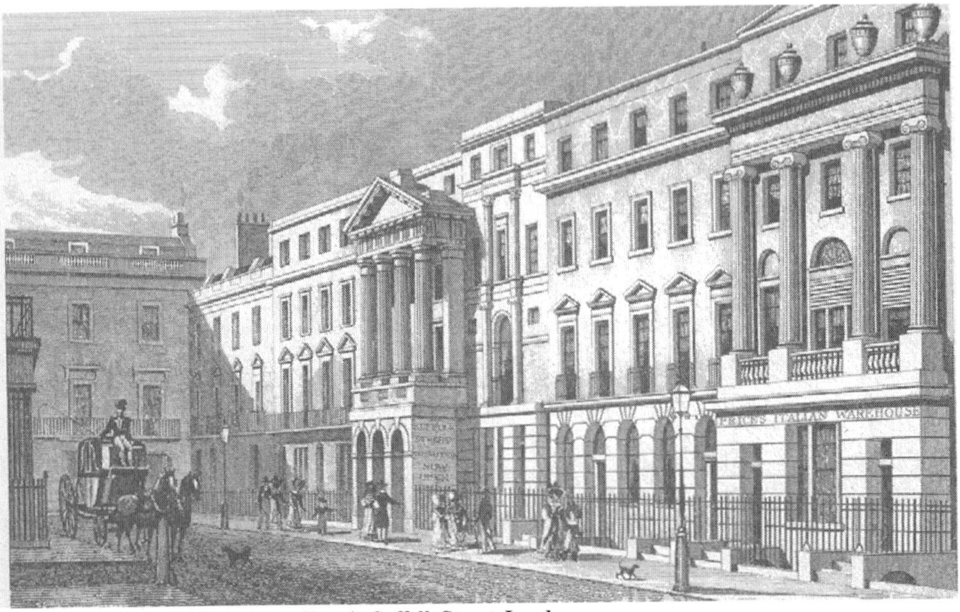

Fig. 31 Society of British Artists gallery in Suffolk Street, London.

(1752-1835). Located in Suffolk Street, a short distance from the original premises of the Royal Academy, the Society aimed 'to promote the English School of Painting' by offering alternative opportunities for artists seeking to escape from the restrictive practices of the Academy.

The second painting owned by Ward illustrates the predominant influence of 17th century Dutch painters on marine art in Britain at this time. Bonaventura Peeters the Elder (1614-1652) was a leading member of this highly influential school of painting. His most arresting works were typically spectacular, depicting river boats in windy weather, or storm tossed vessels by rocky shores. Wrecks, warships, sea-battles, and tempestuous seas are illuminated by the dramatic effects of light and shade heightened by lustrous and intense colour, making his compositions full of movement and imaginative interest. However, the range of Peeters marine works also encompassed serene scenes of shipping in calm waters, topographical detail in depictions of maritime history, and renderings of imaginary events in exotic and fantastical seascapes. In this way, Peeters united marine landscape with ship portraiture that was to define the scope of marine painting for successive generations.

Ward's known affinity with Peeters also suggests a broader spectrum of interests. Both Holland and England were sea powers whose economy depended on access to the oceans of the world. The Dutch East India Company and its counterpart in Britain operated a virtual monopoly of trade. The remit of these Companies, barely imaginable to the modern mind, included the right to trade, wage war, and to colonise foreign lands.[5]

The Anglo-Dutch wars of the 17th century and the naval battles that accompanied them provided patriotic and heroic scenarios for artists to commemorate. Decades later, the social and cultural influence of Holland was duly strengthened with the accession of William III (1650-1702) to the British throne. William III inherited an artistic legacy in maritime painting greatly encouraged by his predecessor, Charles II who had invited the celebrated Dutch artists, the Van de Veldes, (father and son) to paint for the royal court. They arrived in England from Amsterdam in 1672 and soon afterwards worked for the King

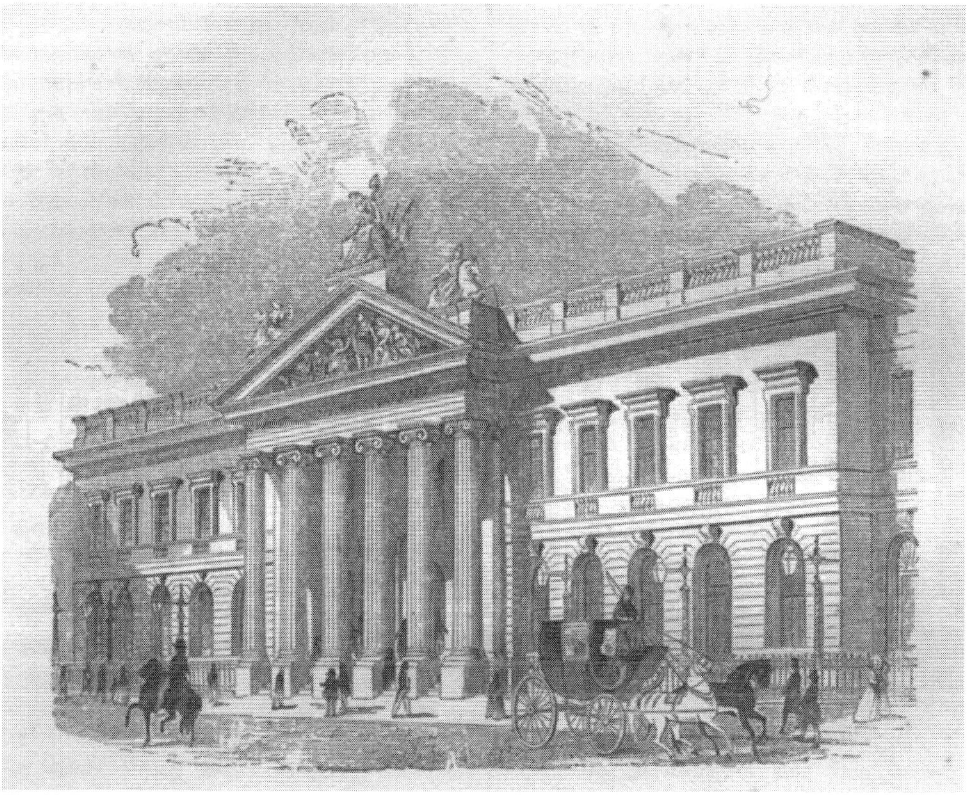

Fig. 32 East India House, London, c.1800.

in a prepared studio at the Queens House at Greenwich until 1694. It was the Van de Veldes who laid the foundations of marine painting in Holland and England for generations of artists to come.

A century later, Dutch vessels were found to be frequent traders in the dockyards of Hull. A major interest in common for both nations was the Arctic whaling industry. This enterprise inspired some of the most celebrated of the Dutch and British marine artists and set a model that Ward was to enrich through his own vision and highly distinctive style.

The third painting owned by Ward was by the marine artist Thomas Whitcombe, (c1760 – c1830). George Chambers (see Ch 1) also admired this painter and owned one of his works. Very little is known about Whitcombe's early life, but he was a frequent exhibitor of sea-pieces, sea-battles, storms, and images of the ports and harbours of Britain, especially Plymouth. He visited Hull between 1805 and 1824 and contributed over fifty plates to the *Naval Achievements of Great Britain from the year 1793-1817*. In total, he produced approximately one hundred and fifty portrayals of Royal Navy engagements. His paintings and drawings, sold in the form of prints, ensured that his work as an artist had a widespread distribution.

It seems highly probable that, given its patriotic importance, "The Naval Achievements of Great Britain" would have found a place on the shelves of the Hull Subscription Library, founded in 1775. Thomas Meggitt (Ward's Master) is listed as a one guinea subscribing member in 1810-1811. The library was a major development in the town, operating from purpose-built premises in 1801 and then from 1854 sharing the exceptionally

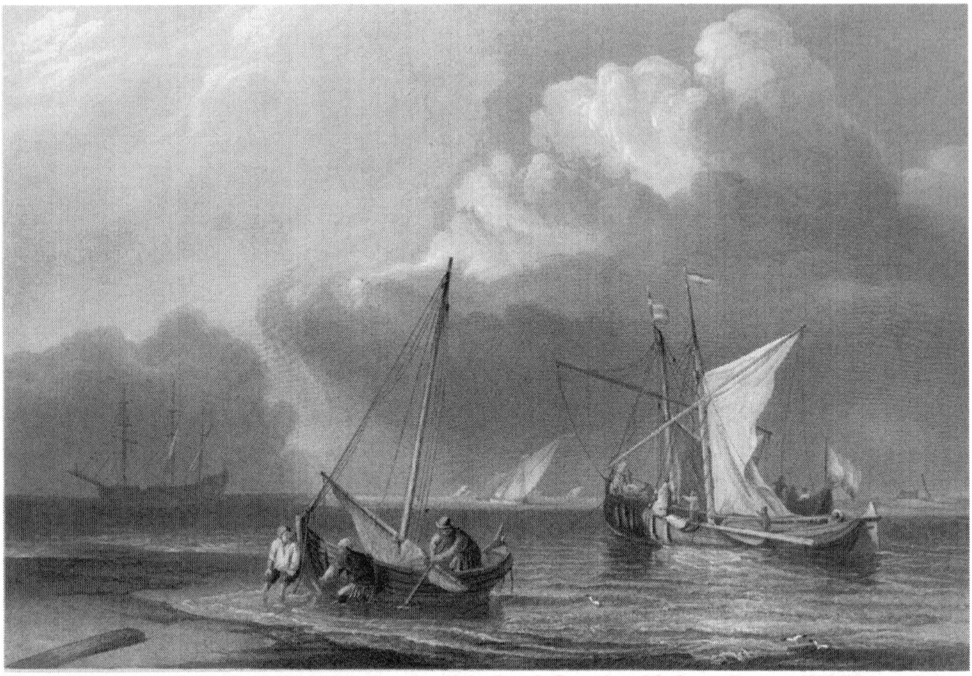

Fig. 33 Willem van de Velde (1633-1707) ***Vessels off the Dutch Coast in a Moderate Breeze.*** **W.Miller sculpt.**

fine new building, the Royal Institution, with the Literary and Philosophical Society's Museum. Its stock eventually grew to some 80,000 items. The Library's aims are colourfully outlined in a contemporary record;

> Many also there are, whose circumstances prevent from procuring a stock of books, the knowledge of which may be necessary to them; and even the more opulent and learned, on whose shelves the best productions find a place, acknowledge the utility of a PublicLibrary, where they can consult such works, as, from their extent or for other reasons are not calculated for a private collection. Nor must we overlook the great advantages derived by society from the solid and useful learning instilled in young persons, who are thus provided with an easy access to what is suitable, and withdrawn from the temptation to a practice, most pernicious in its consequences, that of reading impure and profane books.[6]

In summary, Ward's ownership of the work of four selected artists offers an insight into the development of his own artistic career; Peeters representing the best of the tradition of Dutch maritime painting, Anderson providing a link between the Dutch style and an emerging British tradition, Ovenden offering a reminder of coastal and shore scenes where landscape transforms into seascape, and Whitcombe presenting a model of the heroic historical narrative related to marine printmaking. All of these key concerns are to be found in the development of Ward's contribution to the history of British marine landscape painting.

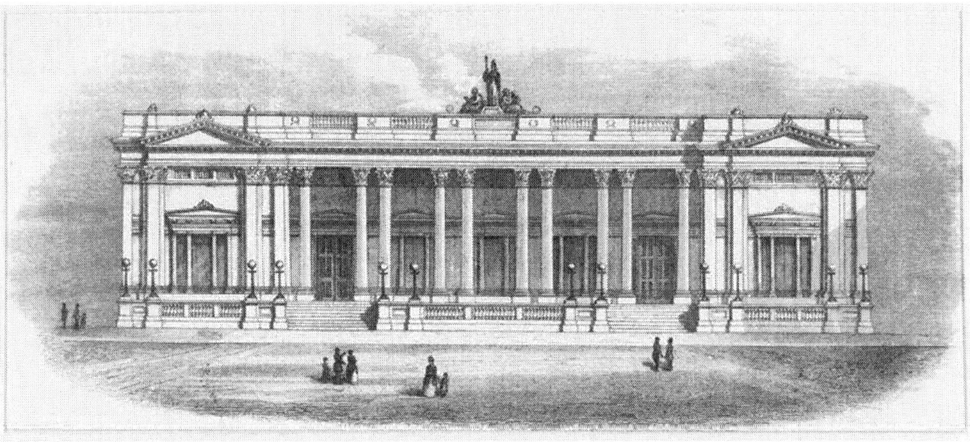

Fig. 34 The Royal Institution, designed by Cuthbert Brodrick,[7] home of the Hull Literary and Philosophical Museum and Subscription Library from 1854.

Marine Painters in Hull: 1800-1835

The leading contender for Ward's early role model must be Robert Willoughby (1768-1843). If Willoughby's career followed the usual pattern, his apprenticeship would have been completed before the end of the eighteenth century. He produced his most ambitious work *Whaleships of the Cooper Fleet* in 1803. It is a large and impressive canvas depicting four whalers in profile and stern view amongst icebergs and floes with figures clambering over them in pursuit of bears and seals; an appealing and evocative image for any marine artist. Willoughby was the principal artist responsible for recording the Hull whaling fleet during its heyday in the first half of the nineteenth century. Other works include topographical pictures of Hull yards including Westerdale's, mast, pump and block maker, close by Savile Street from where Willoughby advertised himself as "house, ship and sign painter".

All the Hull marine painters of the eighteenth and first half of the nineteenth century remained firmly in the artisan, craft based tradition. They were jobbing painters who ran workshops that undertook all the basic tasks of house and ship painting and sign writing as their principal employment. The painting of canvases and panels remained a specialist activity to which the master may have directed much of his time whilst his journeyman and apprentices carried on the daily routine. Some masters offered tuition in drawing, as did Ward in later years. Willoughby himself was practising as a drawing master as early as 1812, giving notice in November of that year that his drawing school would "reopen" at his residence at 8 Castle Row.

Several general drawing masters, as distinct from specialist marine teachers, were also in practice in Hull at this time including William Beilby (1740-1819) the celebrated glass enameller. He was the brother of Ralph Beilby to whom the renowned wood engraver Thomas Bewick (1757-1828) was apprenticed. William moved to Hull in about 1810 and lived there until his death in 1819.

Although not resident in Hull, of particular note is the work of Henry Moses (1782-1870), an artist and publisher mainly working in outline and one of the engravers attached to the British Museum. His example illustrates the way in which leading artists of the day, whether in London or abroad, could exercise systematic influence on young draughtsmen and artists at a distance. This case is significant in at least two other ways; Moses' work is

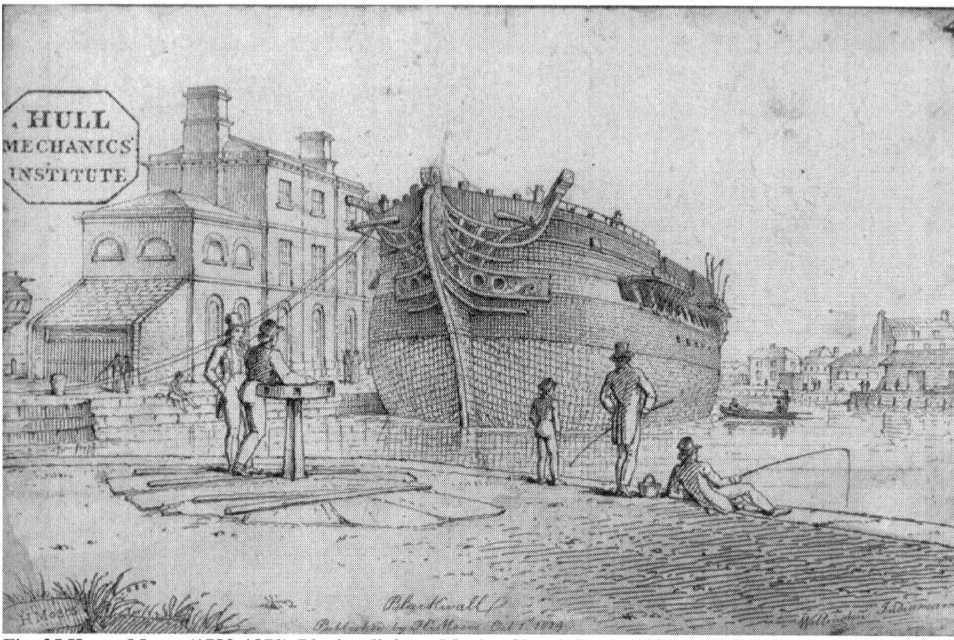

Fig. 35 Henry Moses (1782-1870) *Blackwall,* from Marine Sketch Book (1825 – 1826) published by Ackermann & Co in 1837

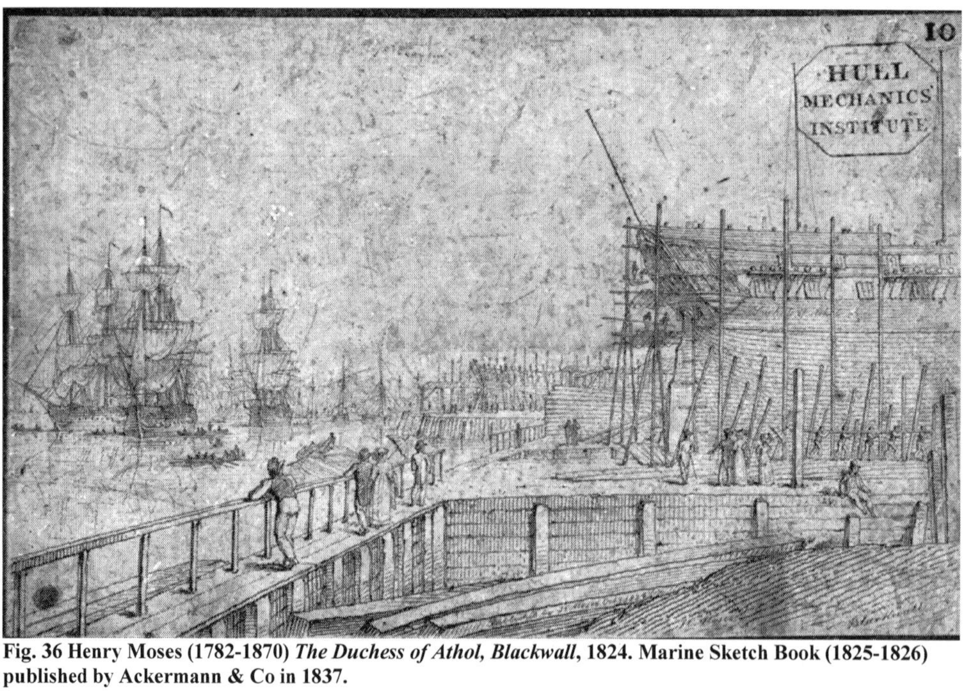

Fig. 36 Henry Moses (1782-1870) *The Duchess of Athol, Blackwall,* 1824. Marine Sketch Book (1825-1826) published by Ackermann & Co in 1837.

closely associated with marine subjects and therefore of particular interest to Ward and rare examples of his teaching aids apparently used when Ward and others were developing their drawing skills have survived intact. They are small prints mounted on board, varnished for protection against wear and tear and bearing the stamp of the "Hull Mechanics Institute".[8]

A contemporary review of Moses' *Sketches of Shipping and Marine Sketch Book*, soon after they were first published in 1824, has this to say;

> <u>Review of New Publications</u>
>
> Sketches of Shipping; Views in Portsmouth Harbour. Drawn and etched by Henry \ Moses.
> The Marine Sketch Book. By the Same.
>
> Whether we consider these publications as perfect examples of the drawing of ships, in every variety of position from which students might derive the utmost advantage, or as fine specimens of art, we are equally disposed to bestow the highest praise upon them. As far as we can judge, every vessel, every mast, and every rope, are as correct as if the ablest seaman in the fleet had handled them; and at the same time the composition of many of the sketches combines the picturesque with the true, in a manner to please the eye, while it informs the understanding. The etching is all that could be wished,— slight, but sufficient; and where the subjects permit, not merely pretty, but interesting.[9]

If this pattern of access to potential sources of support and resources was repeated in the case of other local marine artists of Ward's generation, it becomes clear that a combination of membership of the Hull Subscription Library, attending an evening drawing school, or classes and lectures at the Mechanics Institute, and studying works on view at the Hull Exhibitions of the Fine Arts (1827, 1829, 1835) would be more than sufficient for aspiring marine painters to gain key skills and expertise, especially when firmly grounded in related crafts such as painting, gilding, varnishing and sign writing.

Let us now take a closer look at John Ward's contemporaries exhibiting at Hull between 1827 and 1835 during his formative years. In this way, we may uncover further clues about possible influences as he sought to extend his skills; '(as an)....opportunity is afforded, not only to the artist to improve his studies, but to the man of taste to indulge his passion for the Arts, and to the young and uninitiated to find the means of incitement to become acquainted with them.'[10]

Marine subjects submitted by artists not already noted include George Arnald (1763-1841) who turned to marine views and sea battles later in his career. Elected as an Associate of the Royal Academy in 1810 and styling himself as "Painter to the Duke of Gloucester", he won a commission for a painting of the Battle of the Nile two years before exhibiting at Hull. One of the key vessels in that action and subsequently at the Battle of Trafalgar was HMS *Bellerophon.*[11] Arnald's painting exhibited at Hull of *The Bellerophon, in her present state, a 74-Gun Ship, to which Napoleon surrendered*, appears to refer to her subsequent uses as a convict ship lying at Sheerness, a subject also depicted by Henry Moses (qv) in his Marine Sketchbook. The "Billy Ruffian" as she was commonly called became a prison ship in 1815. A planned or ironic coincidence of Arnald's decision to show this work at Hull was that Robert Hartley, the twenty five year old son of the Hull innkeeper of the "Sir John Falstaff" had recently been executed for stabbing Captain Owen of the Bellerophon whilst awaiting transportation. Catalogued next to Arnald's second exhibited

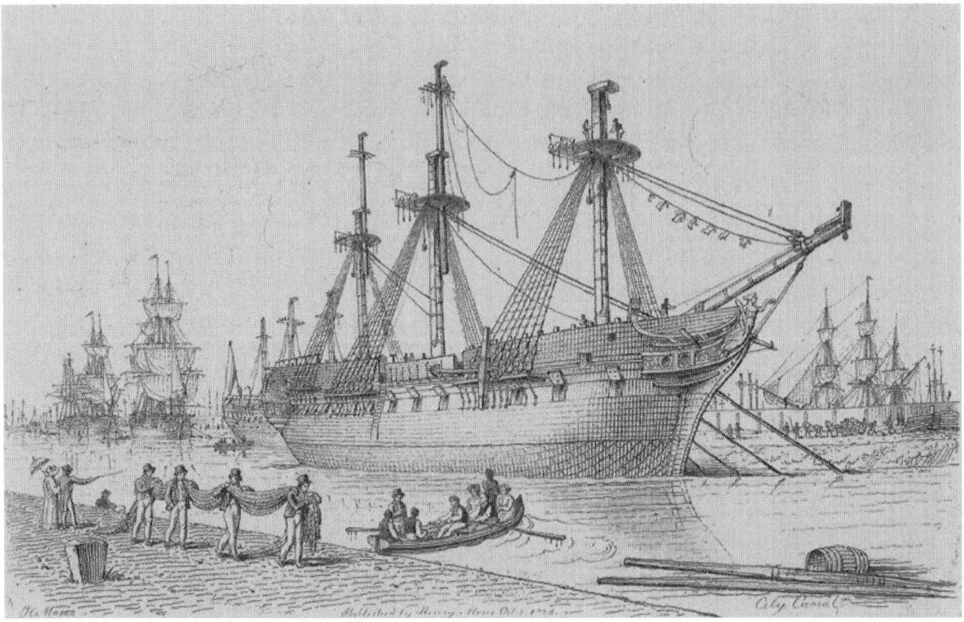

Fig. 37 Henry Moses (1782-1870) ***The City Canal*** **1 October 1824 The City Canal was built in 1805 to relieve the congestion of moored ships in the Thames. Running parallel with the West India Docks, it crossed the Isle of Dogs to provide an improved link between Wapping and Blackwall.**

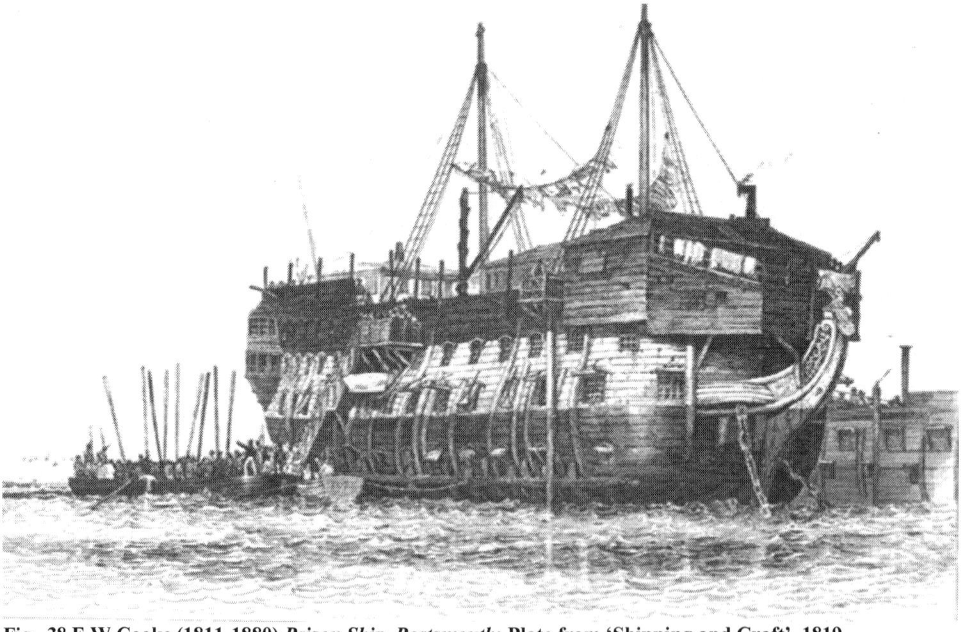

Fig. 38 E W Cooke (1811-1880) ***Prison Ship, Portsmouth*****; Plate from 'Shipping and Craft'. 1819.**

work was another work of local significance; a landscape in oils by his daughter, Anne, *Charles I Demanding Entrance at the Beverley Gate, Hull, April 23rd 1642.*

Thomas Miles Richardson (1784-1848), a leading landscape and marine artist in both watercolour and oils, also contributed three works to the Hull (1827) exhibition. Richardson had co-founded the "Northumberland Institution for the Promotion of the Fine Arts" that held its first exhibition five years earlier. Shortly after exhibiting at Hull, he founded and financed the "Northern Academy of Arts" in Newcastle. His close ally and friend, Henry Perlee Parker (1795-1873) sent two works to Hull including a scene from Sir Walter Scott's *Heart of Midlothian.*

One might expect mutual support and contacts between Hull and Newcastle to have taken place between artists and founders of the respective Institutions for the Promotion of the Fine Arts. A number of Newcastle artists benefited from participation in the Hull exhibitions no doubt taking advantage of the frequency of sea passages to Hull. The lack of any general reciprocal involvement by Hull artists probably reflects the more restricted range of the local men. There were no landscape or history painters of note in Hull and the most able marine artists concentrated on painting local vessels leaving Newcastle ships to the artists of that town.[12]

Richardson began the annual Newcastle exhibitions by adding a room to his house. Five years later in 1827, much grander architect designed premises were built by Richardson and Parker to establish 'The Northern Academy of Arts'. Two octagonal rooms were provided and top-lit to avoid dark corners, a design doubtless influenced by Nash's layout for the Suffolk Street Galleries of the Society of British Artists (see Fig 30). The Newcastle 'rooms' could be re-arranged so as to provide one open space. This provided the setting for a Richardson-Parker 1,350 feet diorama (a variant of a panorama with lighting effects) with a moving platform to carry spectators from one scene to the next. Its subject was a continental coastal bay with vessels, viewed through the archway of a cavern. The Newcastle diorama exhibition opened in 1829 at the same time as the Hull panorama was being staged.[13]

At the Hull Fine Arts Exhibition of 1829, there were approximately seventeen works with titles suggesting coastal, river, and marine landscapes amongst the two hundred and forty two exhibits. More artists were represented than previously; eighty-seven plus twenty-two 'Honorary' (in total, eight were women) compared with seventy five artists plus nineteen 'Honorary' in 1827. The majority of contributors gave no further details other than their names, resident town, or address. For the first time, John Ward styles himself as a "Marine Painter" exhibiting six works, all but one for sale.

The ensuing years up to the 1835 Hull Fine Arts Exhibition saw the completion of the New Public Rooms, a prestigious building that allowed the organisers to divide the exhibits into five rooms beginning with watercolours and oil pictures. A third room (probably both watercolours and oils) preceded a fourth for watercolours and sculpture. A fifth room had the smallest number of exhibits, twenty in all, and seems to have been allocated for the local drawing masters and their pupils. Half of the works shown were by women and with very few exceptions, the artists represented in this room were resident in Hull. John Ward exhibited nine paintings, all for sale; *Frigate preparing to Anchor; Views on the Humber (3); Stoneferry; Storm after Powell; The Whale Fishery; Shipping, the Calm; View of Mr. Gleadow's Warehouse on Fire, taken from the Garrison Jetty.*

Exhibiting for the first time at Hull was W J Huggins (1781-1845) who, together with one of his sons, submitted four marine subjects. The work of Huggins (Snr), formerly a sailor with the East India Company, became known through aquatints and engravings and on account of his interest in nautical detail may have been known to Ward. The noted biographer Samuel Redgrave (1802-1876) was, however, rather dismissive; "In 1834 he was appointed marine painter to William IV who esteemed his work rather for its correctness than its art".

Perhaps the most striking feature of the way in which the Hull exhibitions had developed over the eight years from 1827 to 1835, was the rise in numbers and prominence of watercolour paintings. This growth reflected the way in which watercolours were being recognised as works of art in their own right. Between 1800 and 1835, 'waters' became increasingly successful in challenging both the prejudices of patrons and collectors and the dominance of history and portrait painting in oils, the latter being the principal medium and subject matter for works accepted at the Royal Academy. What had previously been considered to be lowly 'stained' or 'tinted drawings' became increasingly popular, not only for their affordability and portability but also for their intrinsic merits. They were particularly well suited for capturing the effects of light and atmosphere of the British climate and were especially effective for marine landscape painting. Emerging from this innovation was an identifiably British school of living painters who were challenging the ascendancy of continental painters both ancient and modern.[14]

The rise of the professional watercolour artist at this time was greatly assisted by the growth of watercolour societies and alternative venues to the Royal Academy that developed both in London and in provincial centres such as Hull. The question then arises as to how or whether John Ward was influenced by this major development amongst his contemporaries. The Society of Painters in Watercolours (now the Royal Watercolour Society) held its first exhibition in 1805. The manifesto of its exhibition in 1821 clearly expresses the ambitions and mood of the times;

> Painting in Water colour may justly be regarded as a new art, and in its present application, the invention of British Artists. Within a few years the materials employed in this species of painting, and the manner of using them, have been equally improved by new chemical discoveries and successful innovations on the old methods of practice. The feeble tinted drawings, formerly supposed to be the utmost efforts of this art, have been succeeded by pictures not inferior to oil paintings.[15]

The immense public interest in watercolours and the desire by amateurs and professionals to explore this medium is demonstrated by a manual entitled *The Art of Painting in Watercolours*. Dated 1818, it is described as the 18th edition and was the personal property of Michaelangelo Lowther (1808-98) a Hull-based artist and drawing master, contributor to the Hull exhibitions and son of Phineas Lowther (1780-1856), also an artist and drawing master. This copy is inscribed in ink beneath the title label; "sold by Phineas Lowther No.5 Saville St. Hull , Artists Repository, price one shilling".[16]

The manual is a forty-two page booklet, without illustrations, describing the preparation of pigments, mixing and application and concludes with two brief sections "Painting on glass" and "Painting in crayon". It was one of a series of volumes published at a shilling each by James Whittle and Richard Holmes Laurie, London. These were; *The Painter's Companion*, *The Art of Drawing*, *The Art of Drawing in Perspective*, *The Art of Painting in Miniature*, *The Artist's Assistant*, and *The Art of Painting in Oil*. Also from Whittle and Laurie were; *Sandby's Etchings and Landscapes* and *Figures* (10s 6d), *The School of Art (Drawing book)*(15s) and *A new drawing book containing a variety of designs from Ibbetson, Chamberlin, Angelica Kauffmann etc (7s 6d).*

Among the three hundred and fifty eight exhibits at Hull in 1835, around half were watercolours. They were selected from the one hundred and twenty two artists and sculptors who submitted their work, many of whom were (or about to become) pioneers of what is now referred to as the "Great Age of British Watercolours"; e.g. Duncan, Crome, Carter, Nicholson, Copley Fielding, Gastineau, Prout, Varley, Carmichal and Laporte. This roll call of some of leading watercolourists of the 1830's included former presidents and founders of the main watercolour societies that flourished in the early nineteenth century. Several of these artists were closely associated with marine landscapes, if not exclusively so. A few painted in both watercolours and oil; Thomas Miles Richardson (qv) and J W Carmichael (1799-1868) in particular.

John Wilson Carmichael visited Hull in 1827 and completed his *Shipyard at Hessle Cliffs* in 1829. It is now in the Ferens Gallery. Born in Newcastle, he was press ganged at the age of twelve into the navy aboard a powder-ship of the fleet whose Captain encouraged him to draw (Villar 1995). After the ending of hostilities c.1815 he was apprenticed as a shipwright in his home town. The enlightened owners of the yard, themselves amateur artists, gave him further encouragement and introduced him to Richardson (ibid), very probably as his drawing master.

By the time of Hull's first exhibition in 1827, Carmichael had set up his own studio and launched his career as an artist. His first works were historical sea battles and by the age of seventeen had completed a major commission for Newcastle Trinity House of the Bombardment of Algiers. At the time of the first Hull exhibition, he had married and when his first child was baptised signed himself as a 'Drawing Master'. By the third Hull exhibition, he advertised himself as 'marine painter and teacher of drawing,' had launched his illustrated publication of *Views on the Tyne*, and moved his studio next door to the Northern Academy of Arts. Carmichael sent four canvases to the 1835 Hull exhibition; *Leaving Port*, *Morning*; *Sea Piece*, *Calm*; *Sea Piece*, *Storm*, and *Making the Harbour*, and *Early Morning, Moonlight*; all were for sale. Several years later, he made a watercolour copy of Ward's lithograph of the *Dandie Dinmont* published in 1848 (see Fig 12).[17]
Carmichael moved from London to Scarborough in 1863 and continued to paint coastal scenes of the town and its harbour.

We do not know whether Ward visited Newcastle or to what extent he may have been influenced by Carmichael or other artists connected with the Newcastle Institution for the Promotion of the Fine Arts. The parallels with Carmichael's career as an artist do, however, offer interesting comparisons with Ward's own artistic development over the years of the Hull and Newcastle exhibitions from 1823 to 1835. Carmichael expresses his own debt to the Northern Academy in these terms;

> Sept 23, 1829
>
> .....I am glad to have an opportunity of acknowledging the great benefit which I have derived from the sight of pictures painted by the best of the British Masters....to which...I attribute the advance I have made in the Fine Arts, with also the opportunity of offering my own productions for sale.
>
> Quoted in Villar (1995)

We also do not know whether John Ward visited the Royal Academy in 1831 to see his own work hung for the first time in this highly prestigious exhibition. Had he done so, he would have witnessed a feast of works of art from the leading artists of the day; 1234 exhibits of which 478 were portraits. Forty-five members of the Academy were represented among 655 non-members of which the aspiring 'marine painter' was one.

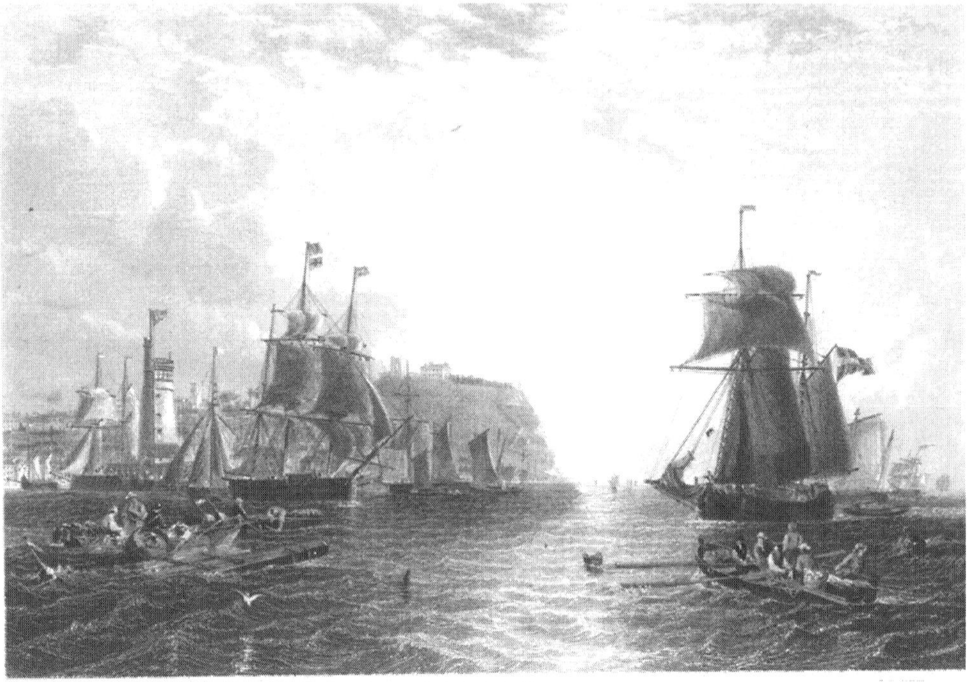

Fig. 39 J W Carmichael (1799-1839) *Scarborough* 1 Oct 1851.

Ship Prints, Drawing Manuals and Guides for Marine Painters

So far, the progress of Ward's career has been in described mainly in terms of his rise from artisan painter to artist through the chronology of his oil paintings. In Chapter One, brief mention was made to his work as a printmaker. This aspect of his art became increasingly evident and led eventually to his project to compile a series of marine prints and a manual for marine artists. This commitment to printmaking was a substantial and significant feature of his later career. We know that he owned two presses for printing lithographs and that his posthumous studio sale included several thousand prints. These works have provided evocative and compelling images of marine subjects before the advent of photography and are of a quality that rivals many of his contemporaries. In their own way, they are the equal of his work in oils by the manner in which his underlying mastery as a draughtsman is brought to the fore. What were the origins of his attraction to marine printmaking and how did he acquire the necessary skills?

If we are looking for a source that may have influenced the design of Ward's, Manual, we need seek no further than Philip Le Comte's *Vyftig Afbeeldingden van Schepen en Vaartuigen* published in Amsterdam in 1831 (see Figs 39 - 41). This consists of fifty lithographic illustrations preceded by sixty pages of explanatory text and shows a whole range of ship types, from cutters and schooners to a man-of-war and a paddle steamer with an occasional plate giving details of rigging. The presentation is very simple and in common with most of Ward's prints all vessels are shown in profile or three quarter view with small craft in the offing to add to the pictorial content. The overall effect of Le Compte's prints is very similar to Ward's except that the former have a coarser stippling and lack the delineation of fine detail so characteristic of Ward. We know nothing about Le Comte himself except he was a Knight of the Order of William, a rare and highly prized honour originating in the Netherlands in 1815.

Close contact between Hull and the Low Countries make it likely that Ward could have seen a copy of Le Comte's book or some of the illustrations from it. However Ward was trying to convey far more detail of the form and dimensions of the various vessels with a series of schematic views to which are applied numbers and letters. However, no sheets have been discovered which give a key to these sections, rigging plans etc and it is likely that Ward was leaving the key to the very end of the project, to be made after completing the set of illustrations, an ambition thwarted by his premature death.

There had been many earlier publications in England which provided general source material for artists including Rudolf Ackermann's *Lessons for Beginners in the Fine Arts* (1796). Such publications consisted mainly of plates of landscapes and classical subjects for copying.[18] Very few were intended specifically for marine artists, although some, including John Varley's (1778-1842) *Treatise on the Principles of Landscape Design with General Observations and Instructions to Young Artists* c1816 and another from one of his pupils, David Cox's (1783-1854) *Treatise on Landscape Painting* published in 1814, featured marine and river scenes. Plates from these and other manuals could be hired as exemplars from Ackermann's shop and gallery in the Strand, London or were sold individually to drawing masters in the provinces. Many of the manuals and sketchbooks available in the early decades of the nineteenth century provided 'progressive studies' for watercolour painting to cater for the growing popularity of this medium.

Marine Architecture was the subject of John Charnock's (1756-1807) exhaustive three volume study published in 1800-1802. Although not intended as a drawing manual, it nevertheless provided a definitive compilation of ninety three engravings and aquatints of vessels together with technical drawings, titled as; *An Enlarged and Progressive view of the Nautical Regulations and Naval History, Both Civil and Military of all Nations, Especially of Great Britain......from the earliest period to the present time.*

A notable exception to these general trends was *Liber Nauticus and Instructor in the Art of Marine Drawing*, published by Dominic and J.T. Serres. Part One (1805) comprises an explanatory text and seven plates of men-of-war, profile and three quarter views, and studies of water in different weather conditions (see Fig. 45). Part Two (1806) has fifty one plates of developed compositions of mercantile and naval vessels each with a descriptive legend. In Part One, Serres (1759-1825) sets out; 'An Address to the Amateurs of Marine Drawing.'

> .....Many are the obstacles to the attainment of a proficiency in drawing marine subjects particularly as it is not only requisite that a person desires of excellence in this Art should possess a knowledge of the construction of a Ship or of what is denominated Naval Architecture together with the proportion of masts & yards, the width, depth & cut of the sails &c but he should likewise be acquainted with Seamanship.
> ..... (the present publication)..will I hope convey a general & accurate idea of a Ship and its Component parts, even to such as are unacquainted with these floating monuments to British Power. The 2nd part of this work which was designed by my Father will be found to contain specimens of all the different kinds of ships & vessels which are made still further interesting and amusing by the introduction, in the background of scenes taken from Nature and characteristic of Ships.

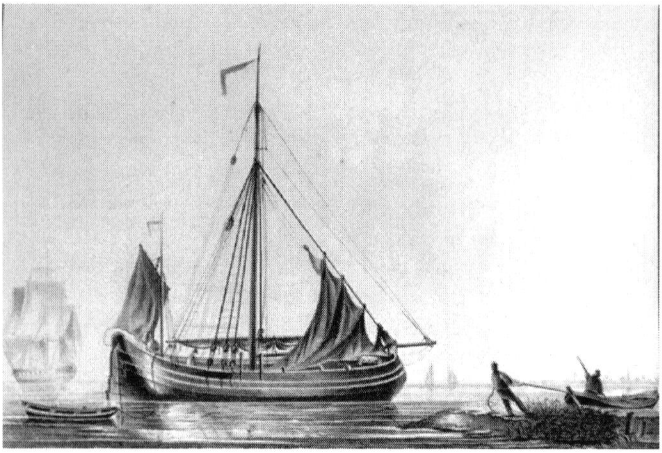

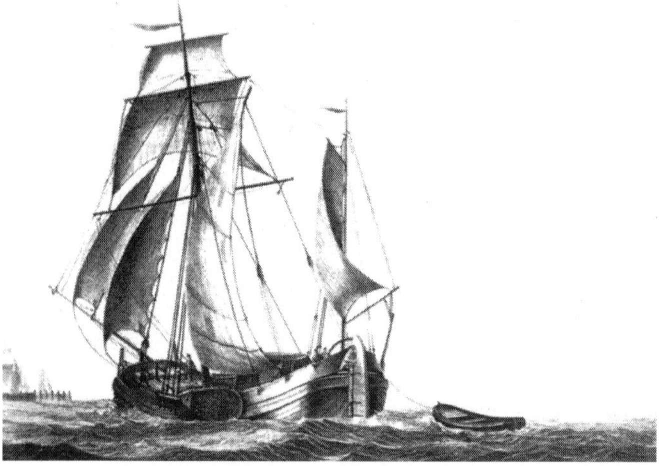

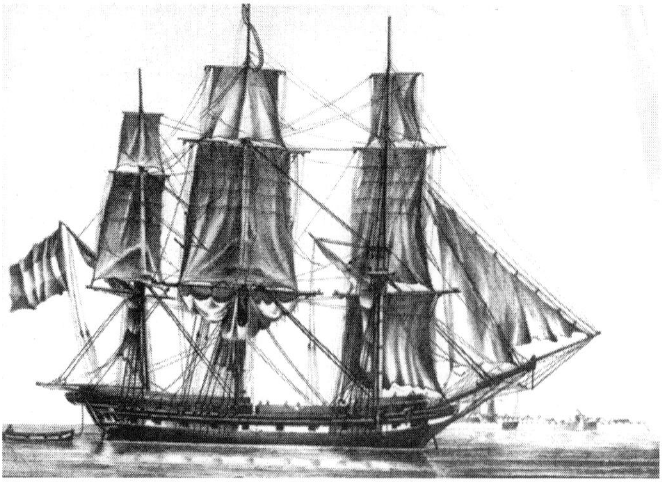

Figs. 40, 41, 42. Philip Le Comte *Pictures of Ships and Vessels*, lithographs, 1831

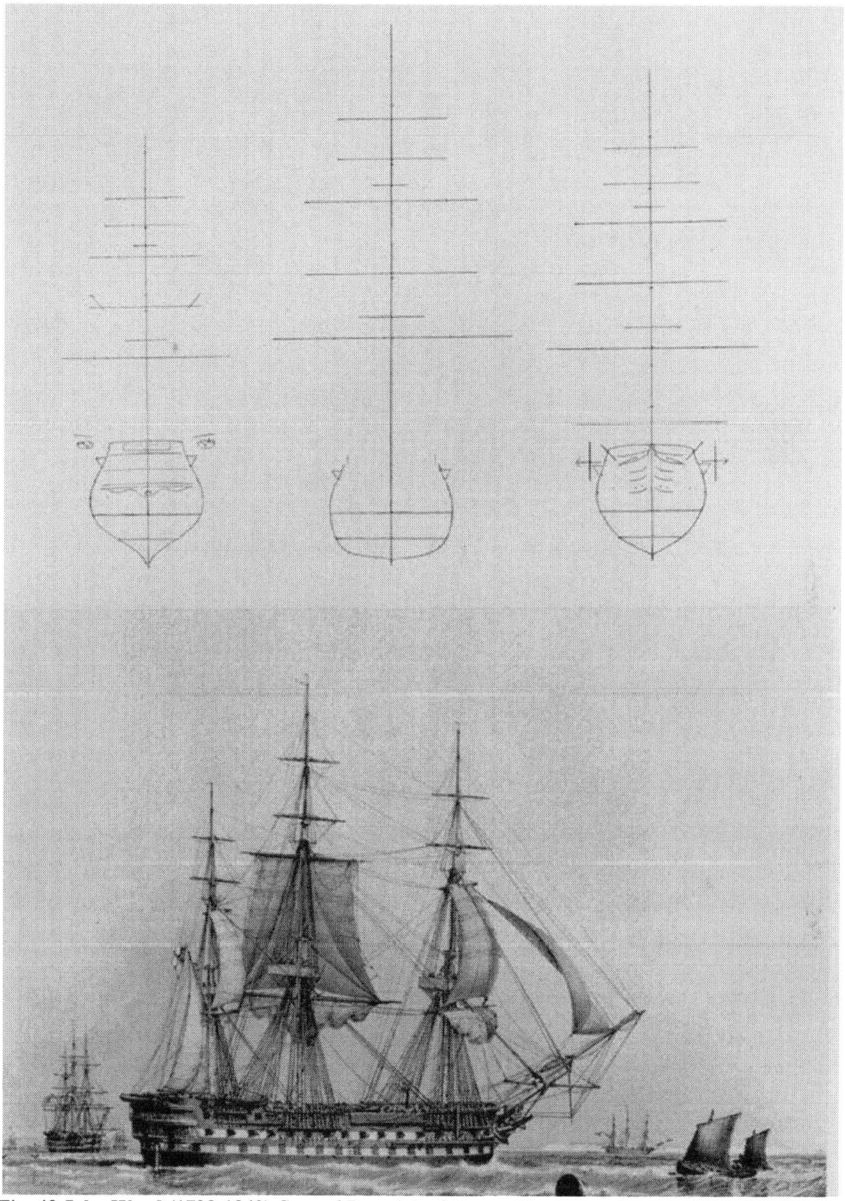

Fig. 43 John Ward (1798-1849) ***Second Rate Asia, 84 guns. Hove to, main topsail aback, canvas hauled up*****. Lithograph. Hull Maritime Museum.**

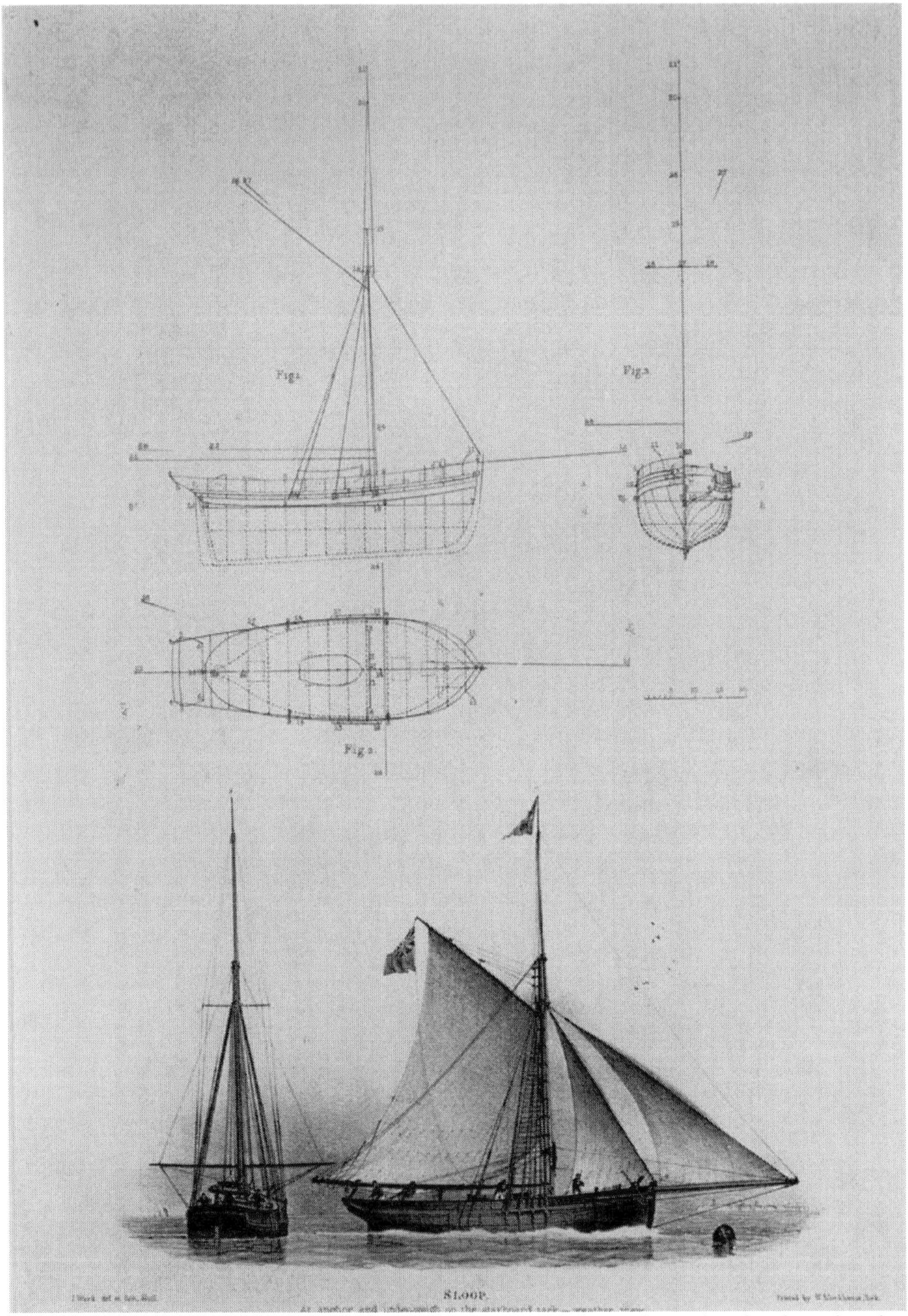

Fig. 44 John Ward (1708-1849) *Sloop. At anchor and under-weigh, on the starboard tack-weather view.* Lithograph. Hull Maritime Museum.

J.M.W. Turner's (1775-1851) *Liber Studiorum* published over a lengthy period between 1807 and 1819 includes seascapes but this series of etchings and engravings are essentially studies in composition. The images reveal little detail of rigging and construction and are quite unhelpful as a source for the novice marine artist though providing a gallery of vessels in a variety of positions, in calm and storm, which the already experienced painter might find useful (see Figs. 46,47).

Samuel Prout (1783-1852) who exhibited at Hull in 1829 and 1835 was amongst the first to produce manuals for young artists, mainly to support his extensive practice as a drawing master in his early career. This series of publications comprising etchings of panoramic shore and estuary scenes were published in a variety of titles including; *Picturesque Delineations in the Counties of Devon and Cornwall* (1812), *Rudiments of Landscape in Progressive Studies* (1813) and *Studies of Boats and Coast Scenery for Landscape and Marine Painters* (1816).

The types of prints that Ward favoured for his own project were "lithographs". This was the medium also used in Prout's manuals and sketch books from c.1820. Perhaps the crowning achievement of this series of publication was Prout's *Microcosm: The Artist's Sketchbook of Groups of Figures, Shipping and other Picturesque Objects*, comprising twenty four tinted lithographs, printed by the master printer Charles Hullmandel in 1841 (see Fig.48).

Illustrated books on marine subjects also provided images to copy; copying being the main means of instruction for aspiring marine artists. James Ralf's *Naval Chronology* published in parts c.1820, offered sixty plates including several engraved by F. C. Lewis (1779-1856), a contributor of four works to the Hull exhibition in 1827 together with his eldest son J. F. Lewis, RA (1805-1876).

Another compilation of prints of ship types is the well known series by the English painter and engraver, Edward William Cooke (1811-1880). Published in parts from March 1828 to December 1829, his *Fifty Plates of Shipping and Craft* comprise etchings of merchant and naval craft, typically shown in a London setting or beached. Each print is simply titled and there is no explanatory text (see Figs. 37 and 48,49).As well as picturesque groupings there are also profiles with minimal backgrounds which may have helped Ward develop ideas for his own guide. Cooke's work may have been the immediate stimulus for Le Comte's publication though the latter's presentation is closer to G. Groenwegen *Verscheide soarten van Hollandse Vaartinge*, first published at Rotterdam in 1786 and last issued in 1801.It had twelve illustrations with simple views of ships and no attempt at making a picturesque scene.[19] Whereas some of these images are attractive compositions that include the fine nautical detail notably lacking in Turner's *Liber Studiorum*, it is likely that Groenwegen was an influence on Cooke, at least those plates with the simpler views.

Another influence on marine printmaking was undoubtedly Louis Francia (1772-1839) watercolourist and marine painter who supplied drawings to the Cooke family of engravers. Francia published *Marine Sketches*, comprising four lithographs in 1822, a copy of which E W Cooke purchased in 1830.[20]

In 'Shipping and Craft' there are a number of images which are primarily picturesque. Overall, however, Cooke produced representations of vessels that were fastidiously correct in their technical detail. The collection was aimed at the connoisseur and those with a strong maritime interest (ship owners, mariners and naval officers etc.) rather than being an attempt to instruct the marine artist; understandable perhaps when one considers that Cooke was but seventeen at the time. There is certainly material useful to the developing artist but no systematic sequence of ship types nor any attempt to show the

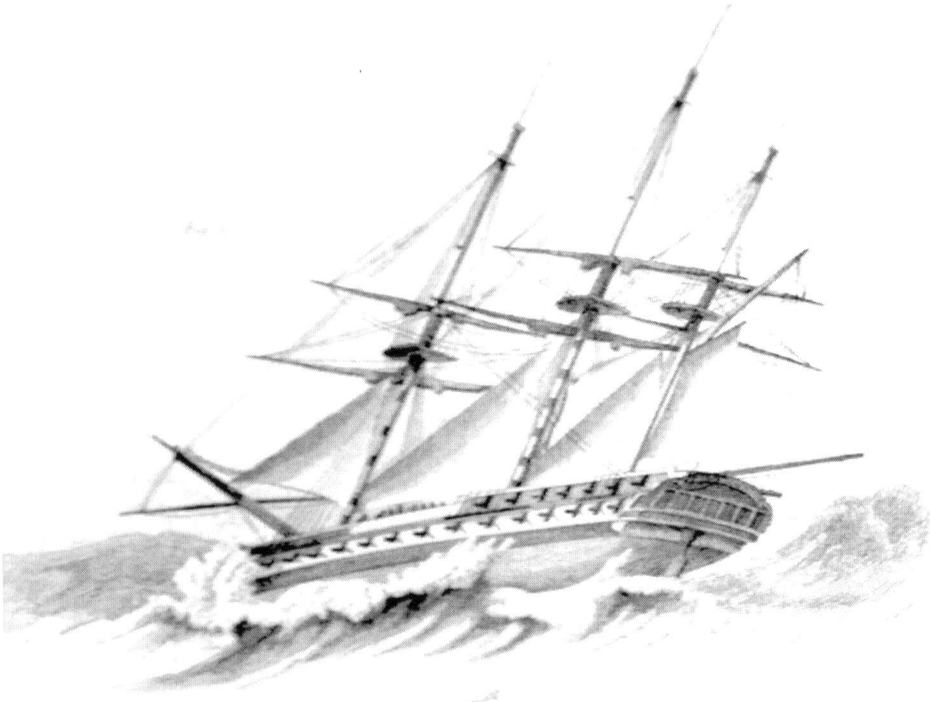

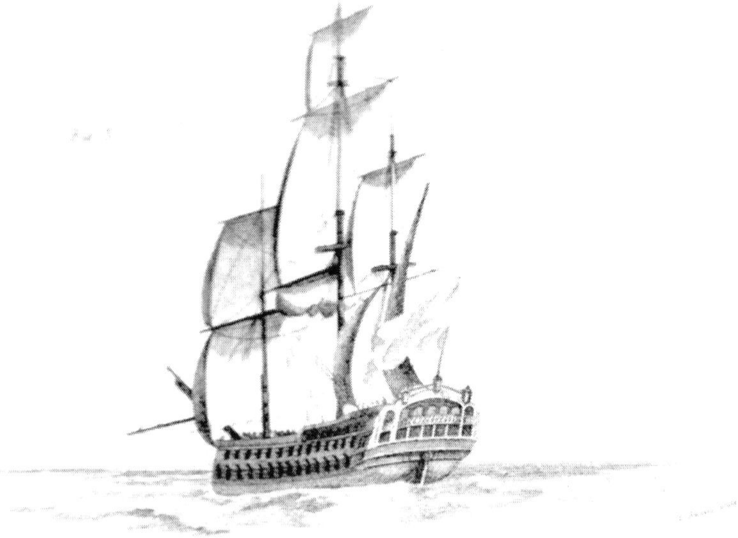

Fig. 45 Detail from Plate XV, Dominic and J T Serres, *Liber Nauticus* Pt.1.1805. (Upper image; *ship 'trying'*- lying in a trough or hollow of the sea in a storm; lower image; *ship under jury foremast*- a temporary mast replacing one carried away by a storm or in battle.)

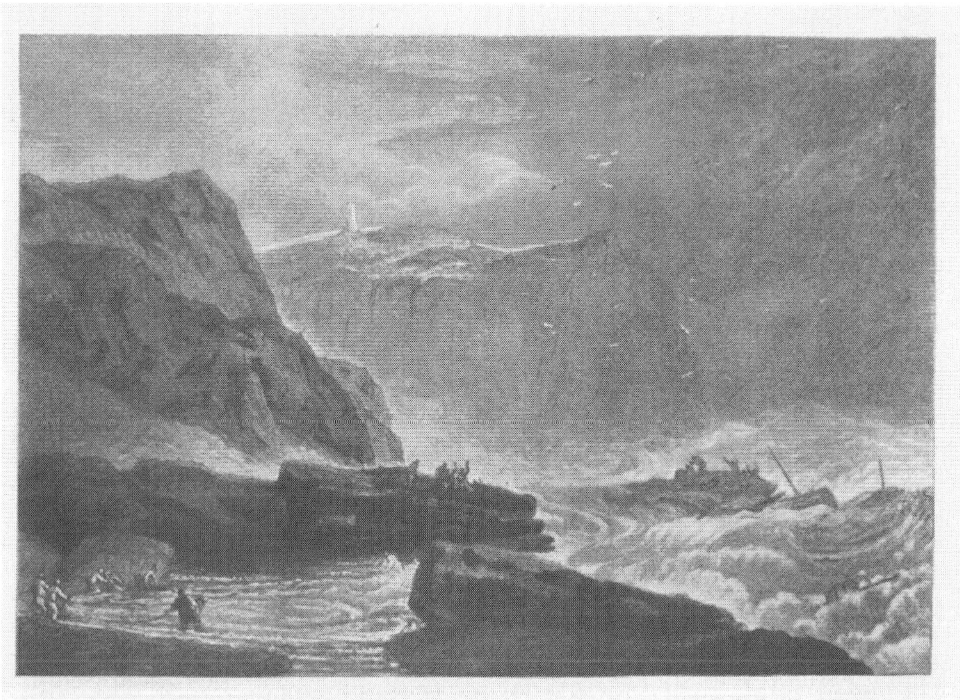

Fig. 46 J M W Turner (1775-1851 *Yorkshire Coast*, 'Liber Studiorum'.

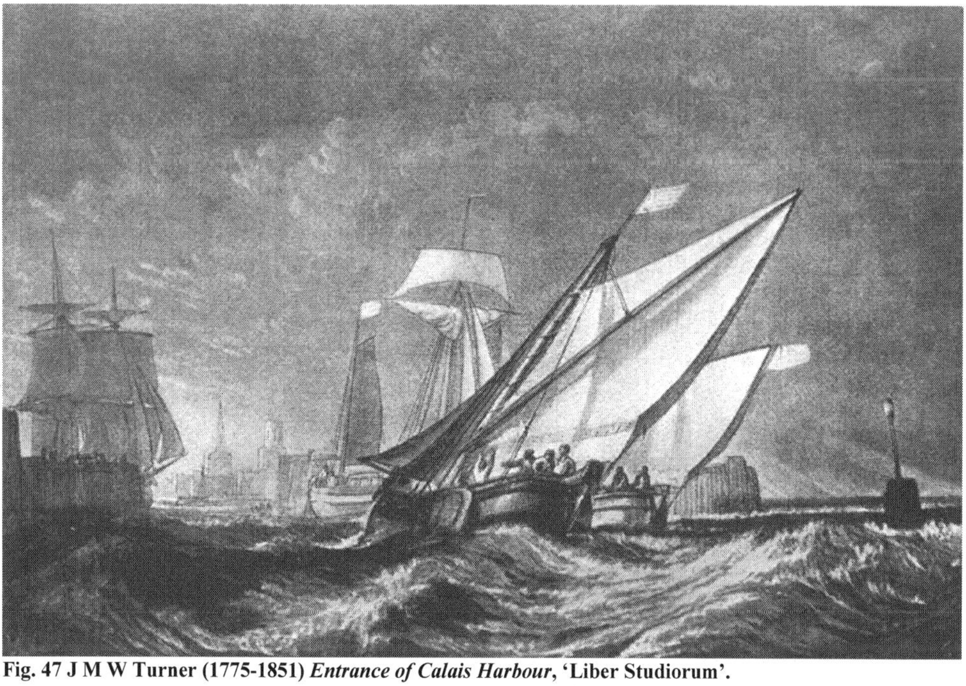

Fig. 47 J M W Turner (1775-1851) *Entrance of Calais Harbour*, 'Liber Studiorum'.

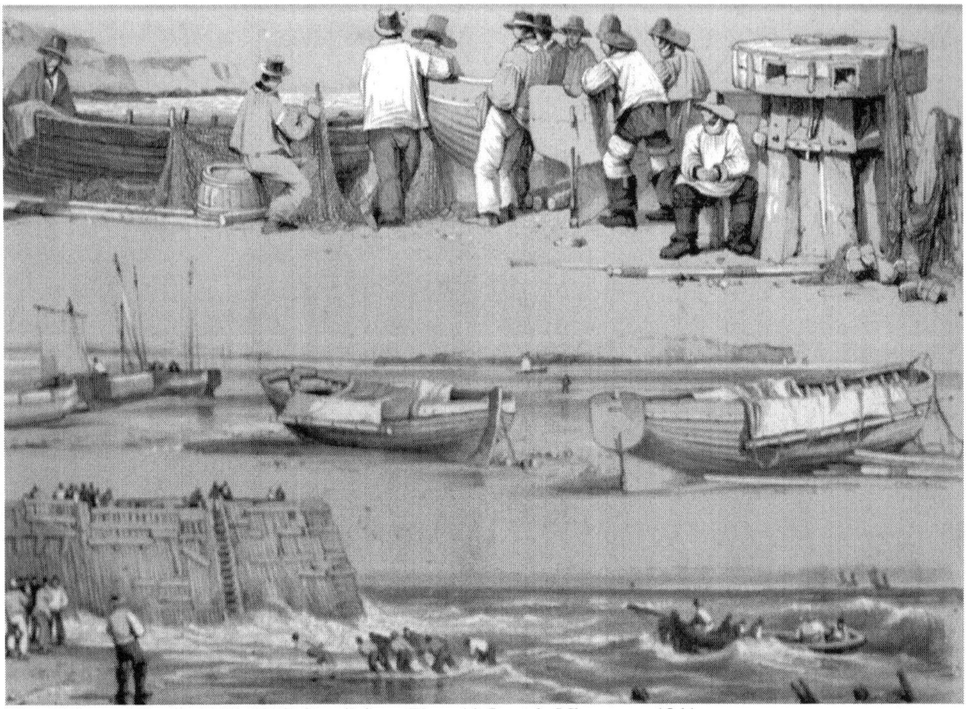

Fig. 48 Samuel Prout (1783-1852) Detail from Plate 11 *Prout's Microcosm* 1841.

proportions of masts and yards and the contours and appearance of each vessel's hull at different angles.

Clarkson Stanfield's (1793-1867) *Coast Scenery in the British Channel* published seven years later in 1836, contains forty plates of maritime subjects, several of which were cut by the renowned engraver of marine views, W B Cooke (1778-1855), the uncle of E.W. Cooke. Again, these scenes were mainly of marine and topographical landscapes with an emphasis on effects and composition.

Probably the best known manuals of marine painting are the pocket handbooks written by J.W. Carmichael. *The Art of Marine Painting in Watercolours* was first issued in 1859 and sold in prodigious quantities but it is concerned with the methodology of sketching and painting and the 'mood' of the sea and sky rather than the technical details of vessels and their rigging. There is little detail offered of individual vessels except for a profile view of a collier brig and another of a frigate each with the sails named. The sample images are, like the plates in *Liber Studiorum*, a variety of compositions in storm and calm and with different cloud formations. Carmichael also published *The Art of Marine Painting in Oil Colours* in 1863, which ran to at least eighteen editions. These two works by Carmichael were of course produced several years after Ward's death. None of the works produced before or since comes anywhere near matching Ward's ambition of providing the marine artist with comprehensive details of each type of craft or attaining the quality of execution of the individual prints, and it is a great pity that the project was never brought to completion.

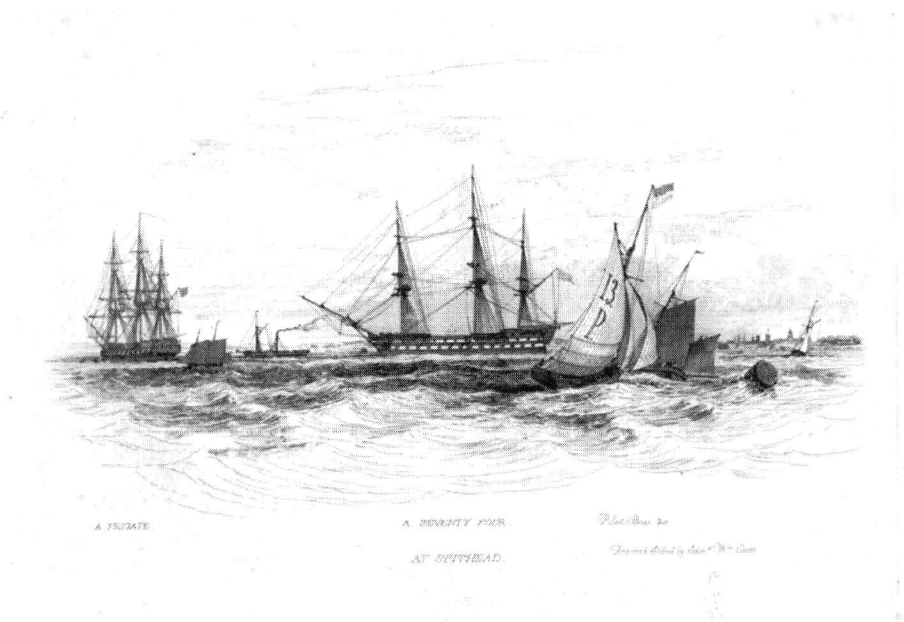

Fig. 49 E W Cooke (1811-1880) Plate from *Shipping and Craft*; *A Seventy Four, Frigate, Pilot Boat & etc at Spithead*, 1829.

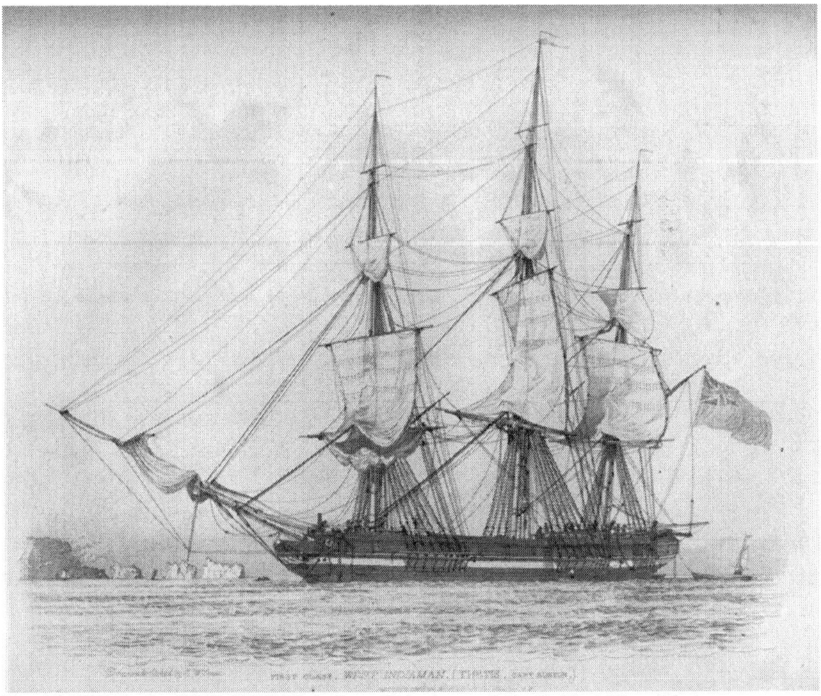

Fig. 50 E W Cooke (1811-1880) Plate from *Shipping and Craft*; *First Class West Indiaman (Thetis. Capt. Burton.) Getting Under Weigh off The Needles, Isle of Wight*. 1829.

'Objects Illustrative of the Fine Arts': John Ward and the Rise of Lithography

The likely trigger point for Ward's Marine Manual was the invention of lithography. This new medium radically altered his ambitions, made additional sources of income available, and created a broader clientele for his work. Making lithographic prints meant that he could produce multiple copies of his paintings or drawings cheaply and quickly. Producing a large exhibition piece in oils on canvas might well take up to two years or more to complete. To reproduce it by using the existing method of engraving a small copper plate would typically take several months. Although multiple copies could be made, copper was a soft metal and rapid wear was inevitable. Whilst more durable steel plates largely replaced copper in c.1820, they were less amenable to subtleties of line and gradations of tone.

Both of these methods required cutting metal that demanded special skills. Such techniques were quite unlike those of a painter who relied on lines and free-forms laid on rather than gouged out of a surface. Mistakes in engraving were virtually impossible to rectify. Paintings and drawings were much more open to corrections and modifications. Lithography, literally meaning "drawing on stone" was a painterly medium whose techniques favoured draughtsmanship and experimentation. The resulting prints, in the hands of gifted craftsmen under the direction of the artist or by artists themselves, were exquisitely evocative of the scenes they portrayed. Whilst lacking the uniqueness of originals, they were, and still remain, works of art in their own right.[21]

This revolutionary technique transformed the circulation of images before the advent of photography. The lithographic process was developed by Alois Senefelder (1771-1834) at the end of the eighteenth century and was patented by him throughout Europe. His standard guide *A Complete Course of Lithography* appeared in English in 1819. The technique of 'stone-printing' or 'polyautography' involved drawing the required image on a high grade limestone block using a greasy, wax based solution ('tusche') or crayon. The image then attracted ink when rolled over the surface of the moistened stone. Paper was placed over the inked stone and printed in a press.

Lithography was around seven times cheaper than copper plate engraving and three times faster for making prints. In this way, artists could reach a wider audience than the occasional connoisseur or patron to satisfy a growing demand for visual records of real or imagined places or events. Various types of printing press were developed for lithography and we know that Ward had two in his studio at the time of his death. This arrangement would have enabled Ward to produce proofs in his own studio without referring to specialist lithographers, the majority of which were based in London.

Prints were very considerably cheaper than an original work of art. They could be produced after the artist's death or for as long as the plates lasted. They could be conveniently sold in books or folios and did not depend upon access to galleries or the salons of the privileged few. They could be bought at stationers, circulating libraries and newsrooms, and from print sellers in shops or from barrows on the street. Artists could supplement their income from publishers, and their customers could satisfy a growing appetite for cultural pursuits. Just as they do today, certain works of art gained celebrity status and their popularity increased through easy access to copies at a fraction of the cost of an original. A whole class of skilled craftsmen emerged to support a burgeoning industry.

Soon after the discovery of lithography, Alois Senefelder visited England and by 1801 had sold his patent to a London publisher. Contacts were made with various artists to invite them to use this new medium of drawing on stone. In 1801, Benjamin West (1738-1820), the serving President of the Royal Academy, was one of the first to take up the

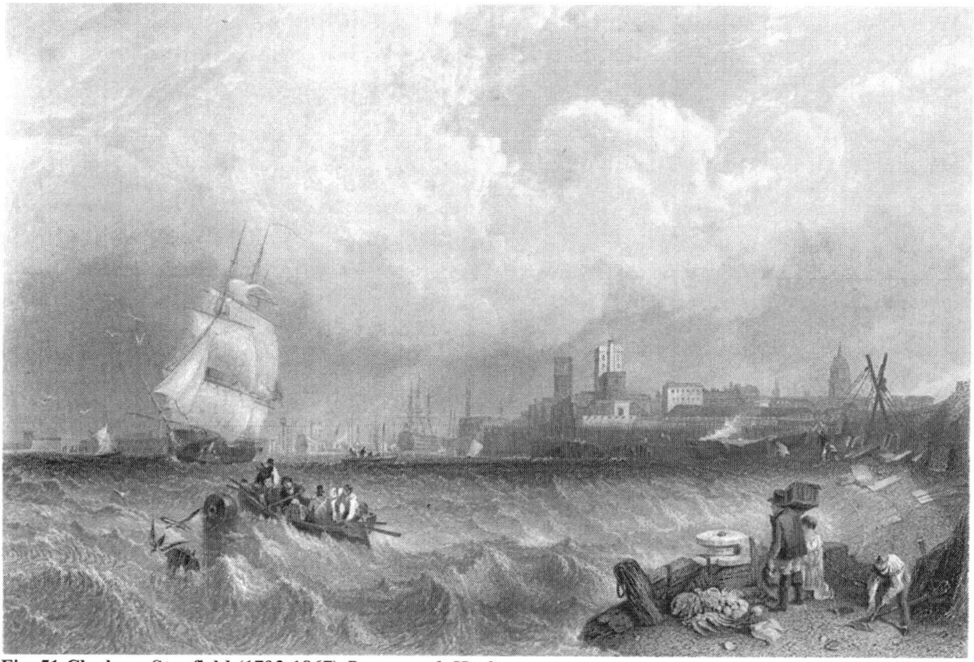

Fig. 51 Clarkson Stanfield (1793-1867) *Portsmouth Harbour.*
During the early nineteenth century, Portsmouth Dockyards were one of the largest industrial sites in the world and the focal point for the maintenance and building of ships for the Royal Navy. It seems highly likely that John Ward would have visited Portsmouth Dockyards to gather material for his Marine Manual.

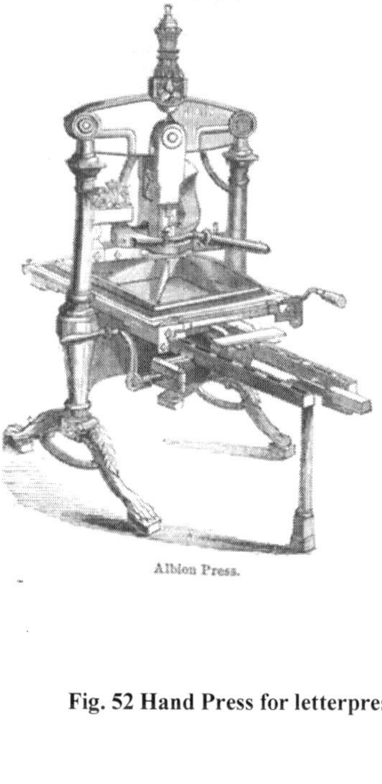

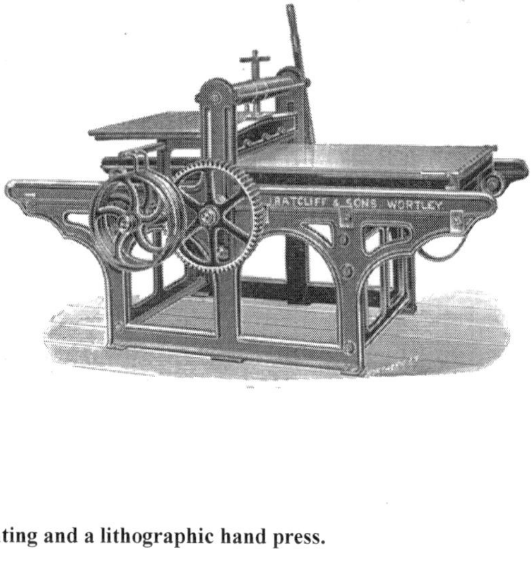

Fig. 52 Hand Press for letterpress printing and a lithographic hand press.

invitation. This opportunity was quickly followed by other artists including Henry Fuseli (1741-1825) who was represented (as a "Deceased Master") by four works at the Hull 1827 exhibition. One of the works shown, *The Night-Mare* (sic) was the subject of one of the earliest English lithographs published in 1802. However, it is not clear whether the exhibit shown at Hull was a lithograph or one of the four versions of the original oil painting that achieved celebrity status after its first showing at the Royal Academy in 1782.

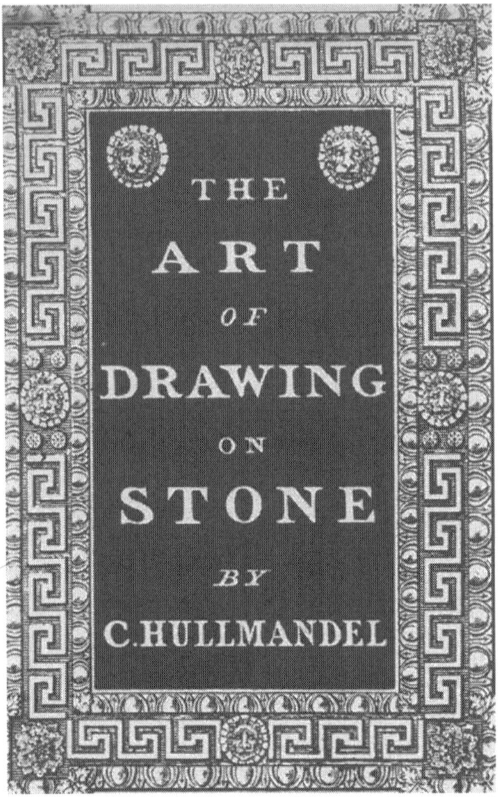

Although sets of lithographs began circulating in England from 1801 onwards, it was not until c.1818 that Charles Hullmandel (1789-1850) set up his lithographic press. He revitalised interest in the medium by the quality of the effects he was able to demonstrate. His *The Art of Drawing on Stone* published in 1824 became a classic text. By 1841, Hullmandel had developed techniques for printing coloured lithographs that either reduced or dispensed entirely with the previous practice of hand colouring by using overlays of four or five tinted stones.[22]

This development further strengthened interest in lithography as a popular medium for several of the early British watercolourists including Francis Nicholson (1753-1844) one of the founders of the Society of Painters in Watercolour and its President in 1813 who directed much of his time and attention to lithography. From c1820 onwards he produced an estimated 800 drawings on stone from which thousands of prints were made for sale or for teaching his pupils. His *Lithographic Impressions from Sketches of British Scenery* published in 1821 also included a lithographed portrait of the artist.

An indirect influence on John Ward may have arisen through the background connections of Nicholson's nephew (possibly his pupil), George Nicholson (1787-1878) who was employed for a time by the Howard family at Castle Howard as a teacher and picture restorer. Nicholson Jnr. was living in Silver Street, Hull when he submitted nine works in oils and watercolours to the Hull exhibition in 1835. Some years previously, he had published topographical lithographs of Yorkshire scenes in 1821 and 1822.

The growth of lithographic printers in London from one in 1814 to twenty five a decade later, gives an indication of the likely influence on Ward of the potential of lithographs. By the time of his death in 1849, the number of litho printers in the metropolis had grown to around ninety workshops.

One of the leading lithographic publishers and printers, ranking in importance alongside Hullmandel and Ackermann (qv), was the firm of Day & Haghe (fl.1833-1867). Louis Haghe (1806-1885) was trained in Belgium as a watercolourist and draughtsman, producing lithographs at the age of seventeen. By 1825, he was working with the printer

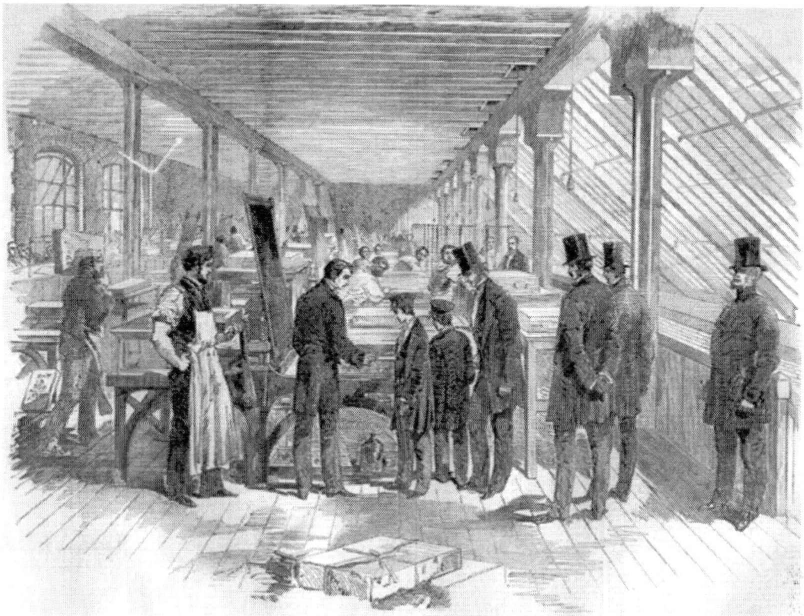

Fig. 53 Visit of the Prince of Wales and Prince Alfred to Day & Haghe, April 1856, *Illustrated London News* vol. xxiii p.488. A lithographic stone is shown in the foreground whilst William Day shows the young princes around the newly extended workshop; "The Royal party then passed through the draughtmen's room, and inspected many lithographs in progress, chiefly incidents of the late war, both naval and military, and some more peaceful subjects, the most remarkable being the drawing for the small edition of Roberts's well known work on the 'Holy Land'.

William Day in London to produce lithographs for various publications. This partnership of artist and printer continued until 1852 when Haghe returned to painting in watercolours.

Haghe's knowledge of this medium and mastery of lithography combined with Day's expertise in tinted stone printing led to some of the finest topographical lithographs of the early nineteenth century. Haghe's sympathetic understanding of watercolours led to the ground breaking collaboration with David Roberts RA (1796-1864) - like Ward, originally apprenticed as a house painter and decorator - to produce *The Holy Land*, *Syria*, *Idumea* and *Arabia* published in twenty parts between 1842 and 1845.

Haghe was the lithographer of choice for many artists and publishers including the marine landscape painter, Henry Barlow Carter (1804-1868) who came to Hull c1830. His *Dutch Brig on the Humber* (1838), now in the Ferens Gallery, is typical of his style and choice of subject matter. Three years earlier, he showed fifteen watercolours at the Hull exhibition in 1835 including views on the Humber by which time he had married the daughter of a Hull family and established his studio and drawing school in Scarborough. In 1840, the local entrepreneur and publisher S W Theakston (1810-1875) commissioned Carter to provide illustrations for one of the first fully illustrated guides to Scarborough and Louis Haghe to lithograph selected scenes. Theakston advertised the Carter-Haghe lithographs for sale in various editions as 'in the Style of Roberts' Holy Land'.[23]

There was no lithographer who had made his mark in Hull so it was quite natural for Ward to turn to William Monkhouse (1812-96).He had quickly established a reputation in York with his print depicting the fire at York Minster in 1840 and his series of *Churches of York* in 1842, just at the time when Ward had decided to devote the bulk of his time to his marine manual. Monkhouse set up in 1836, moving into 4 Lendal in 1840 with a lithographic press his father is said to have bought for him from Day and Haghe. The son of John Monkhouse who had been gardener to the Dean of York Minster he was also an art critic and a friend of the artist William Etty, a native of the town. He and his brother Thomas Monkhouse were great philanthropists to the town and were largely responsible for establishing the "York Industrial and Ragged School". In 1864 he gave up printing to devote himself to photography and in 1866 along with Edward Taylor (architect) and William Hargrove (1826-1918), proprietor of the *York Herald*, set up the "Fine Art and Industrial Exhibition", which again points up the Victorian determination to marry art and design to industry.

His chief associate in the early days of the Lendal establishment was Francis Bedford (1816-94) who was intimately concerned with the 'Minster Fire' print and the church series and quite possibly also embarked on the early stages of the project with Ward. However, around this time he joined Day and Son in London after presenting a letter of recommendation from Monkhouse. Like the latter, Bedford eventually turned to photography and returned from a visit to the Middle East with the Prince of Wales in 1862 with a collection of glass photographic plates. Of incidental interest, Francis John Monkhouse, son of Thomas and nephew of William, was also a printer and lithographer with his own business in York. He married Sarah, daughter of Charles Appleton, architect, of Anlaby, near Hull in 1854 and met a grisly end when he was robbed and murdered twenty years later.[24]

John Ward's rise to local prominence through his marine paintings in oils was steadily achieved alongside the routine business of house and ship painting. At some point during the 1830's he chose to become more of an artist than a jobbing painter. Lithography offered the chance of making up for lost revenue and the prospect of exploring an entirely modern medium. He must also have seen the opportunity of re-directing the enormous flow of picturesque views of landscape towards the potential offered by marine subjects. At the core of his concerns was draughtsmanship rather than effects, unlike many of his contemporaries who chose to pursue the drama of the latter in their marine paintings and prints. Having also experienced the toil of combining self teaching with innovation, Ward moved towards passing on his knowledge to others who were following the same path by offering his services as a drawing master and securing his expertise in a permanent form by means of a manual.

'Floating Monuments of British Power': Ward's Manual of Naval and Merchant Vessels

Handsome ship portraits continued to appear in the 1840s by many artists, but the flow was much reduced compared with the productive years of the previous decade. A number of small panels were produced by Ward at this time that relate to the subjects which also appear in his lithographs. For example, *HMS Britannia at anchor with the Fleet* and the *Maese*, *Amazon*, and *Dandie Dinmont* were panels painted in either 1848 or 1849 (see lithograph, Fig.57). Clearly, he was using the drawings and studies, including watercolours, for his lithographs as material to be re-worked into the sort of seascapes that he had initially derived from the work of William Anderson.

Also painted around this time is a very simple profile portrait of the *Rosetta*, one of W & C L Ringrose's brigs in the Dutch trade. This work is reproduced as a lithograph but reversed left to right. In this print version, the image is used to exemplify the brig as a ship - type and is not otherwise identified.

It appears that the majority of his lithographs, apart from a handful of special commemorative prints, were material for his projected manual of marine painting. (see

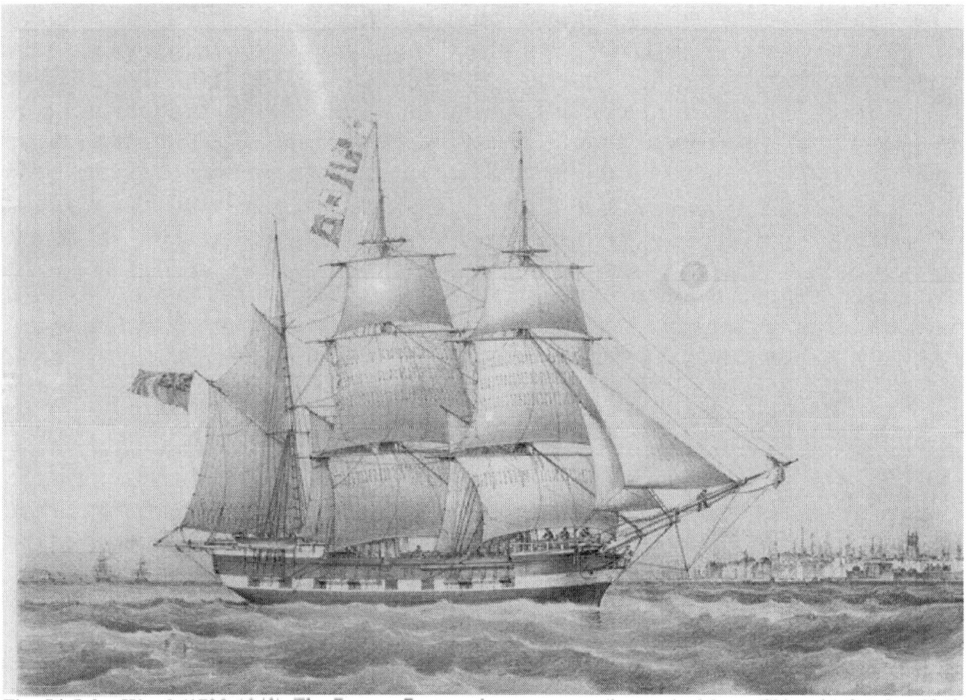

Fig. 54 John Ward (1798-1849) ***The Barque Raymond: commemorating arrival from China 14 October 1843.*** **Lithograph. Hull Maritime Museum.**

Chapter 3). Some of the sheets were sold in batches inside paper covers entitled; 'Marine Studies of British Merchant Vessels' designed and lithographed by John Ward, Hull [M C Peck, printer, Lowgate, Hull]. A series of ten views of naval vessels from a naval cutter to a first rate and a steam vessel was also sold in paper wrappers entitled *The British Navy*. At least one set exists, cloth bound with leather spine and corners, the cover stamped in gold letters with the title *Ward's British Navy*. In addition, the artist's lithograph of the barque *Raymond* is also bound with the latter volume.

This volume like the sets in paper wrappers has two introductory pages with text that begins;

> A series of Ten Views illustrative of the several rates and classes of Vessels in Her Majesty's Navy, Lithographed in a tinted manner from the Drawings taken at the different Naval Establishments, by J. Ward and expressly executed as a work of information and instruction.

The large number of prints involved and the need to maintain a high standard of reproduction clearly rendered the project an expensive one and difficult to bring to fruition without significant patronage.

Unfortunately, we do not know anything about John Ward's visit to the south of England to make his preparatory sketches; neither precisely when nor where he went or how long he stayed, but the results are outstanding. There is, however, a pencil drawing of the paddle steamer *Alban* that is one of the vessels in the series of ten naval prints, signed and dated 'Sept. 5 1841'.[25] This is a clear indication that he was collecting his sketches of these craft some two years before his announcement in the press.

In addition to the prints already discussed, Ward lithographed a group of four views of HMS *Britannia* , each 13in x 9in, at anchor and underway, which are amongst the finest studies of a man-of-war ever produced. (see pages 166 - 173 and front cover).

In 1842, he exhibited stern and bow views of this vessel at the Royal Academy along with pictures of a ninety-gun ship and a first rate of 110. These studies were presumably examples of the original drawings for the large-scale prints of the *Britannia* and his series of ten naval craft confirming that his tour of 'naval establishments' must have been before 1842. Whether this was undertaken solely in 1841 or over a number of previous years we do not know.[26]

His contribution to the Hull exhibition in 1842 of 'Objects Illustrative of the Fine Arts', included bow and stern view of HMS *Britannia,* a sketch in pencil of a thirty-gun frigate, and 'Diagrams and Drawings of Vessels in Watercolour'. To the same event, works by Ward were loaned by several clients and collectors e.g., William Ringrose, *View off Spurn*, George Robinson, *View of Hull*, John Levitt, *Marine View*, and a Mr J James, *View on the Humber*. Two pieces from the Wharton Collection, *View on the Thames*, and *River View and Shipping* were also included.

In the following year, Ward published a print in 1843 to commemorate the barque *Raymond* inscribed, 'The first vessel direct from China'. Also issued in 1843 was the print of the *Columbine* of the Gainsborough Steam Packet Company. There was a regular service along the Trent between Hull and Gainsborough, the steamers berthed at the Hull pier outside the Minerva inn, as can be seen in the oil painting of *The buoy yacht Zephyr* which includes a fine image of the p.s Pelham. Another print appeared in 1845 to celebrate the arrival of the barque *Wanderer*, the first ship ever to leave Hull with a full cargo destined for China. She sailed under the command of her owner, John Priest, and returned with 55 tons of tea, unloaded at London. An oil painting of this vessel recently passed through Christies auction house.

Two years later in 1847, another commemorative print appeared, this time recording the first Grand Regatta of the Royal Yorkshire Yacht Club. It was dedicated to Thomas Richardson the owner of the *Hilda* and winner of the challenge cup. A runner up was the *Whim*, owned by Joseph Gee (one of Hull's major ship owners, including the *William Lee*, already mentioned) Vice Commodore of the RYYC from 1847 to 1851 and a member of the Royal Yacht Squadron.

The iron schooner *Dandie Dinmont* was published as a print c1848 and dedicated to George Cammell, a local ship owner. He had been agent for the *P S Forfarshire*, the ill-fated vessel lost on the Farnes in 1838. A fine canvas of this vessel, painted for Cammell by Ward is now in the Ferens Art Gallery. The *Dandie Dinmont* was printed by Goddard and Lancaster of Hull and a print of the *Vivid* by Goddard in 1845. All the remaining lithographs were printed by William Monkhouse of York.[27] Each copy has the artist's signature inscribed usually in the form; 'J. Ward del. et lith.' indicating that Ward not only originated the design but drew directly on the lithographic stone, or at least corrected the drawing after it had been transferred to the stone

Between 1840 and 1847, Ward exhibited more naval subjects in London, e.g. at the Royal Academy in 1843 he exhibited the *Britannia*, *Pique*, *Greyhound*, and *Nautilus* (all of which feature in the naval lithographs) and at the British Institution between 1843 and 1847 he showed six works. Ward's most ambitious canvas featured HMS Britannia with units of the fleet at Spithead. Signed and dated 1847 and exhibited at the Royal Academy in the same year, it measures 67in x 97in - the largest he ever produced (see Fig.55). For many years, this canvas was in the possession of Sir Edward Bates (1816-1896), the Liverpool

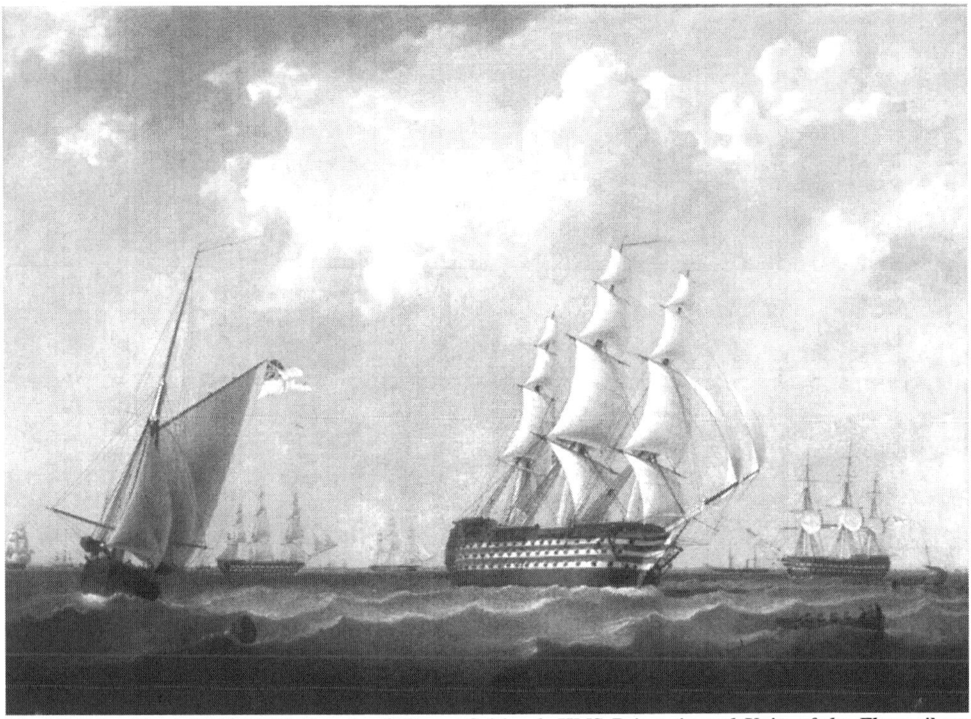

Fig. 55 John Ward (1798-1849) ***Vessels of War at Spithead: HMS Britannia and Units of the Fleet*****; oil on canvas, 67 in. x 97 in. Hull Maritime Museum.**

ship owner and director of the Cunard Steamship Company and son-in-law of the Hull merchant and ship owner, Thomas Thompson. After disappearing into an American collection, the picture has once again returned to Hull and was purchased for the Hull Maritime Museum in 1998.

In his latter years, Ward was probably in contact with Robert Strickland Thomas (1787-1853) a retired naval officer and part-time painter. He joined the service at the age of eighteen and was influenced by Capt. George Tobin, himself an amateur painter, who was a friend of Thomas Luny (1759-1837), an important figure in the history of marine painting in Britain. R S Thomas retired in 1815 with the rank of Lieutenant and settled in Portsmouth supplementing his pension by painting pictures of naval subjects. The two main features of a splendid canvas entitled 'the White Squadron at the Nore' are HMS *Britannia* and a cutter in full sail. The composition is borrowed directly from Ward's Academy piece of 1847 and whilst the stern three-quarter view of *Britannia* is the same as that which appears in Ward's lithograph, it is reversed left to right.

We can conjecture, therefore, whether Thomas copied from Ward's finished work, or maybe through friendship with the Hull artist, had direct access to the original studies. Both men exhibited at the Royal Academy, and in the year that Ward showed his bow and stern views of HMS *Britannia*, Thomas hung his canvas of the *Battle of Navarino*. It may be that they had originally met when Ward visited the south of England in 1841, or earlier, to make his sketches of the various types of warship used both in the preparation of his print series and the Academy piece of 1847. Richard B Spence (fl. 1850-75) also made a

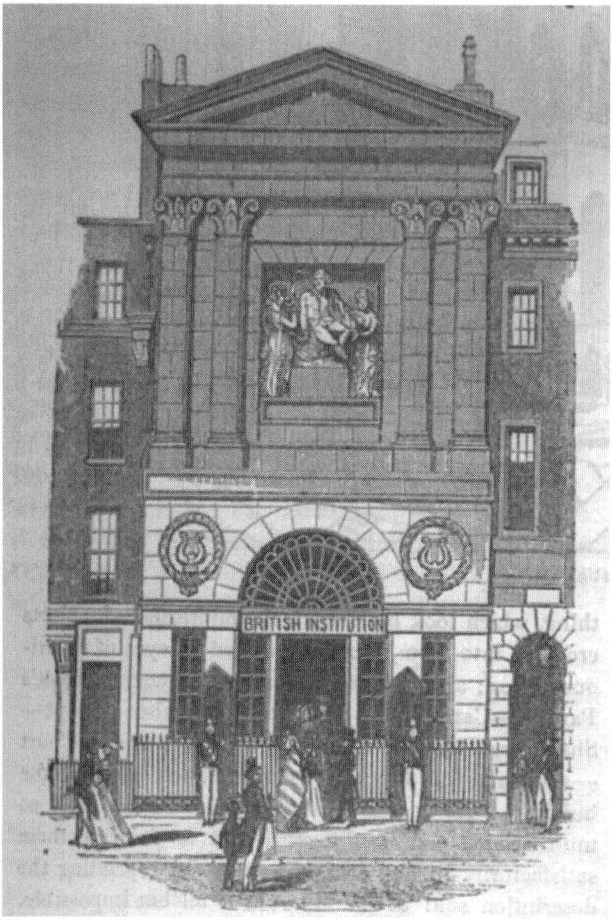

Fig. 56 The British Institution (1808-1869) an alternative venue to the Royal Academy with alternating exhibitions of Old Masters and living artists.

comparable composition, although with a fortified harbour shown in the background and all executed in a racy, somewhat slick manner.

Ward also produced a large number of lithographs of merchant vessels. His intention clearly was to illustrate an example of each type of craft, both sail and steam, which traded out of the Humber and indeed out of any major port in the land. Notable by its absence, however, is the Humber Keel, a classic local sailing barge that appears so often as an ancillary subject in his ship-portraits. It was excluded perhaps because it was unique to the Hull region and not generally encountered very far afield.

The simplest of this series of lithographs show a profile view with the name of the type of vessel below and a short description of the set of the sail and state of the wind. In some cases, the vessel is represented by more than one print when it is shown in different attitudes. The names of the artist and publisher are inscribed on the small sheets (6in x 8in) but are absent from the larger sheets (15in x 10¾in overall) which include the same views but accompanied by a plan view, elevation and transverse section(s) recording the proportions of the mast(s) and yards. A full sheet may show a particular craft in various

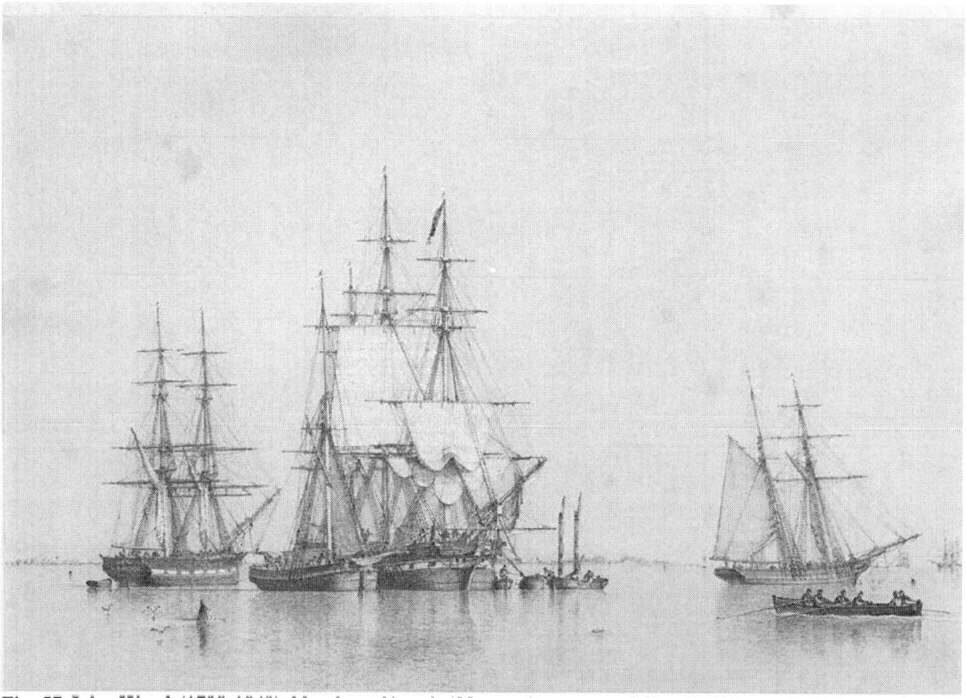

Fig. 57 John Ward (1798-1849) *Merchant Vessels* (Maese, Amazon and Dandie Dinmont). Lithograph. Hull Maritime Museum.

views in the one lithograph, again with title and simple description; usually cream tinted and with the caption *Marine Studies* printed outside the picture area. Other sheets portray ship types in monochrome, lacking a defined picture area and printed one above the other, two to a sheet.

A series of merchant vessels bound in paper covers (13¾in x 19in) is entitled *Marine Studies of British Merchant Vessels*, etc. The selection is preceded by a single introductory page followed by two sheets of monochrome studies, two to a page, and five cream-tinted prints depicting respectively a sloop, brig, and ship in various views, and finally an assemblage of merchant vessels of different types. (see Chapter 3.)

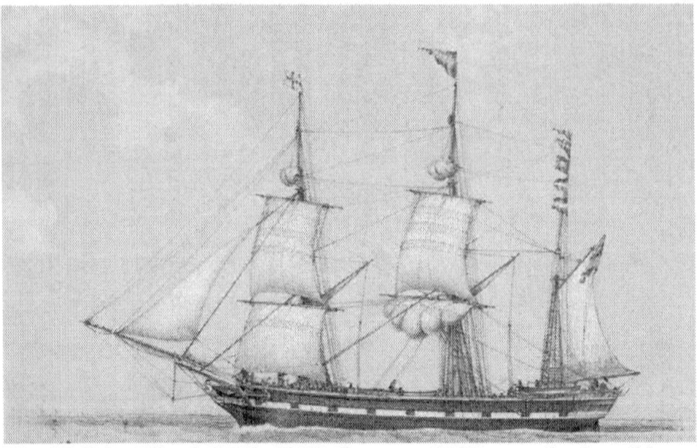

Fig. 58 John Ward (1798-1849) *Barque of 295 tons. Larboard broadside view, showing signals. Scale of feet 0-20*. Lithograph. Hull Maritime Museum.

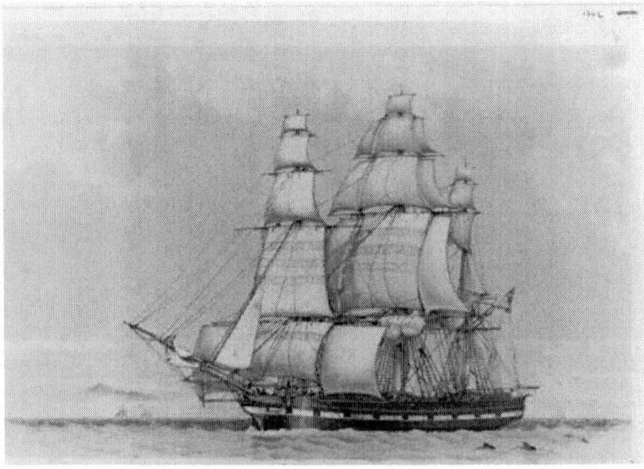

Fig. 59 John Ward (1798-1849) *Ship of 375 tons. In full sail-studding sails low and aloft, wind right aft, a steady breeze*. Lithograph. Hull Maritime Museum.

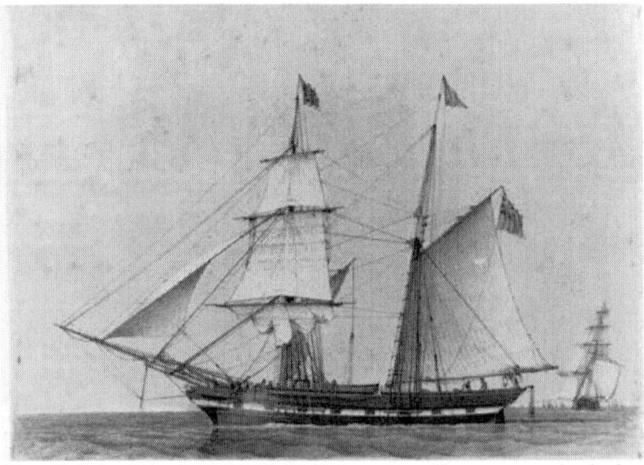

Fig. 60 John Ward (1798-1849) *Brigantine. Hove to, on the larboard tack, off the S. Foreland*. Lithograph. Hull Maritime Museum.

Chapter 3

John Ward's Marine Manual

It is not known when Ward initially formed the idea of a manual of marine painting but the decision to work in earnest and so bring it to fruition is surely marked by his public announcement in 1843. He informs the reader that 'having arranged his draughts and drawings of ships is desirous of giving instruction in marine drawing as applicable to marine painting, and feels confident from his experience as a marine draughtsman to impart such information as will ensure him the support of those anxious to obtain a knowledge thereof' (*Hull Advertiser* 4 January 1843). Commissions for major ship portraits are scarce in the 1840s, most surviving examples are modest in scale and ambition (many include vessels which appear in his lithographs) and his effforts are clearly being concentrated on the lithographic studies. Of the recorded drawings which form the basis of the prints only one is dated, a pencil drawing of the *Alban* signed and dated 'Sept. 5 1841' and bow and stern views of HMS *Britannia* were shown at the Royal Academy in 1842, drawing on the material he had gathered from his visits to Portsmouth. Perhaps taking on William Frederick Settle as an apprentice in 1839 is some indication that he wanted, at this stage in a very successful career, to hand over the more mundane aspects of his workshop to an assistant. A watercolour of the ship *Wanderer* offered for sale in 2009, executed in the same fashion as the various surviving studies for the lithographs, is labelled indicating that it depicts the vessel on 14 May 1840. This was a vessel built and owned by Edward Gibson of Hull in 1835 and not to be confused with the barque *Wanderer* (see below) or the armed schooner of the same name, all pictured by Ward.

Judging by surviving examples and the large numbers of prints offered at his studio sale in 1853 the work of recording all types of vessel with at least one representation (though for some there are two separate prints each with the wind in a different quarter and the appropriate setting of the sails) had been achieved but it is equally clear from the small sample sets sold in paper covers that he was finding it difficult to finance the completion of his project.

The second introductory page which precedes the sequence of 'ten views illustrative of the several rates and classes of vessels on Her Majesty's Navy,' concludes 'These views were originally intended to illustrate a work containing Draughts, Plans and Sections of vessels with their dimensions, displacement and tonnage; forming a guide to drawing for the purposes of painting, and the marine profession generally. That the work has not been published arises not from a doubt of its success or utility but from circumstances which for a time preclude the possibility of bringing so difficult but desirable a work before the public-whose patronage with that of the commanders, builders and artists generally, J.Ward is anxious to obtain'.

From the examples seen over the last thirty years it seems clear that the 'draughts, plans and sections' were probably also completed for all the ship types (though not all have been seen by the present writer) but there is no trace of any explanatory text relating to the key numbers applied to the various parts of the vessel in these schematic views.

Such a major work would have been issued in parts, continuation being dependent on the subscriptions of interested parties. There is no indication of a prospectus being issued, other than the texts already quoted, detailing the scope and content of the manual so it seems that Ward was never able to raise enough support to properly launch his project. The groups of mercantile and naval subjects issued in paper covers were surely not parts produced for subscribers but attractive selections of his prints offered for sale to recoup some of the money he had invested and also with the intention of exciting interest in the manual. The bound set of naval prints, offered for sale in London, also included the print of the *Raymond*, 1843. The print of a barque represents a vessel built in 1845and so must have been produced that year or later. It may not have been just a matter of a lack of financial support but also of problems at the lithographer's workshop, William Monkhouse of York. A significant contribution to some of the best quality prints produced there was made by Francis Bedford who had joined the establishment in 1840 or shortly before but who, sometime in the mid or late 1840s, departed to London. The loss of such an able craftsman may have effectively brought Ward's plans to a halt. The last production of outstanding quality for Ward was the 'The Hull Grand Regatta' of 1847 and the following year the competent but simple design of the *Dandie Dinmont* was executed by the Hull firm of Goddard and Lancaster. In 1845 W.R. Goddard, before the partnership with Lancaster, produced a print of the p.s. *Vivid* for Ward, indicating that he was already seeking the help of local craftsmen while still using the York establishment. The earliest dateable pieces from Monkhouse are the commemorative prints of the *Columbine* and the *Raymond* 1843, the year of his announcement in the Hull press.

These selections issued in paper covers are not dated but in his guide for sign writers published in 1848 he also took the opportunity to display his marine lithographs by printing a different image on the reverse of the plates of letter types. These individually bear the imprint of Monkhouse of York but the likelihood is that the 'The English Alphabet' as a whole was printed in Hull. A portion of the text of the introduction has been discovered on the reverse of one of the studies of merchant vessels (Barque of 295 tons); the wording has beeen lithographed from a clear copperplate hand, no doubt by Ward himself using one of the presses in his studio. Printed in the same year was a lithographic portrait, the only known example lost or destroyed in the 1939-45 war, inscribed 'John Ward, of Hull, Mr.Painter 1848'; possibly intended to accompany the manual.

It must have been a great disappointment not to be able to bring his project to a satisfactory conclusion but his determination to be noticed was undimmed and two years before his premature death, his largest and most ambitious oil painting 'HMS *Britannia* and units of the fleet at Spithead'[1] was displayed at the Royal Academy.

Price

Marine Studies

OF

BRITISH MERCHANT VESSELS,

DESIGNED AND LITHOGRAPHED

BY

John Ward,

HULL.

M. C. PECK, PRINTER, LOWGATE, HULL.

MARINE STUDIES

OF

BRITISH MERCHANT VESSELS.

In submitting the present Series of Views of British Merchant Vessels to public notice, it is respectfully intimated that they are chiefly intended for the use and instruction of those desirous of obtaining correct information in Marine Drawing.

Although it must be admitted that the acknowledged want of such information presents a favourable opportunity for bringing forward so desirable a Work; yet, to render it still more serviceable, in this instance, the proportions of the Vessels, their detail, arrangement, and incidents, have received the most minute attention. And, in order to form a useful and general work of reference to the Student and Artist, with the broadside representations is given a Scale of Feet to assist in determining their respective proportions.

At the same time it is presumed the series will not be unacceptable to those connected with the Mercantile Shipping interests of this country, to whom this Work is particularly and respectfully dedicated by their

Obedient Humble Servant,

JOHN WARD.

HULL, 23, North-Street.

(Series of prints sold in paper covers)

Sloop or Smack, of 160 Tons

Preparing to Sail---Anchor hove short---Calm. Scale of Feet 0-20.

(*Eds:* A true smack, with single mast. Extensively used in the coasting trade.)

Schooner, of 120 Tons

At anchor---Sails loose----light air of wind---Scale of Feet 0-20.

(*Eds:* A topsail schooner, a fore and aft rig with topsail yards on the fore mast; adapted for a wide variety of uses, coastal and short sea trading, carrying passengers, fishing and naval duties.)

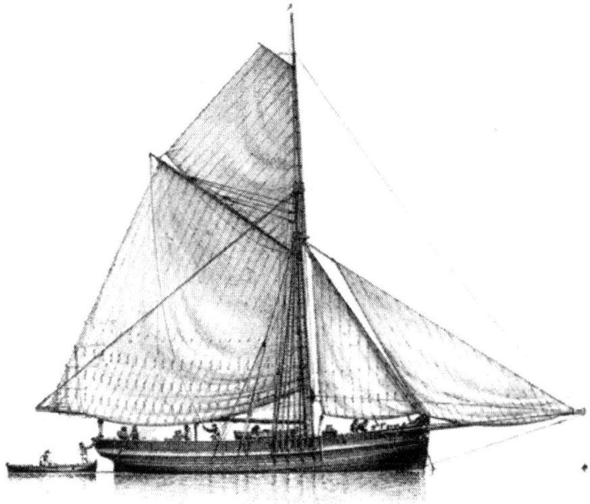

SLOOP or SMACK, of 160 Tons.

Preparing to Sail.—Anchor hove short.—Calm.—Scale of Feet.

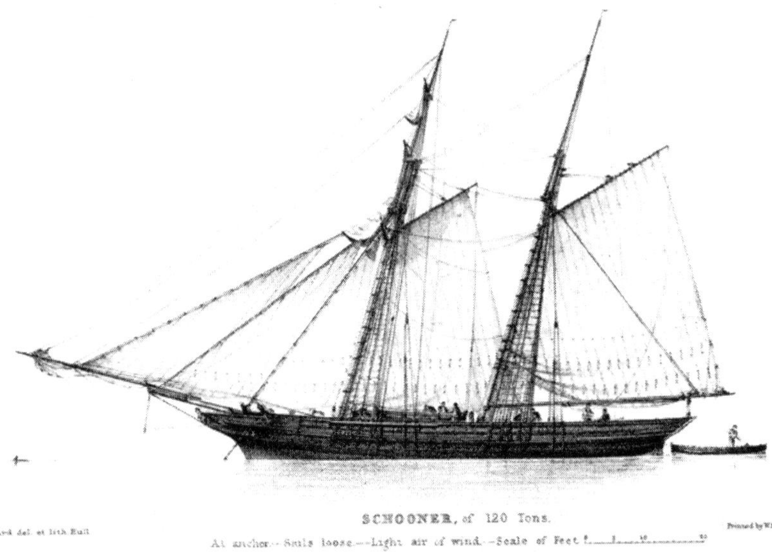

J. Ward del. et lith. Hull

SCHOONER, of 120 Tons.

At anchor.—Sails loose.—Light air of wind.—Scale of Feet

Printed by W. Monkhouse, York

Brig of 223 Tons

Under way---Before the Wind…Yards squared---Scale of Feet 0---20.

(*Eds:* A two masted vessel, square rigged on both; the work horse of the North Sea and Baltic trades.)

Ship of 650 Tons

Riding at Anchor---Sails furled---Wind ahead. Scale of Feet 0---20.

(*Eds:*A three masted vessel, square rigged on each. Suitable for long distance voyages.*)*

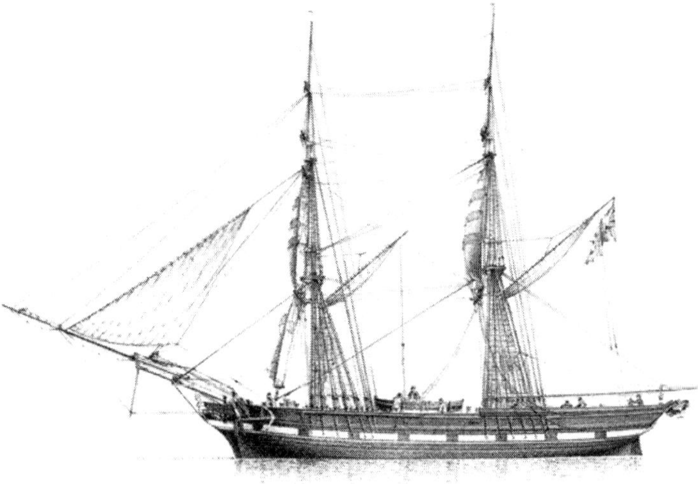

BRIG, of 223 Tons.

Under way — Before the Wind — Yards squared. — Scale of Feet

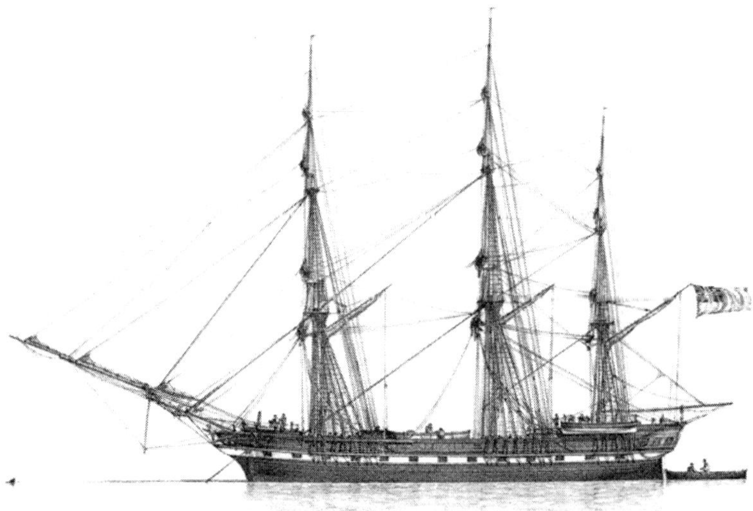

SHIP, of 650 Tons.

Riding at anchor — Sails furled — Wind ahead. — Scale of Feet

J. Ward del. et lith. Hull

Printed by W. Monkhouse, York

Sloop – before the wind.

1. Before the Wind---Larboard bow view.
2. Stern view---at Anchor. Strong Breeze.

MARINE STUDIES.

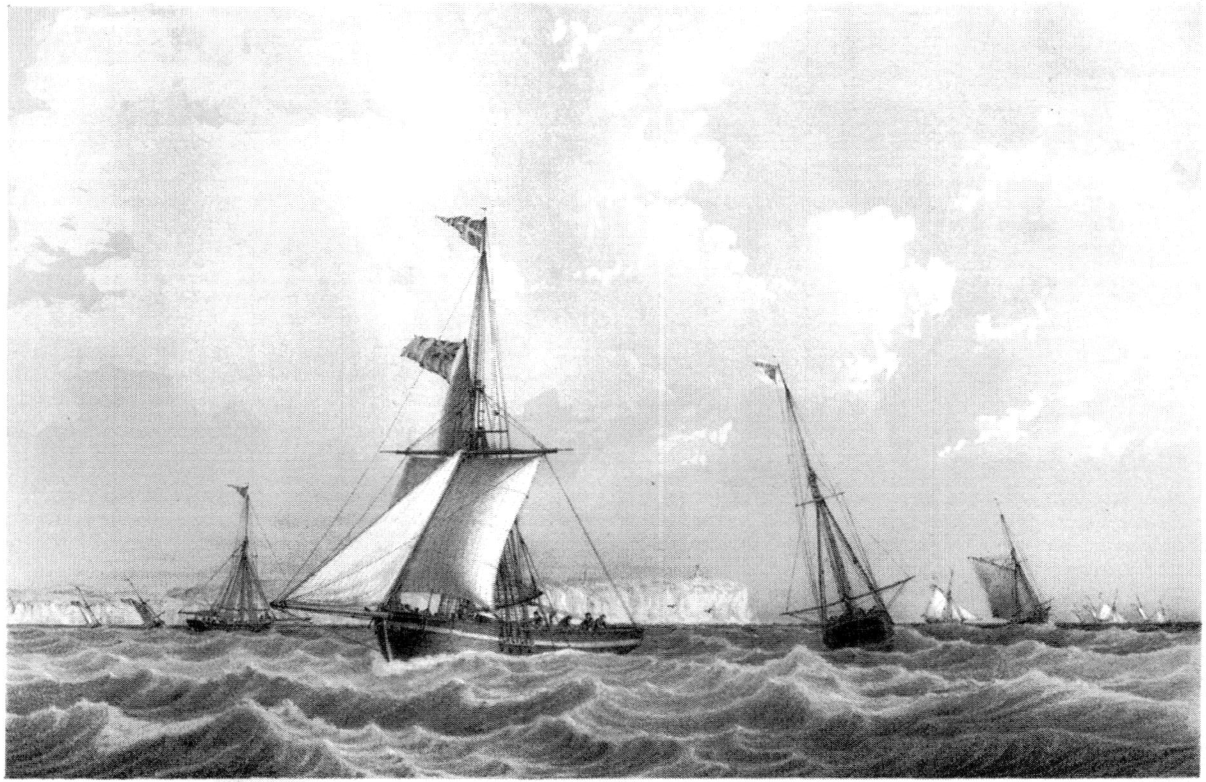

1

John Ward del. et lith. Printed by W. Monkhouse, York.

SLOOP.

1 Before the Wind...Larboard bow view. 2 Stern view...at Anchor. Strong Breeze.

Schooner

1. Before the Wind---Studding sails set.

2. Close hauled. Starboard tack. Light Breeze.

MARINE STUDIES.

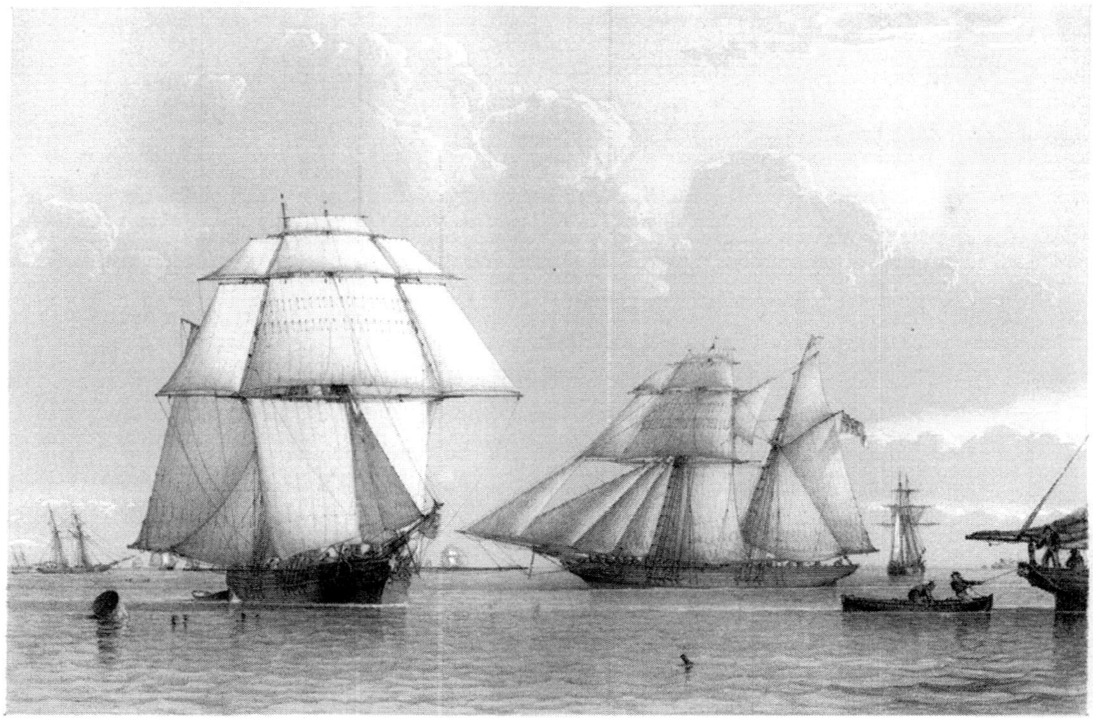

John Ward del. et lith.

Printed by R. Monkhouse York

SCHOONER.

1. Before the Wind _ Studdingsails set. 2. Close hauled _ Starboard tack. Light Breeze

Brig

1. At Anchor---Bow view.
2. Underway---yards braced sharp up. Calm.

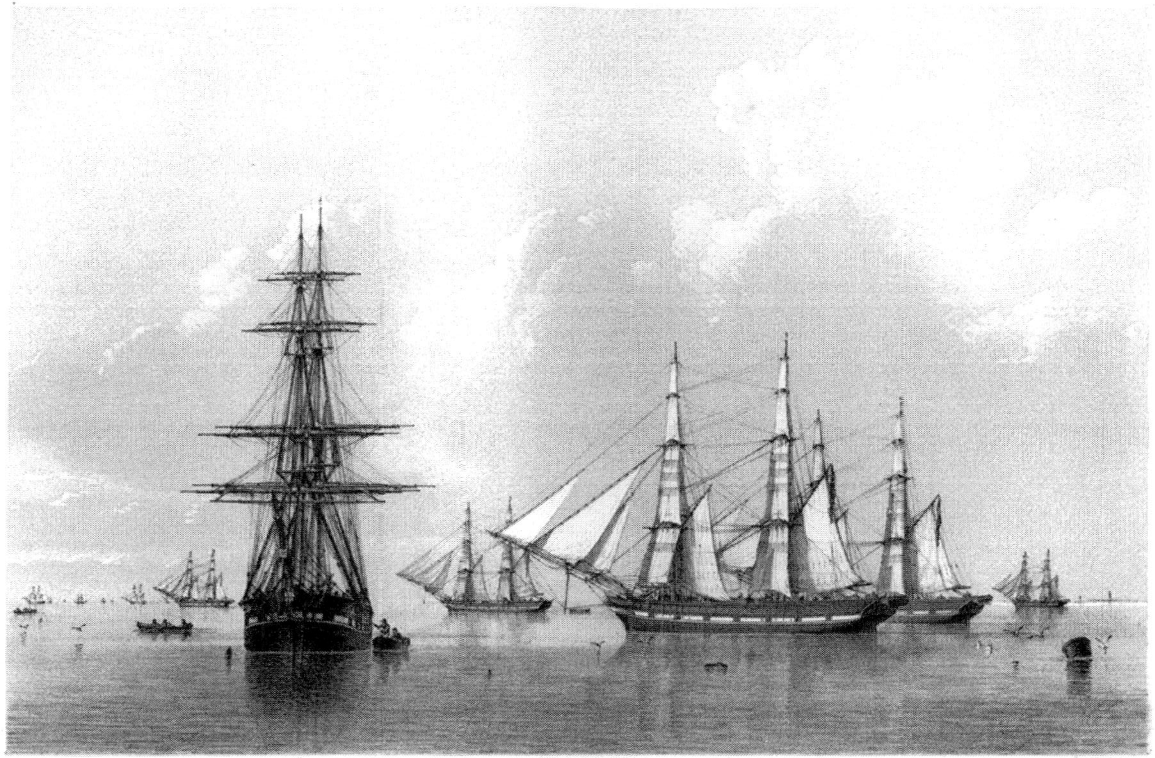

1 2

John Ward del. et lith.

Printed by W. Monkhouse, York

BRIG.

1. At Anchor _ Bow view. 2. Underway _ yards braced sharp up. Calm.

Ship

1. At Anchor---Stern view.

2. Starboard bow view---Wind on the quarter. A Breeze springing up.

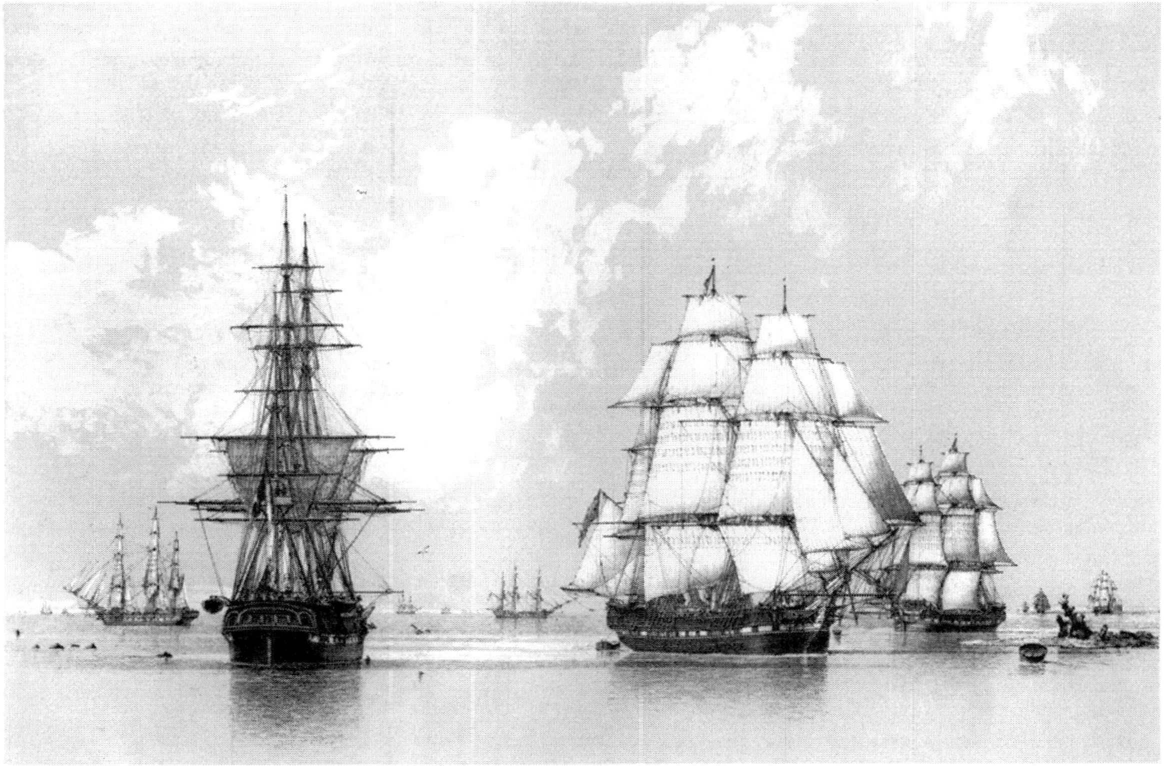

1 2

John Ward del. et lith.

Printed by W. Monkhouse, York.

SHIP.

1. At Anchor. – Stern view. 2. Starboard bow view. – Wind on the quarter. A Breeze springing up.

Merchant Vessels

1. Ship moored to the Buoy….preparing to Sail. 2. Brig at Anchor. 3. Schooner. 4. Sloop. Calm.

(*Eds:* This is the last of the sequence of merchant ships in paper covers. A loose page in the Hull Maritime Museum collection with the printed title THE BRITISH MERCHANT SERVICE was perhaps intended as a half title for a set in paper wrappers, though one would have expected this to read BRITISH MERCHANT VESSELS, to match the cover title, so perhaps it was an alternative which had been discarded.)

MARINE STUDIES

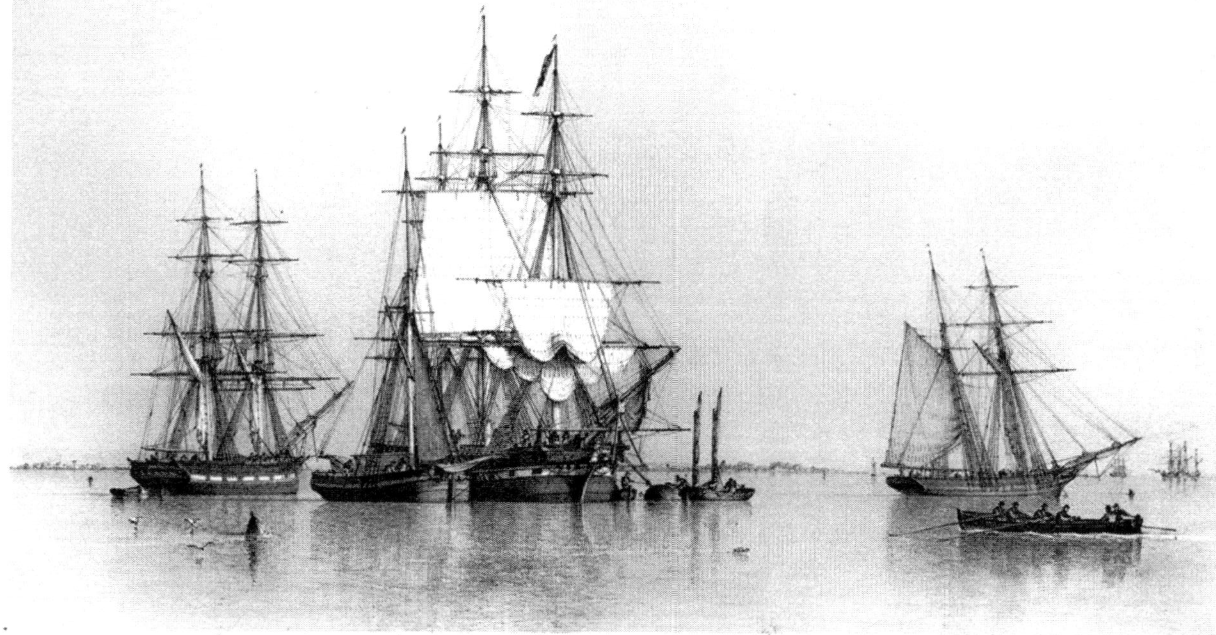

John Ward del. et lith.

Printed by W. Monkhouse, York.

MERCHANT VESSELS.

1. Ship moored to the Buoy – preparing to Sail. 2. Brig at Anchor. 3. Schooner. 4. Sloop. Calm.

Buoy Yacht

(*Eds:* This lithograph (6in. x 8in.) of a cutter seen flying the flag of the Hull Trinity House - a body responsible for pilotage and navigation on the Humber, including light houses, light vessels and buoys; now solely a charitable organisation for mariners , can be identified as the buoy yacht *Ariel* launched at Cowes in 1844.)

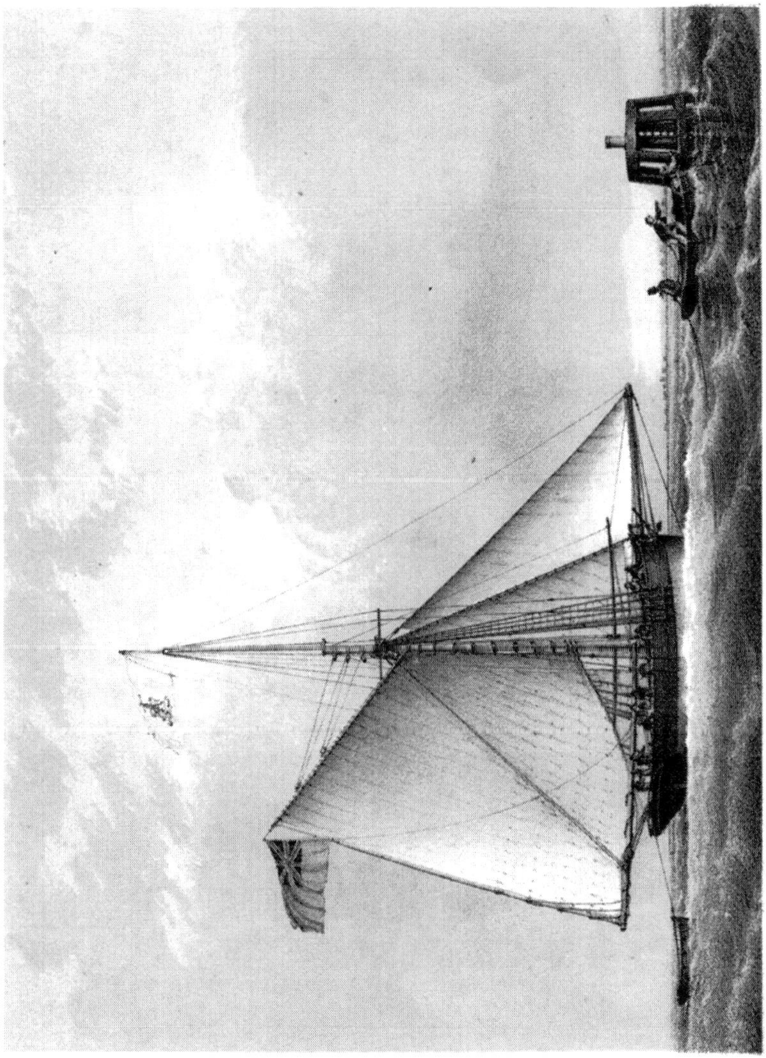

Sloop at anchor

At anchor and under-weigh on the starboard tack---weather view.

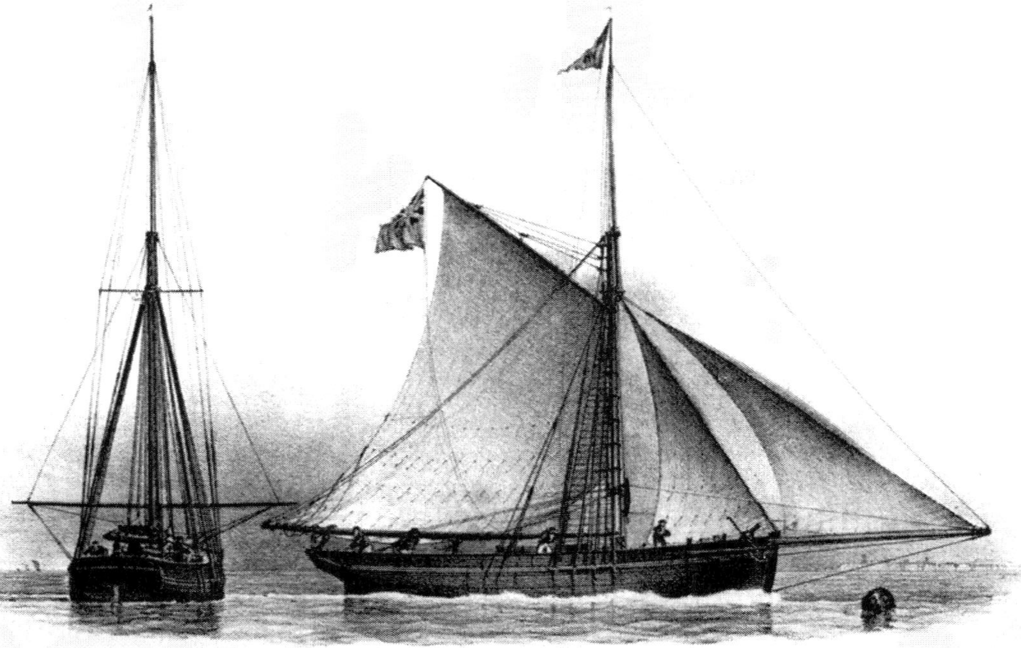

J Ward del et lith. Hull.

SLOOP.

At anchor and under-weigh on the starboard tack — weather view.

Printed by W. Monkhouse, York.

Sloop or Smack of 160 Tons

Preparing to Sail---Anchor hove short----Calm. Scale of Feet 0-20.

(*Eds:* Shown above printed on same sheet as schooner of 120 tons; here printed as a single plate.)

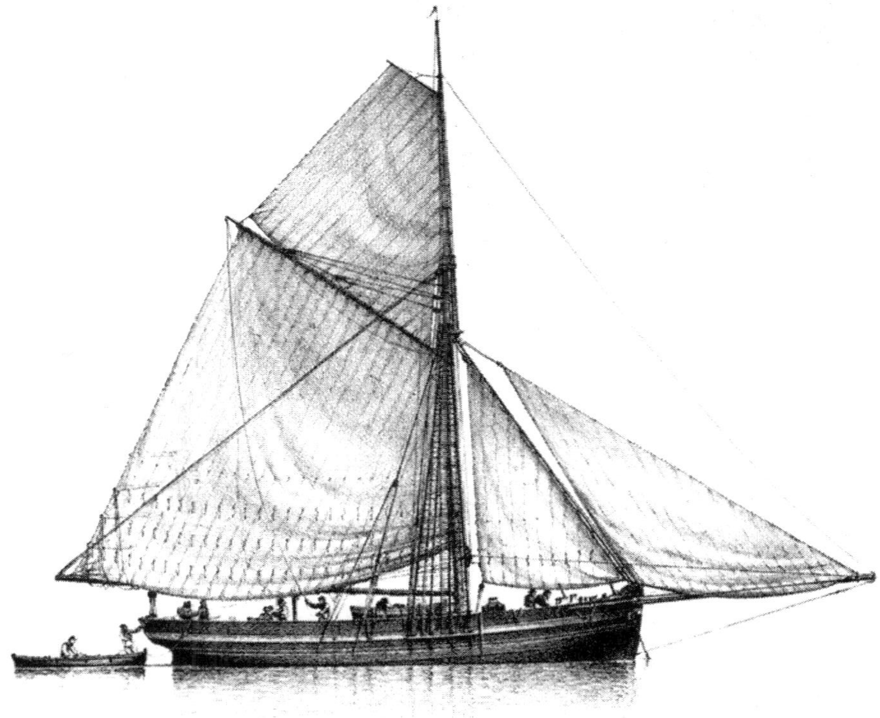

SLOOP or **SMACK**, of 160 Tons.

Preparing to Sail.—Anchor hove short —Calm.—Scale of Feet, 0 5 10 20

Sloop or Smack

Dandy-rigged- going free, off Flambor'o Head

(*Eds:* 'Dandy–rigged' refers to the small mizzen mast; The expression was also used to describe the North Sea fishing smacks which elsewhere would be referred to as 'yawls'.)

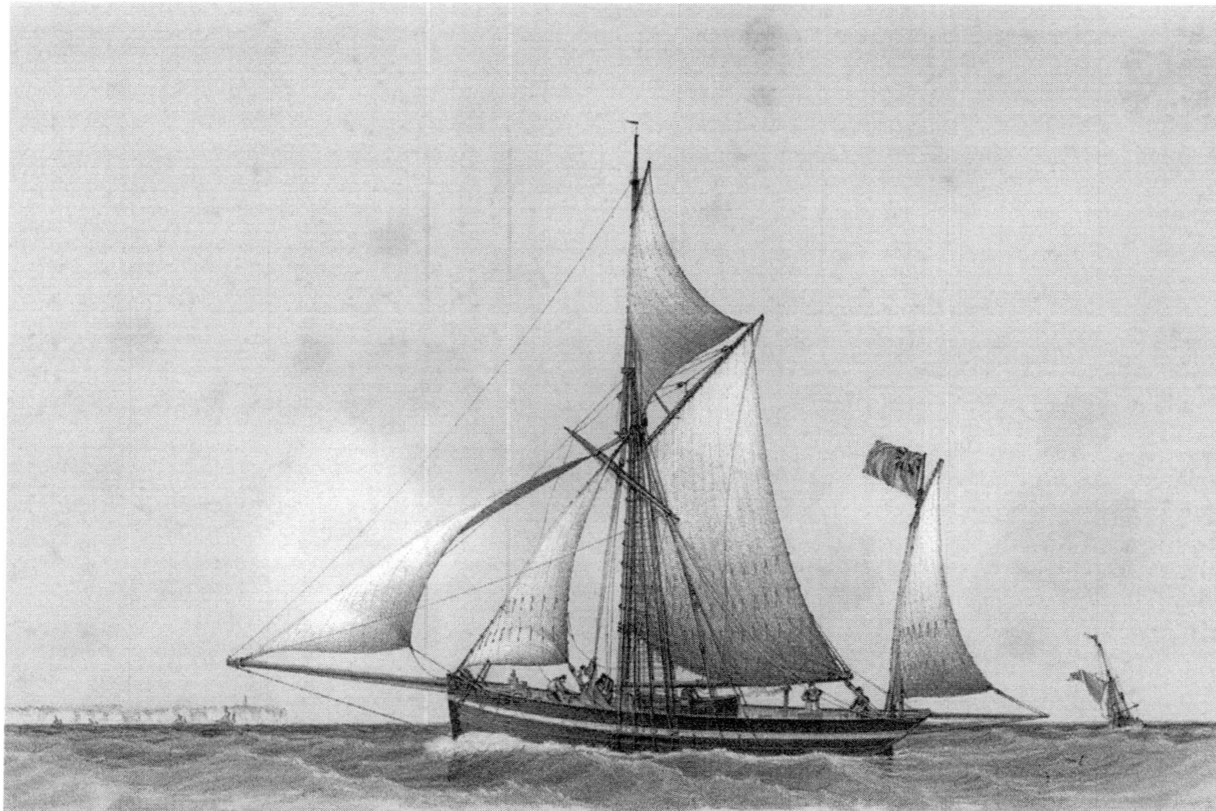

Del. et lith. H.C.

Printed by W. Monkhouse, York.

SLOOP OF SMACK

Dandy rigged,— going free,—off FLAMBOR'O HEAD.

Sloop or Scotch Smack

Getting under-weigh---heaving the anchor---on the Humber

(*Eds:* Note the initial JW on the mast head pennant.)

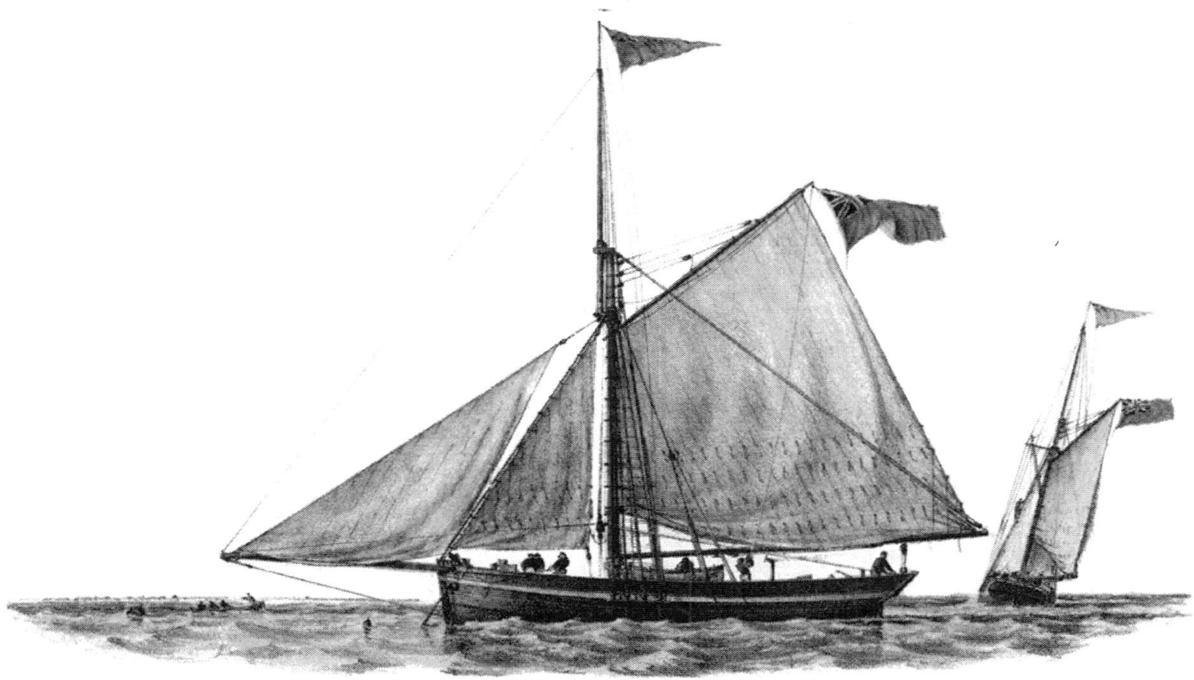

SLOOP OR SCOTCH SMACK.
Getting under-weigh. heaving the anchor—on the HUMBER.

Schooner

Sailing by the wind---on the Larboard tack---Lee view---light breeze.

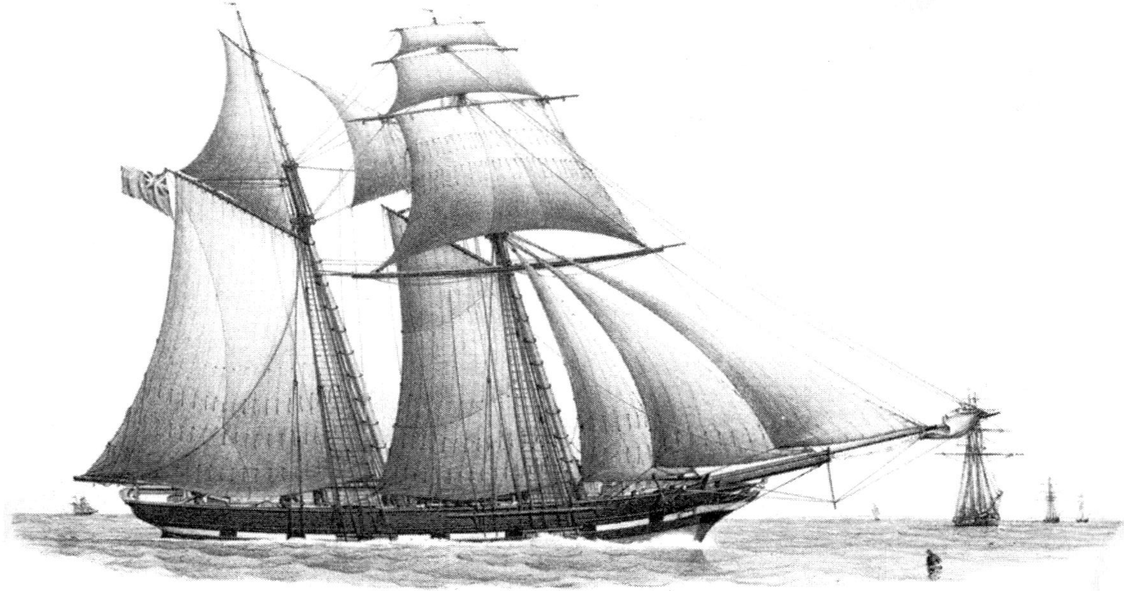

J. Ward del et lith Hull.

SCHOONER.
Sailing by the wind — on the Larboard tack — Lee view — light breeze.

Printed by W. Monkhouse, York.

Schooner of 120 Tons

At anchor---Sails loose---Light air of Wind---Scale of Feet, 0-20

(*Eds:* Already shown on a sheet with the Sloop of 160 tons; here a separate plate.)

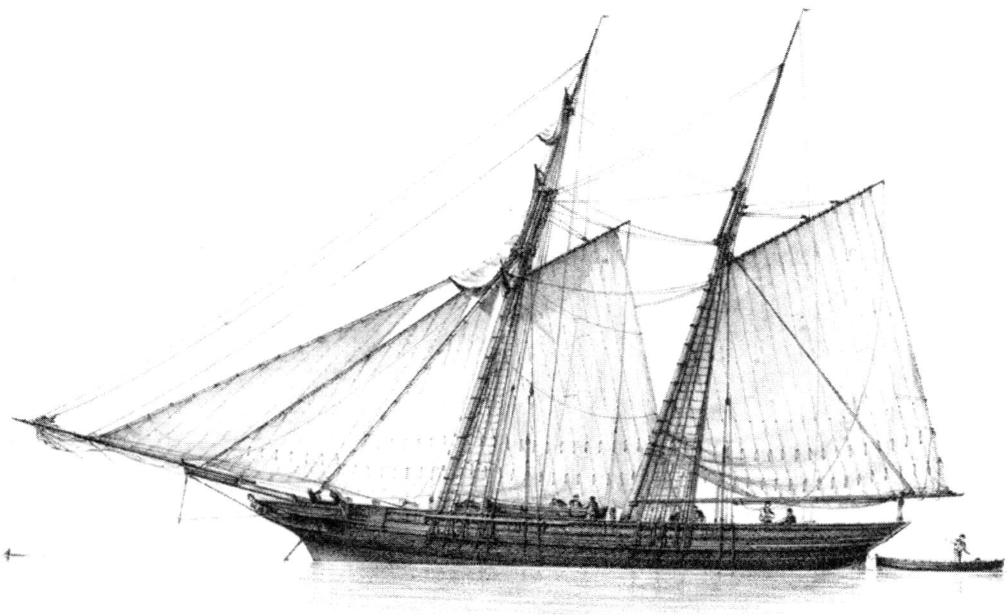

J Ward del. et lith. Hull

SCHOONER, of 120 Tons.

At anchor.—Sails loose.—Light air of wind.—Scale of Feet 0 5 10 20

Printed by W. Monkhouse, York

Brigantine

Hove to, --- on the larboard tack --- off the S. FORELAND.

(*Eds:* Tinted stone grey with gouache highlights.)

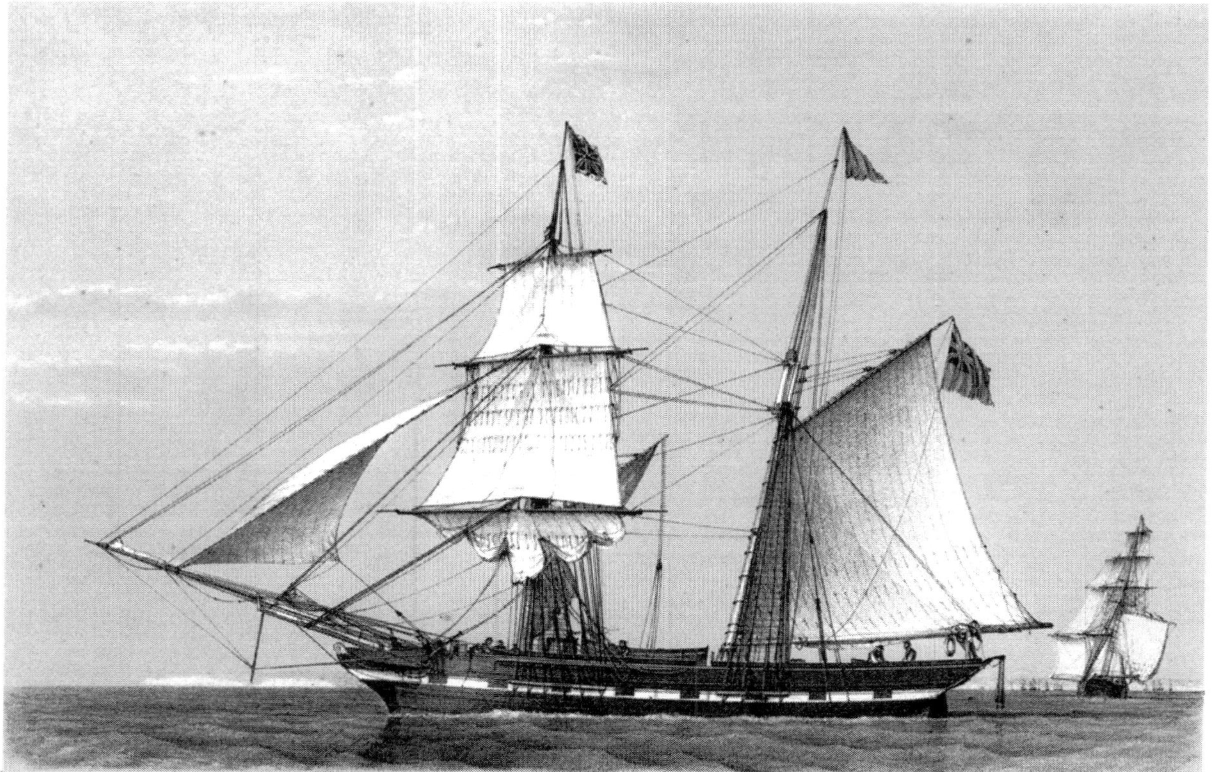

J. Ward del et lith Hull

Printed by W. Monkhouse, York

BRIGANTINE

Hove to,—on the larboard tack—off the S FORELAND

Brig – close hauled.

Close-hauled on the Larboard tack---calm---entering the HUMBER.

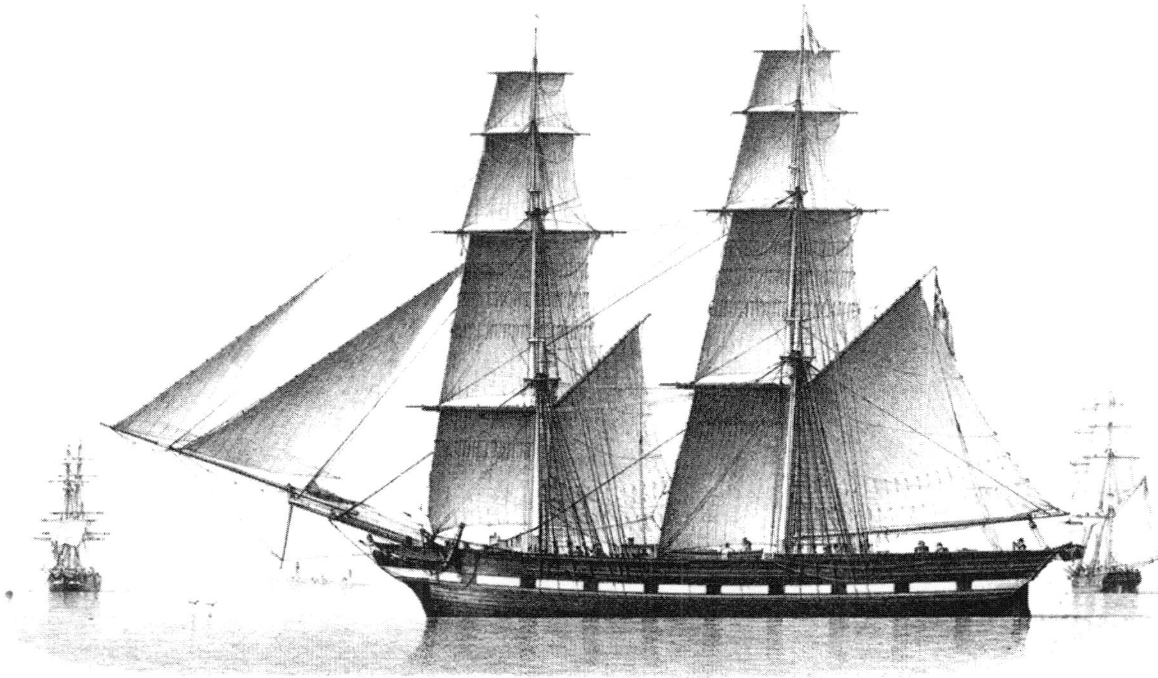

BRIG

J. Ward Del et Lith Hull — Close-hauled, on the Larboard tack — calm — entering the HUMBER — Printed by W. Monkhouse York.

Brig, of 223 Tons

Under way-before the wind-yards squared scale of feet 0-20

(*Eds:* Reproduced above on a sheet with Ship of 650 tons; here printed as a separate plate.)

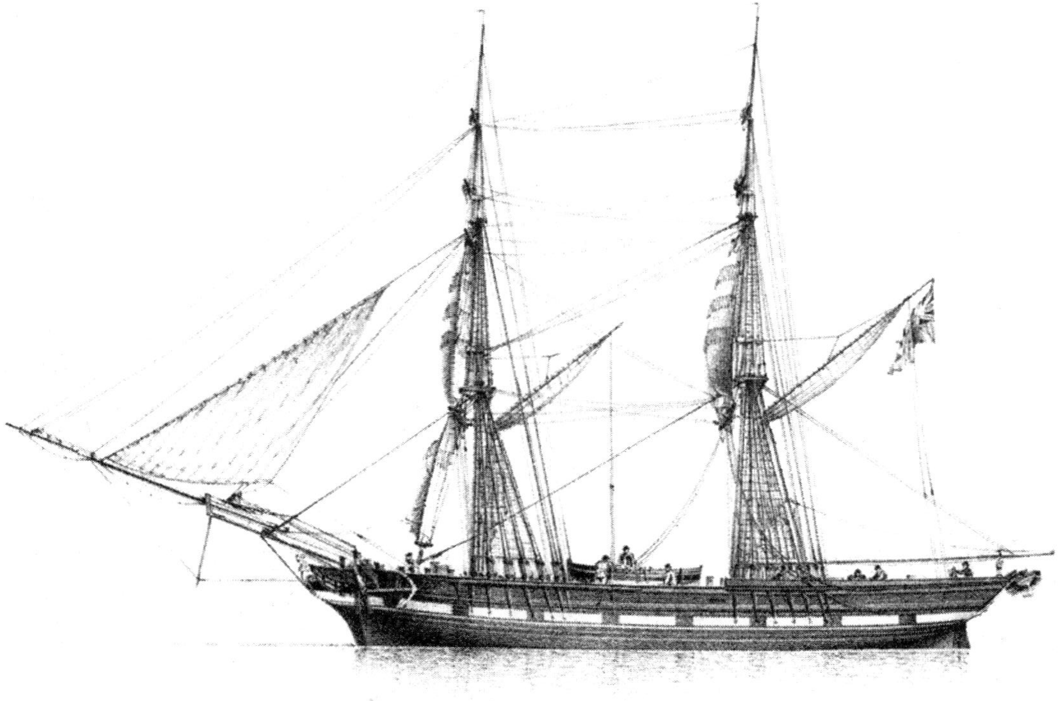

BRIG, of 223 Tons.

Under way.—Before the Wind.—Yards squared.—Scale of Feet.

Barque, of 295 Tons

Larboard broadside view. ---Showing signals.---Scale of Feet 0-20.

(*Eds:* This can be identified from the Marryat code flags and a partially legible name pennant GAR--, as the barque *Gardyne*, built in Hull in 1845.Owned by McTear of Liverpool; she was registered in the latter port but sailed out of Hull; in 1849 was sailing to South America. On reverse is a proof pull of hand written text for introduction to the 'English Alphabet'.)

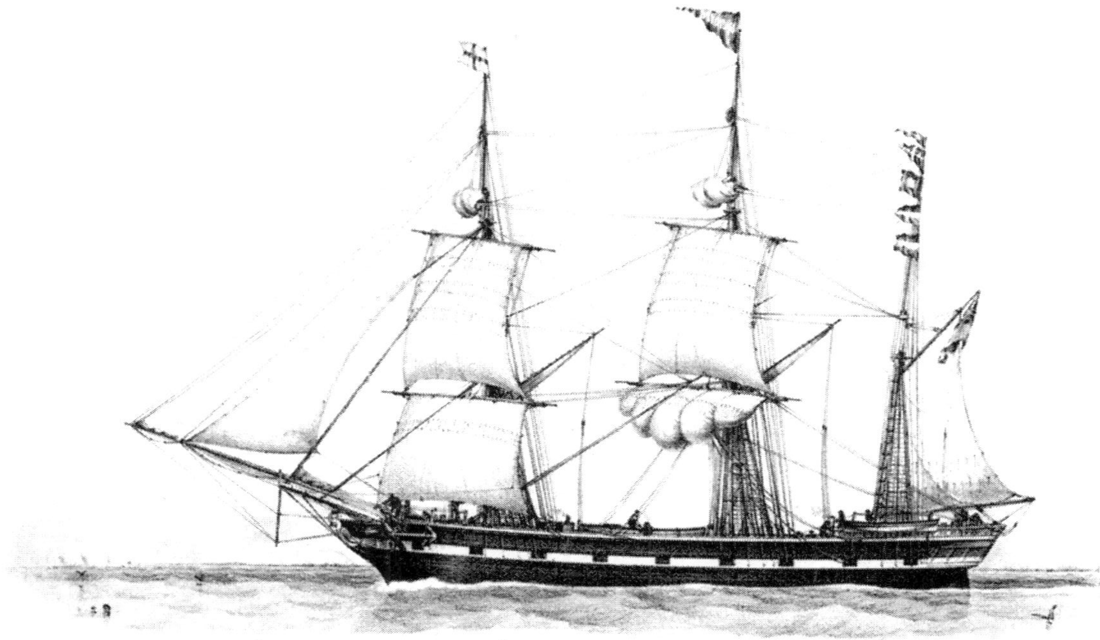

BARQUE, of 895 Tons.

Larboard broadside view. — Showing signals. — Scale of Feet

Ship

Lee broadside view---blowing a fresh gale---off the HUMBER

(*Eds:* Displaying a hoist of code flags which have not been deciphered.)

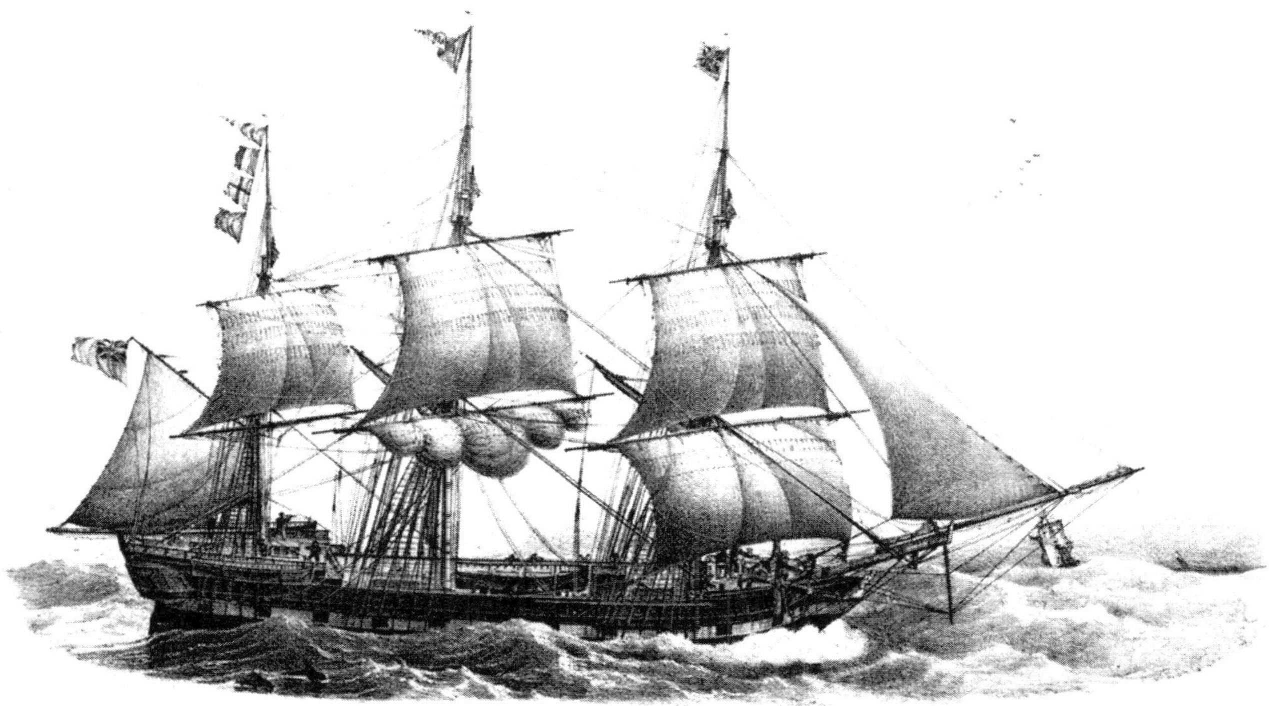

SHIP.

Lee broadside view — blowing a fresh gale — Off the HUMBER.

J Ward Del et Lith Hull

Printed by W Monkhouse York,

Ship, of 375 Tons

In full sail.---Studding sails low and aloft.---Wind right aft.---A steady breeze.

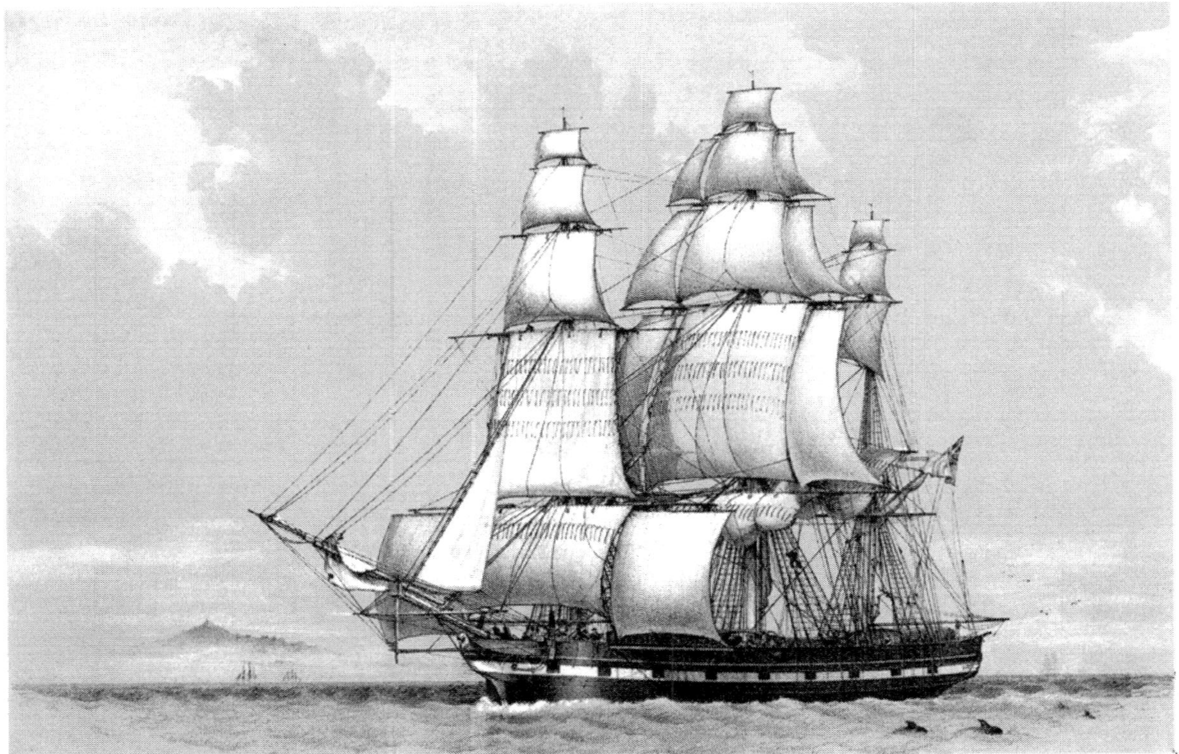

J. Ward del. et lith. Hull

SHIP, of 375 Tons.

In full sail.— Studdingsails low and aloft. — Wind right aft.—A steady breeze.

Ship, of 650 Tons

Riding at anchor.---Sails furled.---Wind ahead.---Scale of Feet, 0-20.

(*Eds:* Also found on dual print version above.)

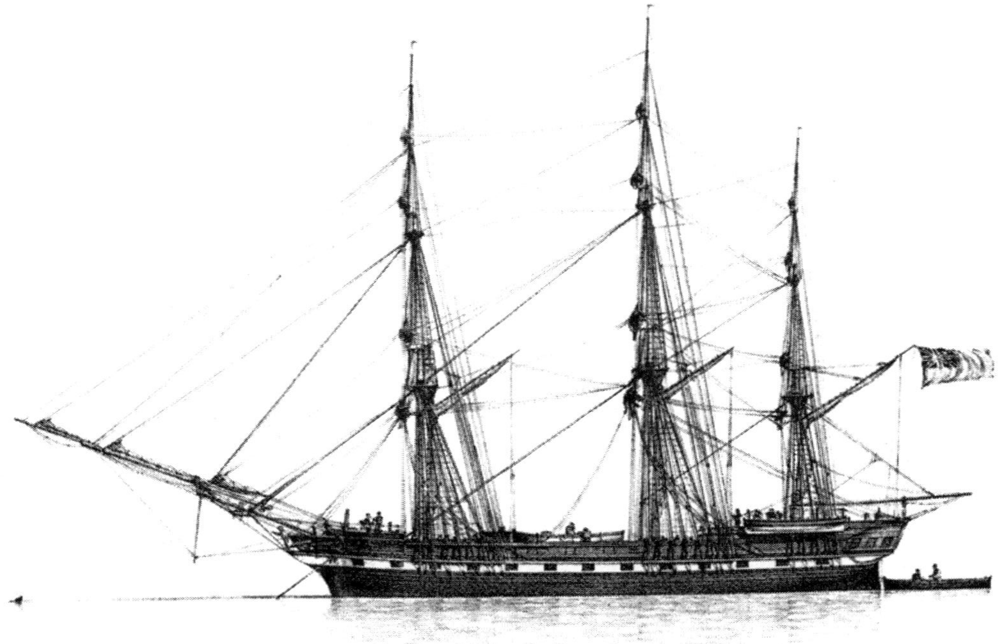

J. Ward del. et lith. Hull

SHIP, of 650 Tons.

Riding at anchor.—Sails furled.—Wind ahead.—Scale of Feet. 0 5 10 20

Printed by W. Monkhouse, York

Paddle Steamer 'Vivid'

Printed by W.R. Goddard, Hull, 7 April 1845; apart from the commemorative print of the *Dandie Dinmont* , by Goddard and Lancaster 1848, this is the only lithograph not from Monkhouse of York.

(*Eds:* This same vessel appears with *Waterwitch* in 1839 aquatinted by W.G. Reeve after Ward's oil painting. Built 1836 for Humber Union Steam Navigation Co. and sold 1841 to General Steam Navigation Co, London, whose house flag appears in this print.)

MARINE STUDIES

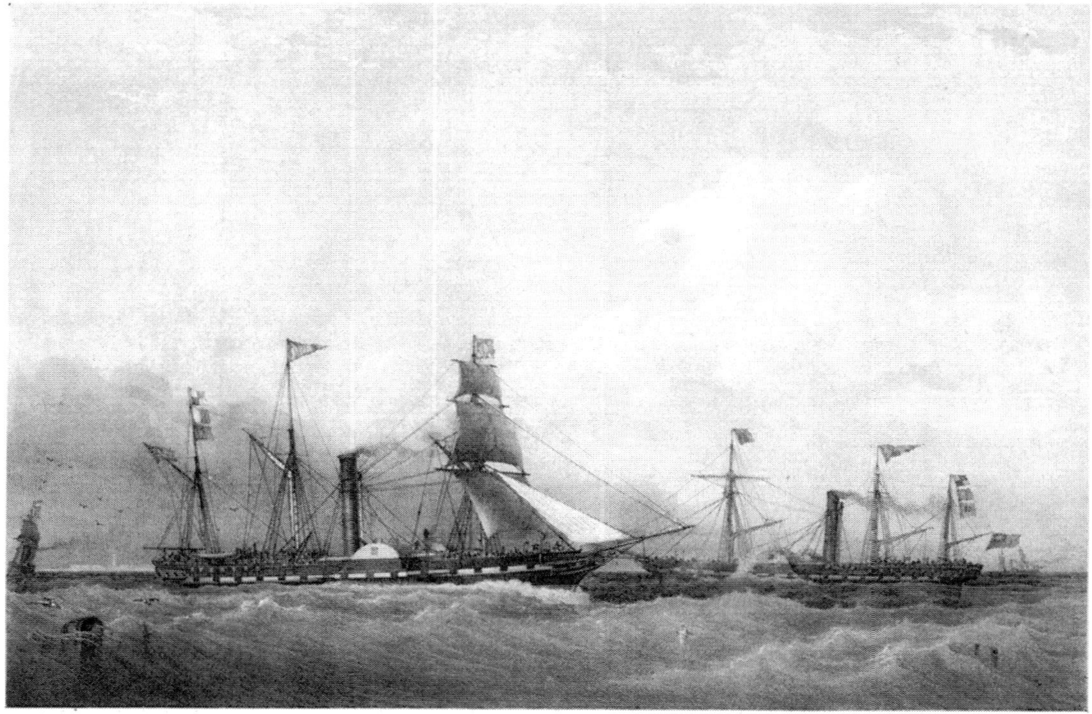

John Ward del et lith. Hull. Printed by W.R. Goddard. Hull.

Untitled

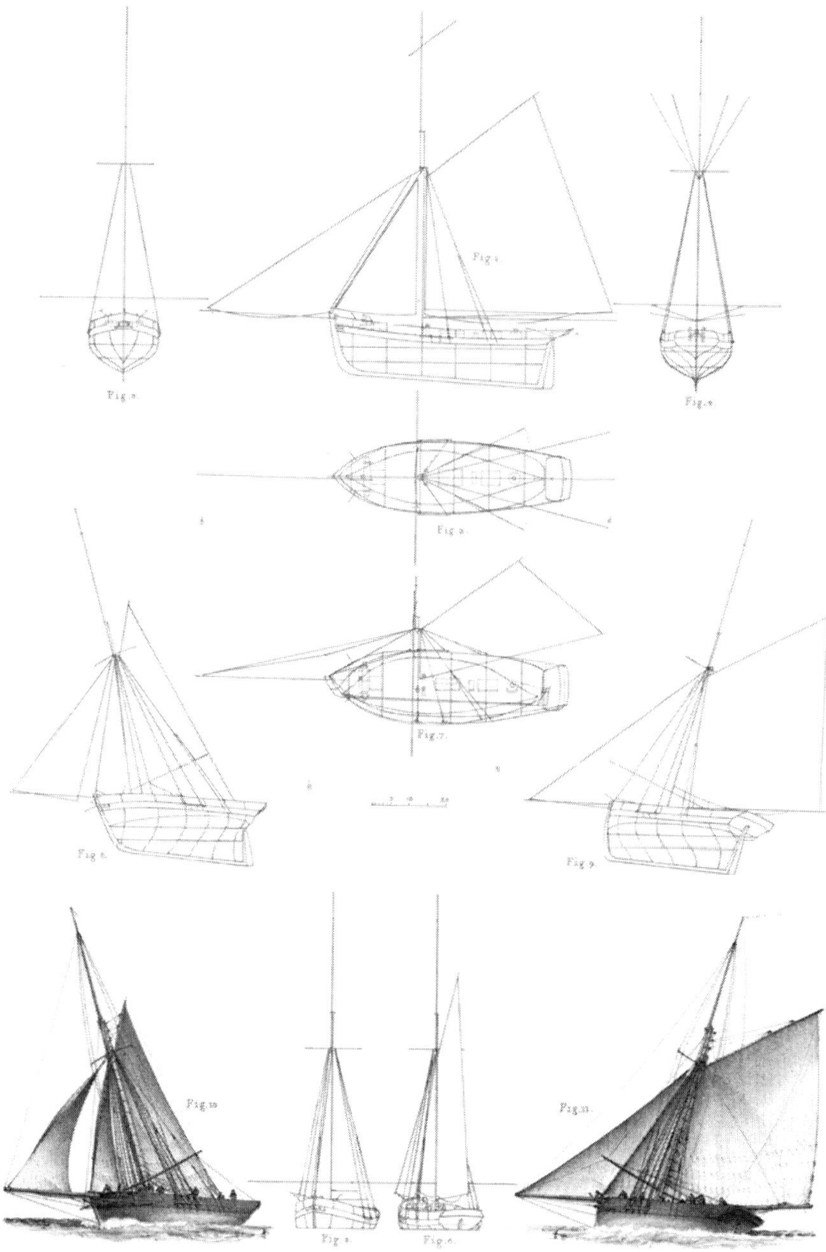
Fig.7.
Fig.9.
Fig.10
Fig.11.
Fig.6.

Sloop

At anchor and under-weigh on the starboard tack---Weather view.

(*Eds:* Note pennant at mast head with artist's initials JW.)

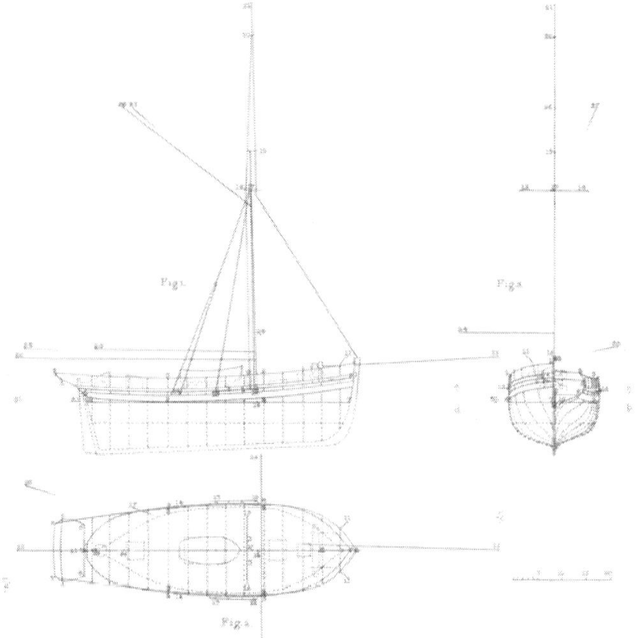

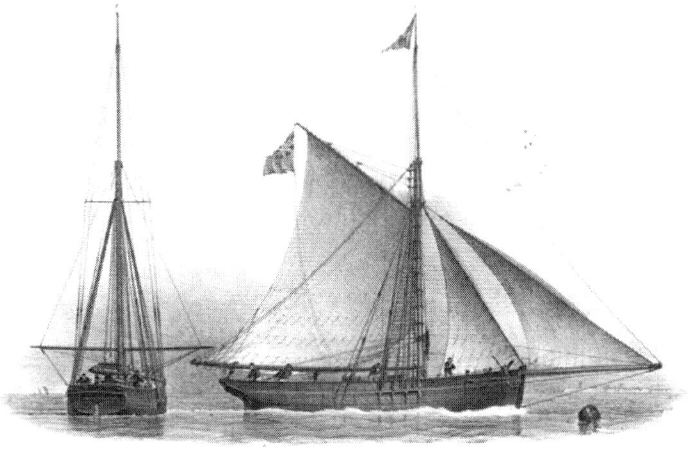

J. Ward, del et lith, Hull

SLOOP.

At anchor and under-weigh on the starboard tack — weather view

Printed by W. Monkhouse, York.

Schooner

Sailing by the wind---on the Larboard tack---lee view---light breeze.

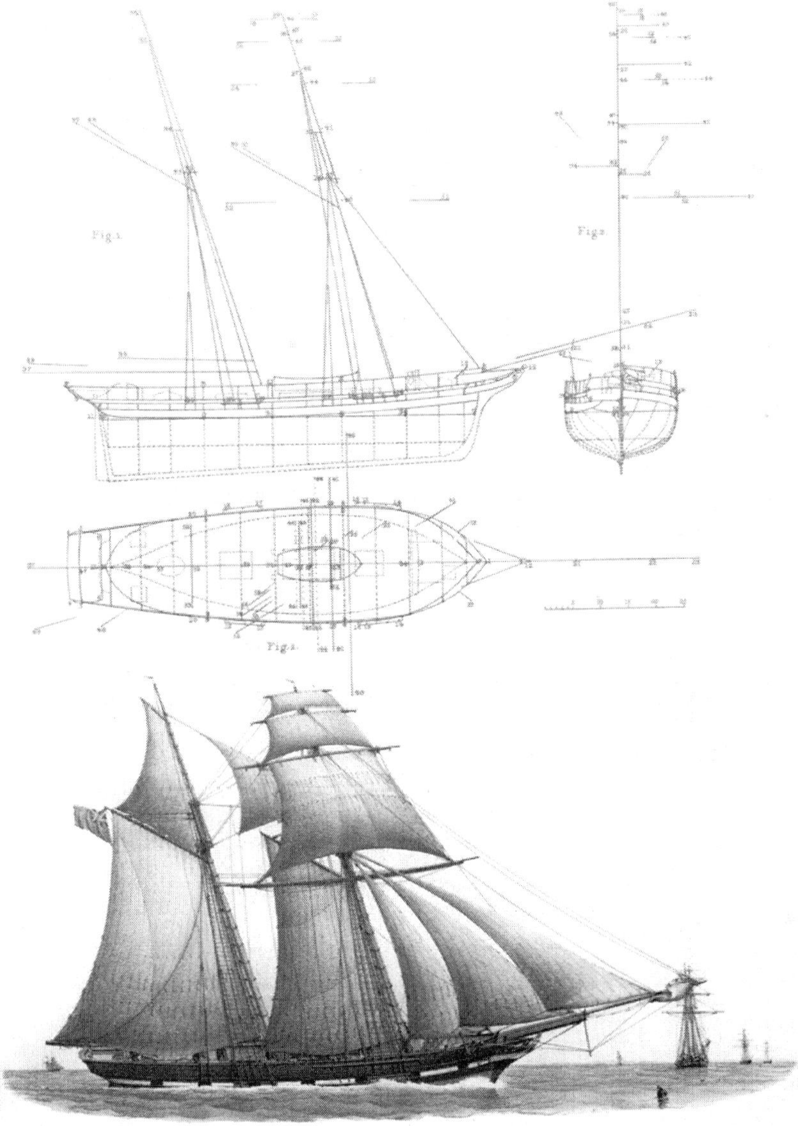

T. Ward del et lith Hull.

SCHOONER.

Sailing by the wind — on the Larboard tack — lee view — light breeze.

Printed by W. Monkhouse York.

Brig

Close hauled on the Larboard tack---calm---entering the HUMBER

(*Eds:* Port broadside view, Spurn lighthouses visible.)

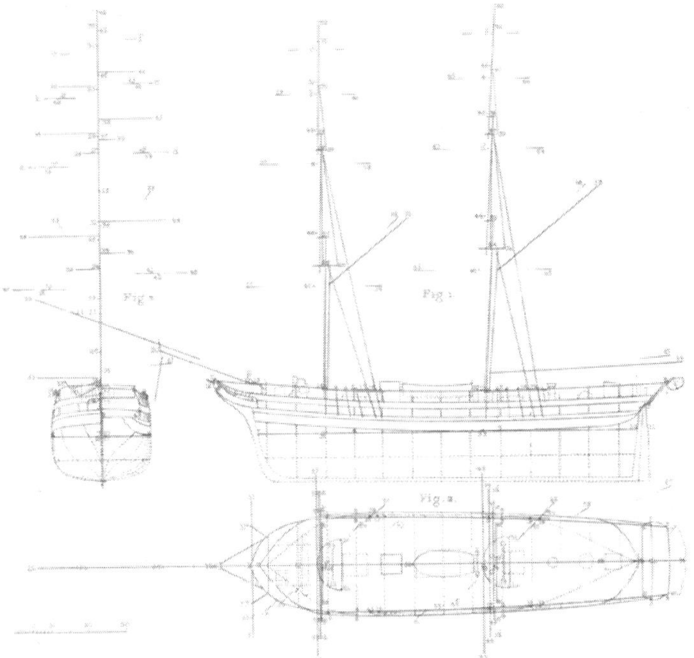

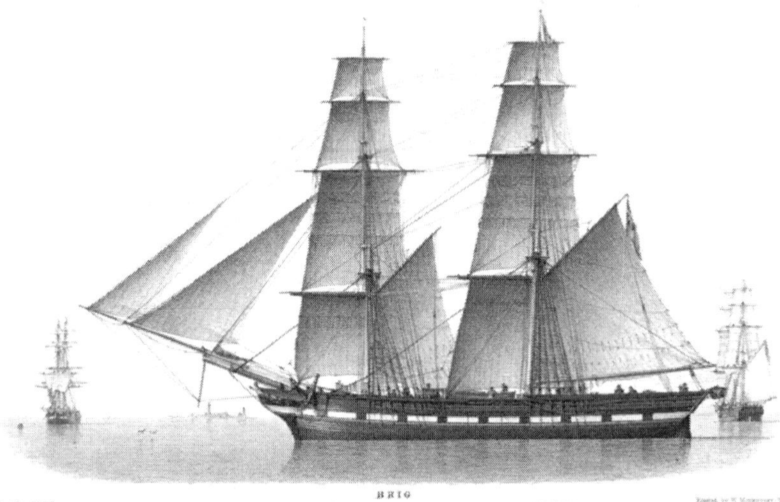

BRIG

Close-hauled on the Larboard tack — calm — entering the HUMBER

Ship

Lee broadside view---blowing a fresh gale---off the HUMBER

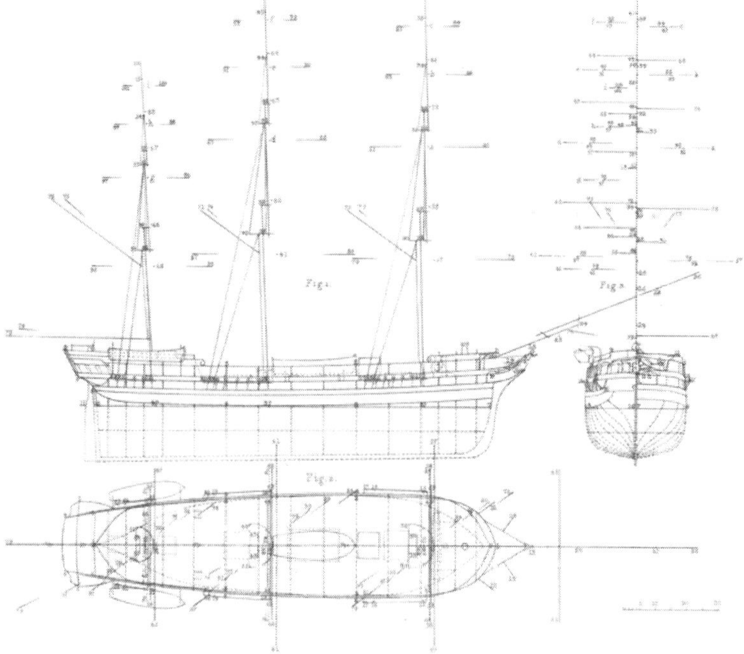

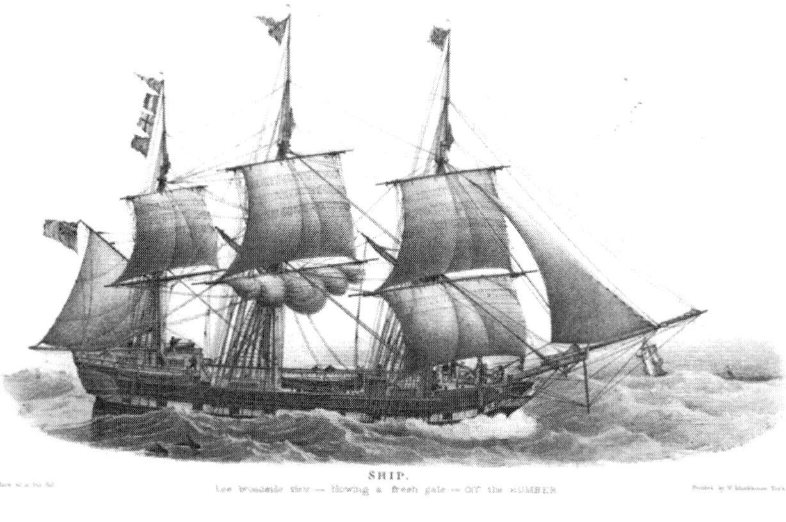

SHIP.

Lee broadside view — blowing a fresh gale — Off the HUMBER

Steamer ‘Vivid’

At anchor---signal for sailing. Blue Peter flag at the Fore---In HULL ROADS.

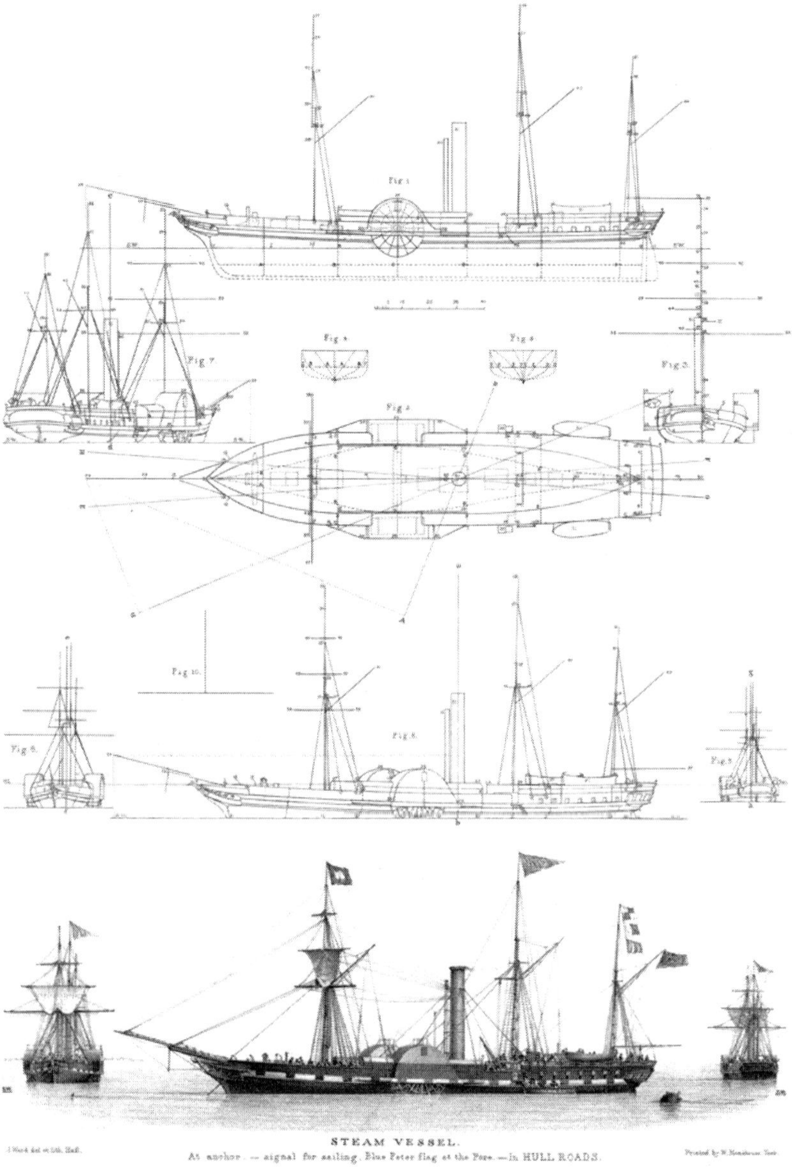

STEAM VESSEL.

At anchor. — signal for sailing, Blue Peter flag at the Fore. — In HULL ROADS.

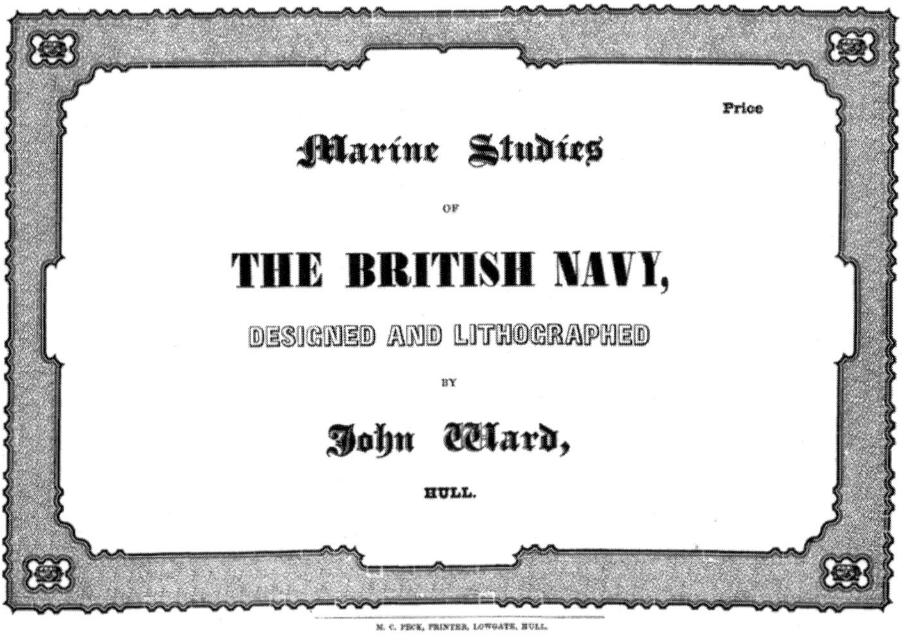

Price

Marine Studies

OF

THE BRITISH NAVY,

DESIGNED AND LITHOGRAPHED

BY

John Ward,

HULL.

M. C. PECK, PRINTER, LOWGATE, HULL.

(*Eds:* The form of the missing cover page would probably resemble the reconstructed version above.)

THE BRITISH NAVY.

A Series of Ten Views illustrative of the several rates and classes of Vessels in Her Majesty's Navy, Lithographed in the tinted manner from Drawings taken at the different Naval Establishments, by J. Ward, and expressly executed as a work of information and instruction.

The series contain the Revenue Cutter; Schooner; Gun-Brig; Corvette of 18 Guns; Frigate of 36 Guns; large Frigate of 50 Guns; 74 Gun-Ship; 84 Gun-Ship; First-rate of 120 Guns; and the Steam Vessel.

To such as have not the opportunity of seeing those bulwarks of the Nation, the Wooden Walls of Old England, the present series will convey a clear and picturesque delineation of some of the most approved vessels at present afloat; and to those desirous of studying Marine Drawing, an opportunity is afforded of obtaining that, which as a work of reference will be highly desirable, every care having been taken with the proportions and detail of each, with their positions, spars, rigging, canvas, &c.

It is necessary to state that in the accompanying Views the Revenue Cutter is represented from the dimensions of the Greyhound; the Schooner from the Wanderer; Gun-Brig from the Nautilus; Corvette from the Vesta; the 36 Gun Frigate from the Pique; 50 Gun Frigate from the Vindictive; 74 Gun Ship from the Bellerophon; 84 from the Asia; the First-Rate from the Britannia; and the Steam Vessel from the Alban.

These Views were originally intended to illustrate a Work containing Draughts, Plans, and Sections of Vessels, with their dimensions, displacement, and tonnage; forming a Guide to Drawing, for the purposes of Painting, and the Marine Profession generally.

That the Work has not yet been Published, arises not from a doubt of its success or utility, but from circumstances which for a time preclude the possibility of bringing so difficult yet desirable a work before the public—whose patronage with that of the Commanders, Builders, and Artists generally, J. Ward is anxious to obtain.

The Cutter

Sailing by the Wind---Starboard tack---Lee bow view---Strong breeze.

(*Eds:* In its original usage, a cutter refers to a single masted small boat with fore and aft sails and a bowsprit. The mast is typically set further back than a sloop. The print found in the bound set, not reproduced here, is titled 'REVENUE CUTTER/ Getting under way- jib and mainsail hoisted-broadside view –light air of wind'. It represents the *Greyhound.*)

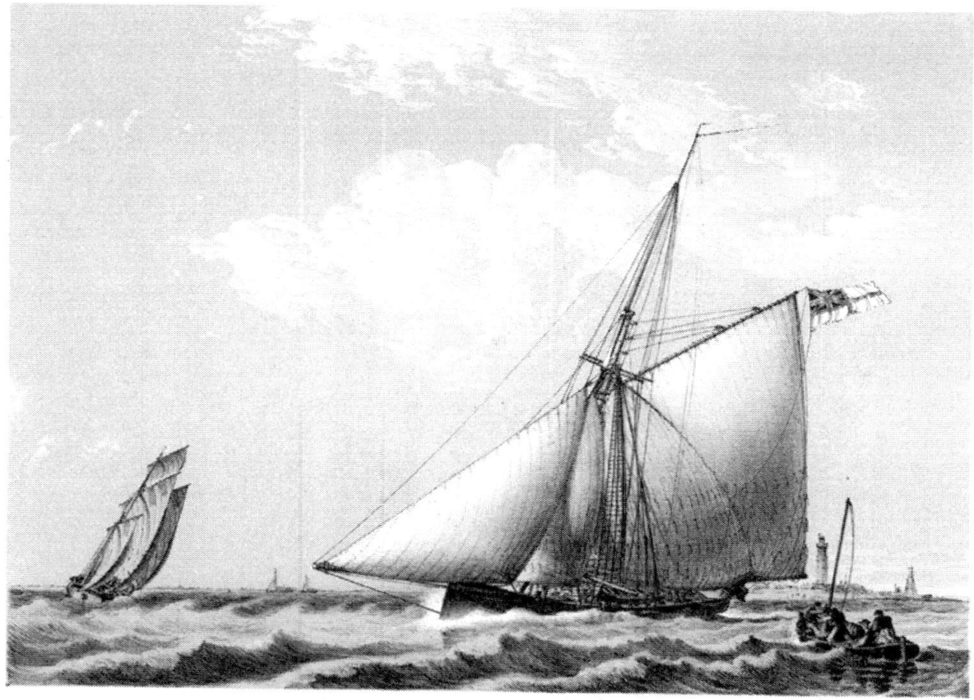

THE CUTTER

Sailing by the wind – Starboard tack – Lee bow view – Strong breeze.

The Armed Schooner

Larboard tack---Broadside view---blowing fresh.

(*Eds:* The *Wanderer* built by Betts of Mistleythorn.)

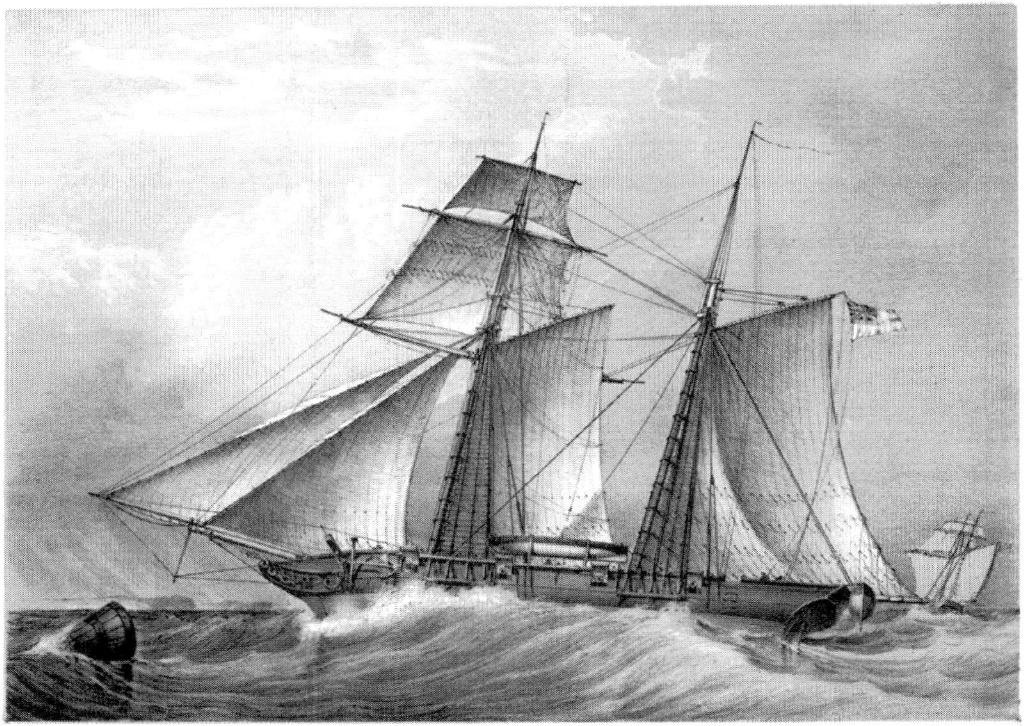

THE ARMED SCHOONER

Larboard tack — Broadside view — blowing fresh.

The Gun Brig

At anchor---Sails loosed---Light air of Wind.

(*Eds:* The *Nautilus* built in 1807 by Betts of Mistleythorn.)

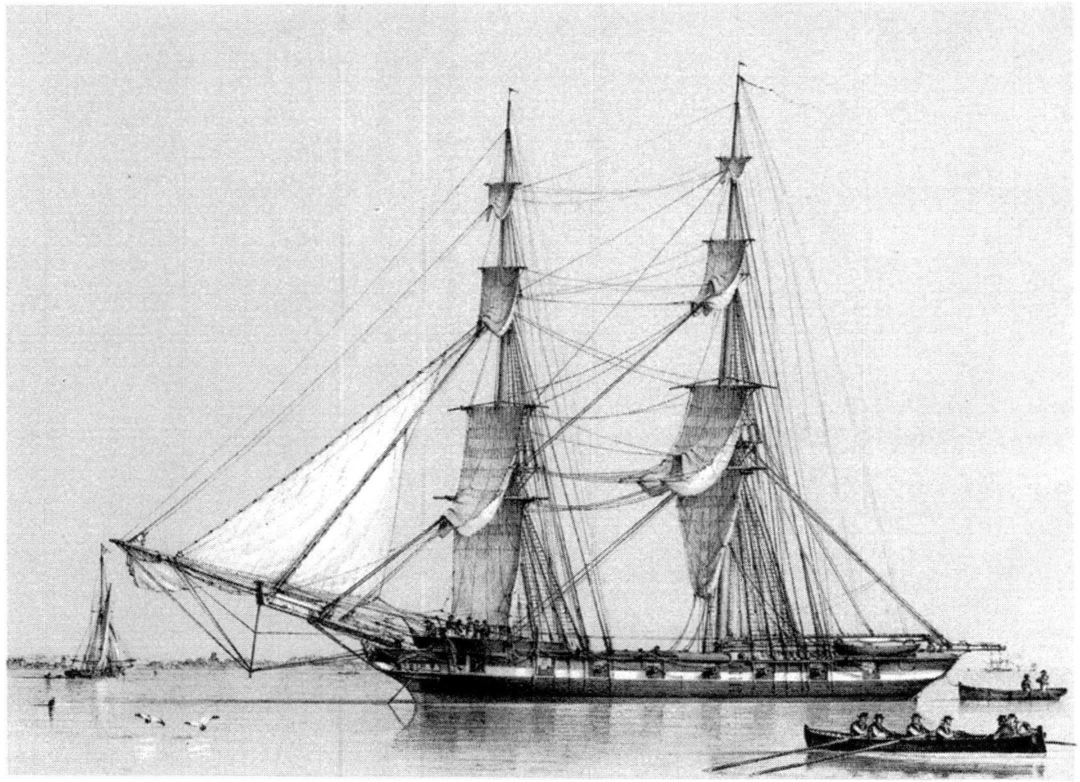

THE GUN BRIG

At anchor – Sails Loosed – Light air of Wind.

A Sixth Rate---18 Gun Corvette

Close hauled---Starboard tack---Weather broadside view.

(*Eds:* The *Vesta* built at Bermuda 1806.)

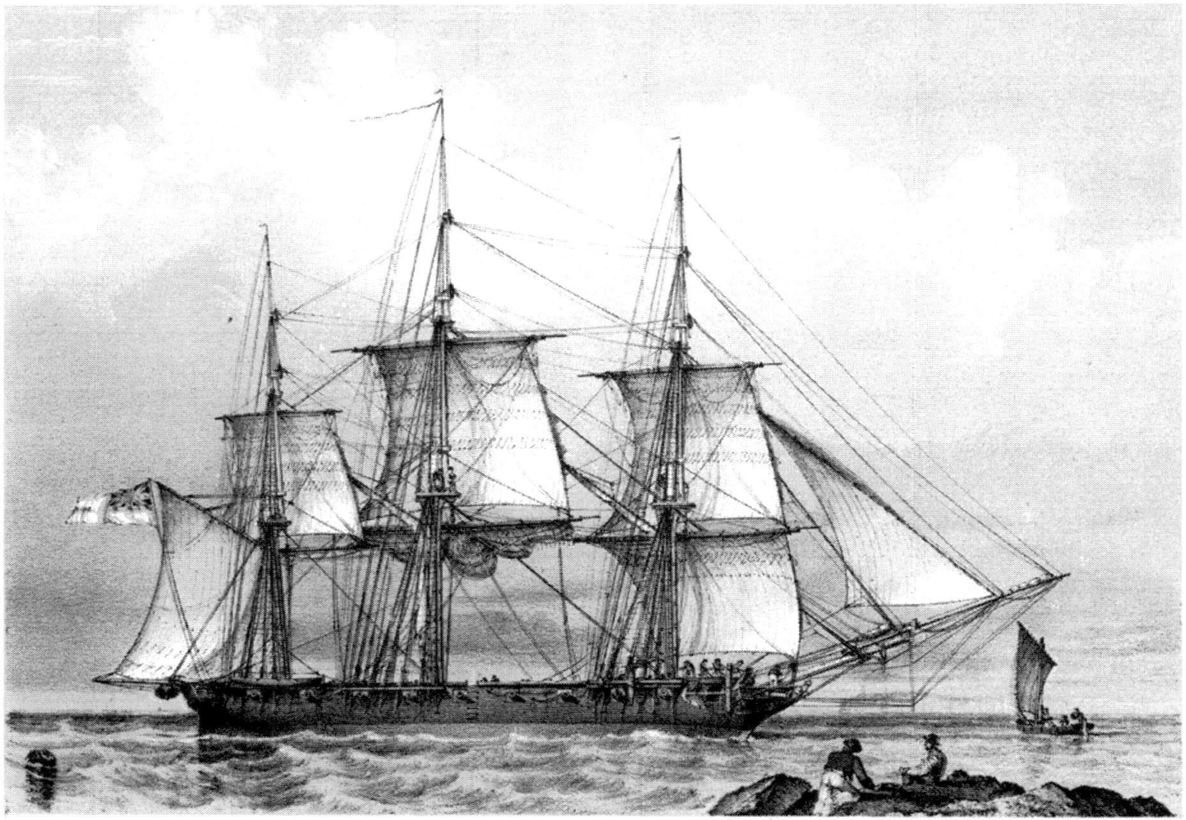

A SIXTH RATE – 18 GUN CORVETTE

Close hauled – Starboard tack – Weather broadside view.

A Fifth Rate – 36 Gun Frigate

Hove to --- Larboard tack --- Lee bow view --- Light breeze.

(*Eds:* The *Pique* launched at Plymouth in 1834, named after a French prize. Notorious for her 'smartness'; 1837 in action against Carlist forces in northern Spain, assisted at bombardment of Petrapavlosk; laid up at Portsmouth 1846-51 and in 1871 became an isolation hospital at Plymouth; sold out of the service 1910.)

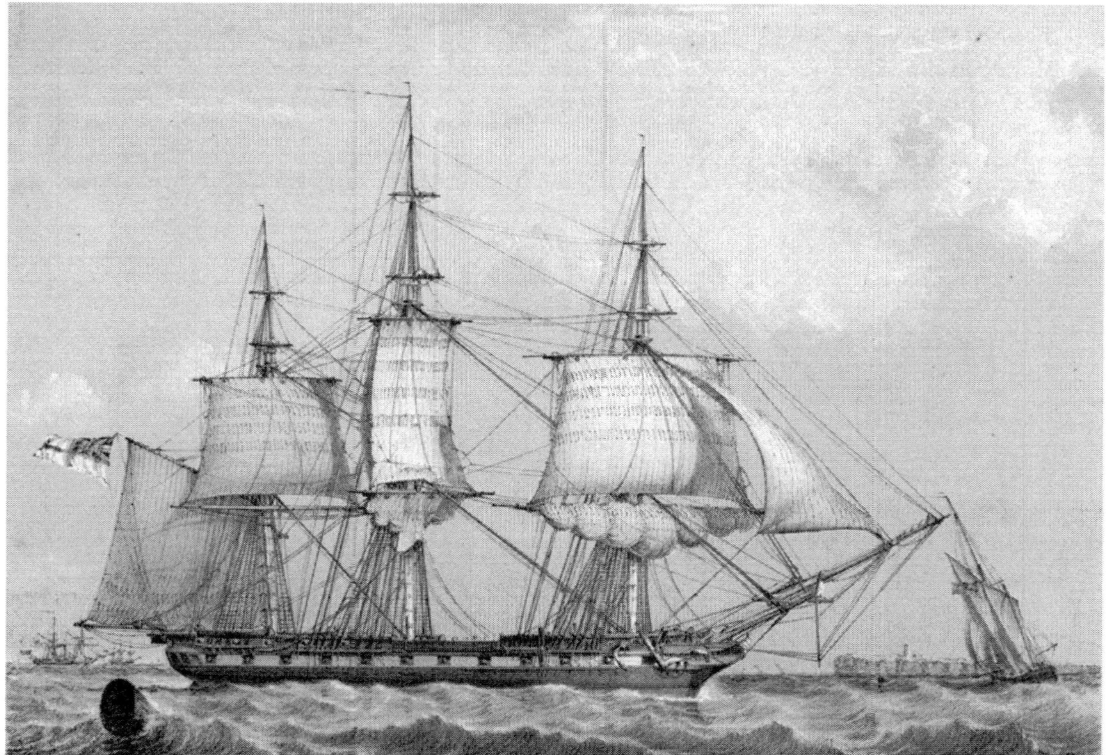

A FIFTH RATE - 36 GUN FRIGATE

Hove to — Larboard tack — Lee bow view — Light breeze.

A Fourth Rate – 50 Gun Frigate

Close hauled---Starboard tack---Weather quarter view.

(*Eds:* The *Vindictive* built as a 74 (third rate) at Portsmouth 1813 and reduced to 50 guns in 1832; in 1865 a store ship at Fernando Po for squadron suppressing slavery; wrecked 1871.)

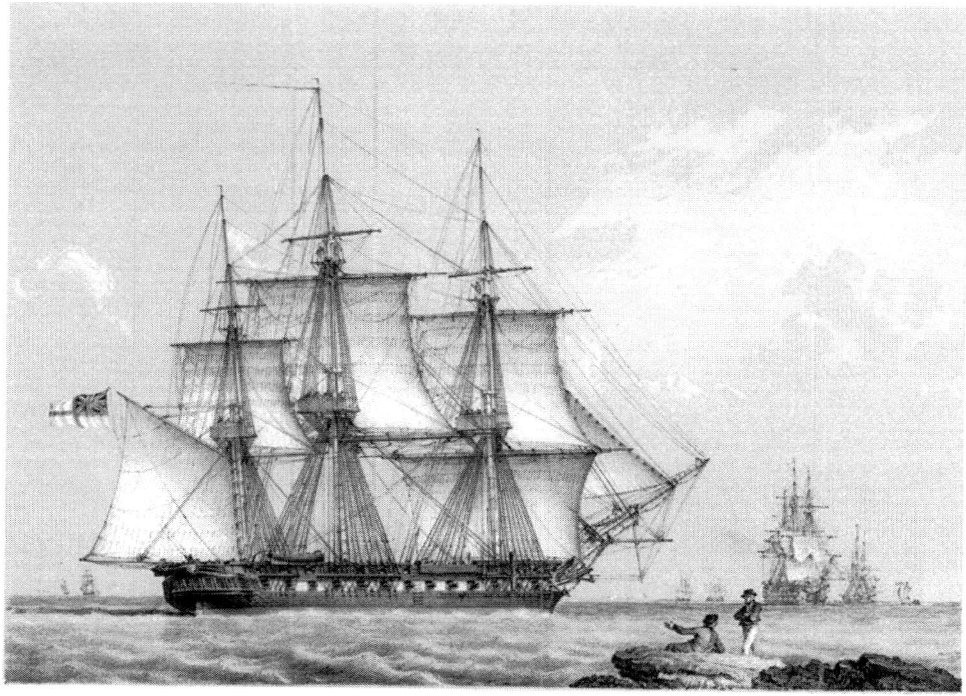

A FOURTH RATE – 50 GUN FRIGATE

Close hauled—Starboard tack—Weather quarter view.

Third rate – 74 guns

Close reefed topsails-larboard quarter view-A gale – Lee shore

(*Eds:* The *Bellerophon*, not the vessel of that name associated with Bonaparte; formerly the *Waterloo*, built at Portsmouth 1818, renamed 1824, and employed for harbour service in 1848.)

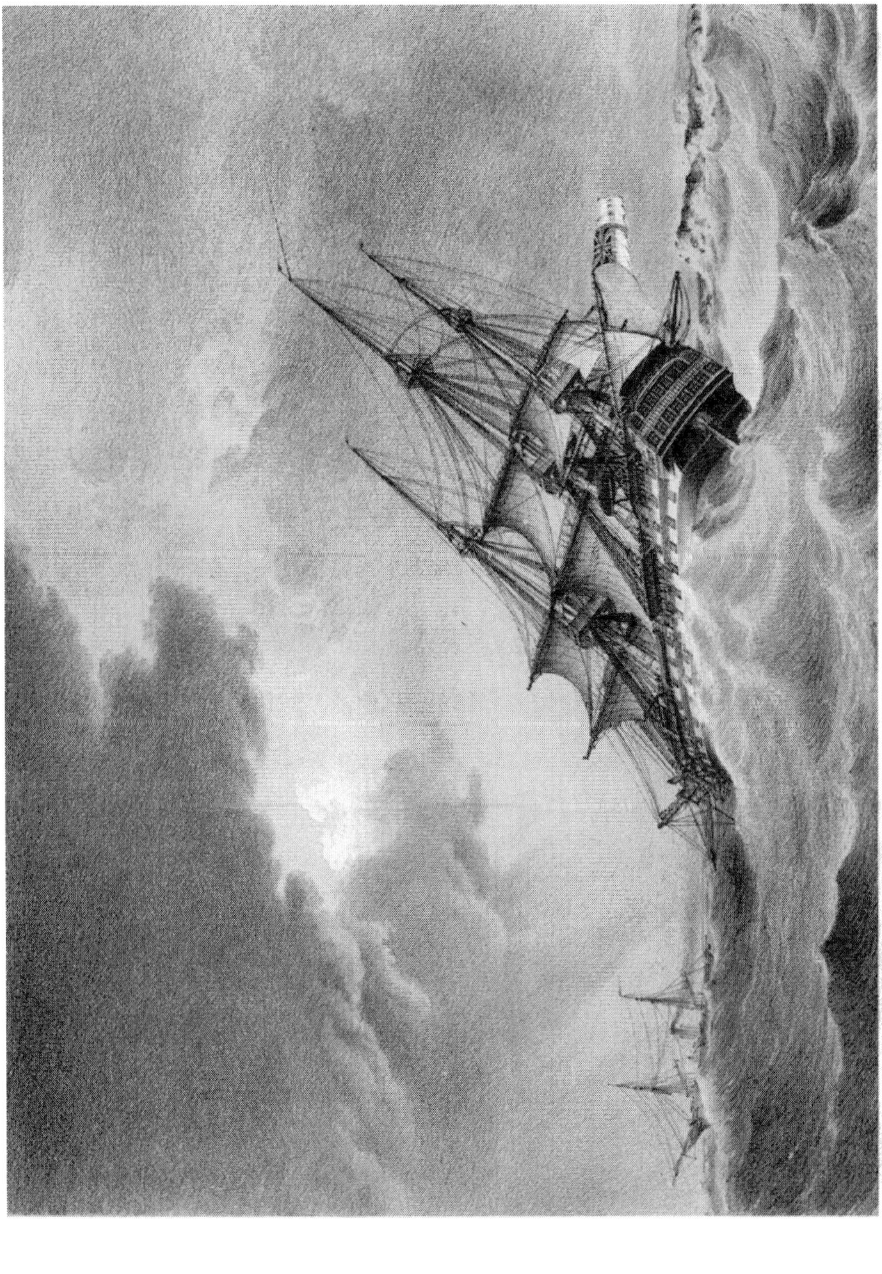

A Second Rate – 84 Guns

Hove to---Main topsail aback---Courses hauled up---Jib sheet eased of.

(*Eds:* The *Asia* a teak vessel built at Bombay in 1824, she was Codrington's flagship at the Battle of Navarino in 1827; in 1840 blockaded Syrian coast and used as a transport in Crimea; in 1859 became a guardship and broken up in 1908.)

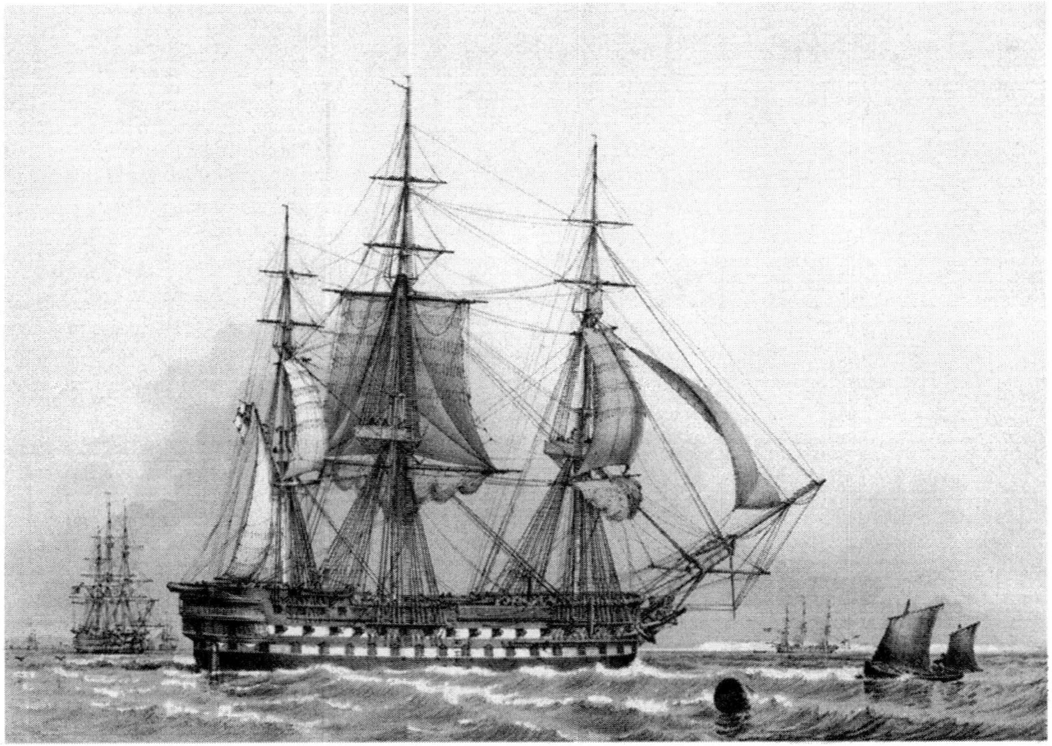

A SECOND RATE – 84 GUNS

Hove to – Main topsail aback – Courses hauled up – Jib sheet eased of

A First Rate – 120 Guns

Going free---Wind abeam---Lee Larboard quarterview---moderate breeze.

(*Eds:* The *Britannia* built at Plymouth in 1820, the flagship at Portsmouth 1836-51; 1859 commissioned as a cadet training ship and eventually gave her name to the 'Britannia Royal Naval College'. She was relieved by the *Prince of* Wales in 1869 and broken up at Devonport the same year.)

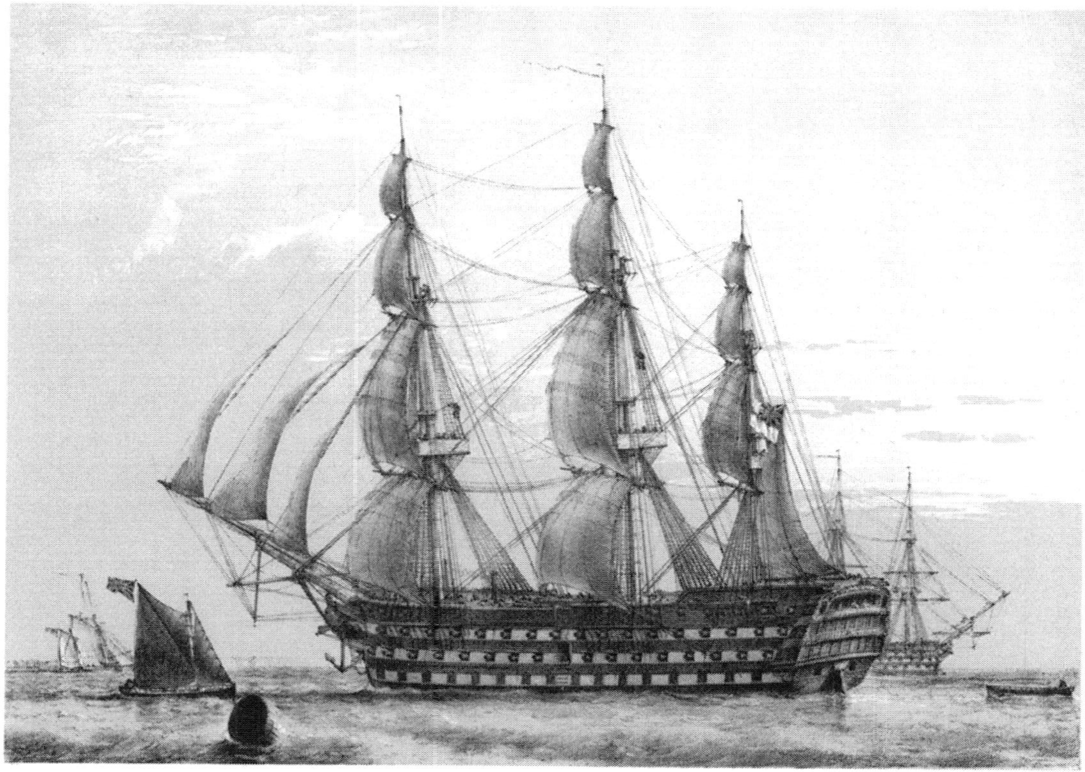

A FIRST RATE - 120 GUNS

Going free – wind abeam – Lee Larboard quarterview – moderate breeze.

Untitled

Port bow view of the First Rate, *HMS Britannia* under way.

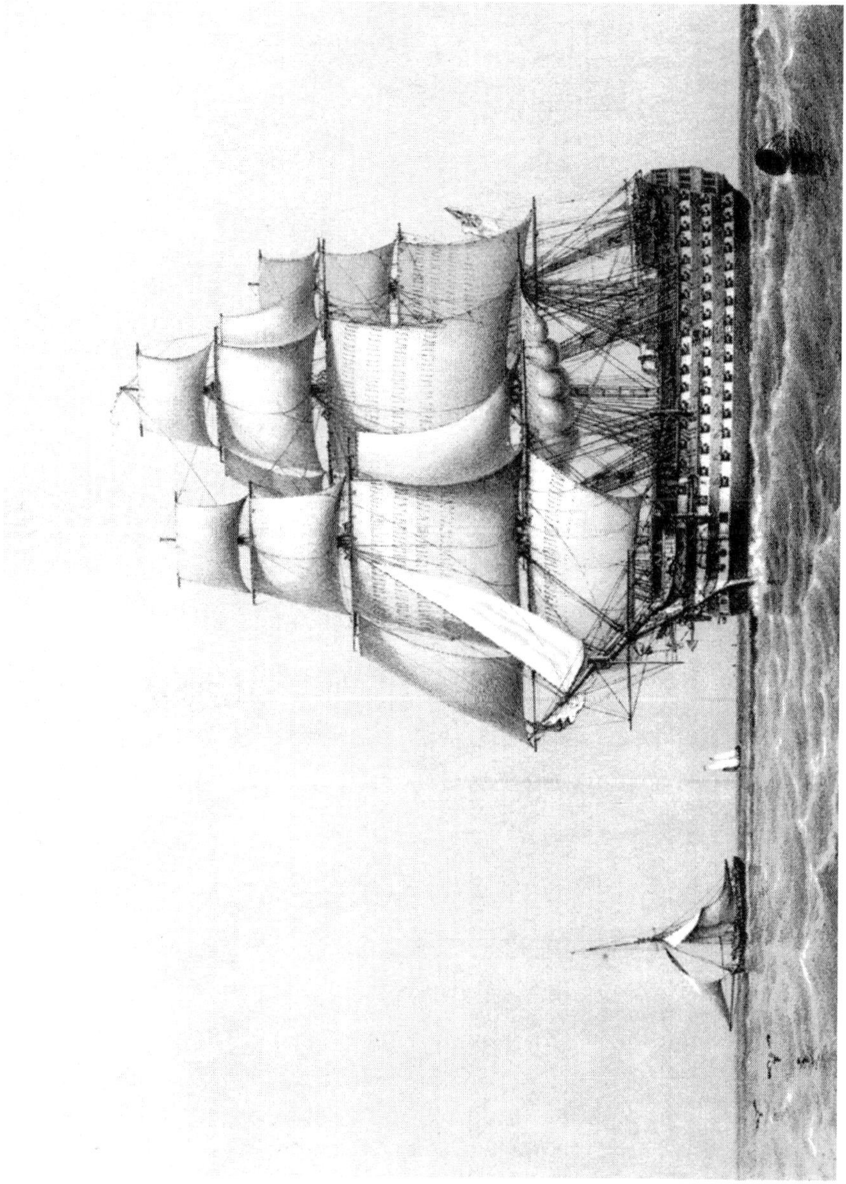

The Steam Vessel

At anchor---Larboard broadside view---Calm.

(*Eds:* The paddle steamer *Alban*; one of the first steamers in the Royal Navy, designed at Deptford as a 10 gun brig and given engines of 80 and then 100 n.h.p. Lengthened at Chatham 1839 and remained in service till 1860.)

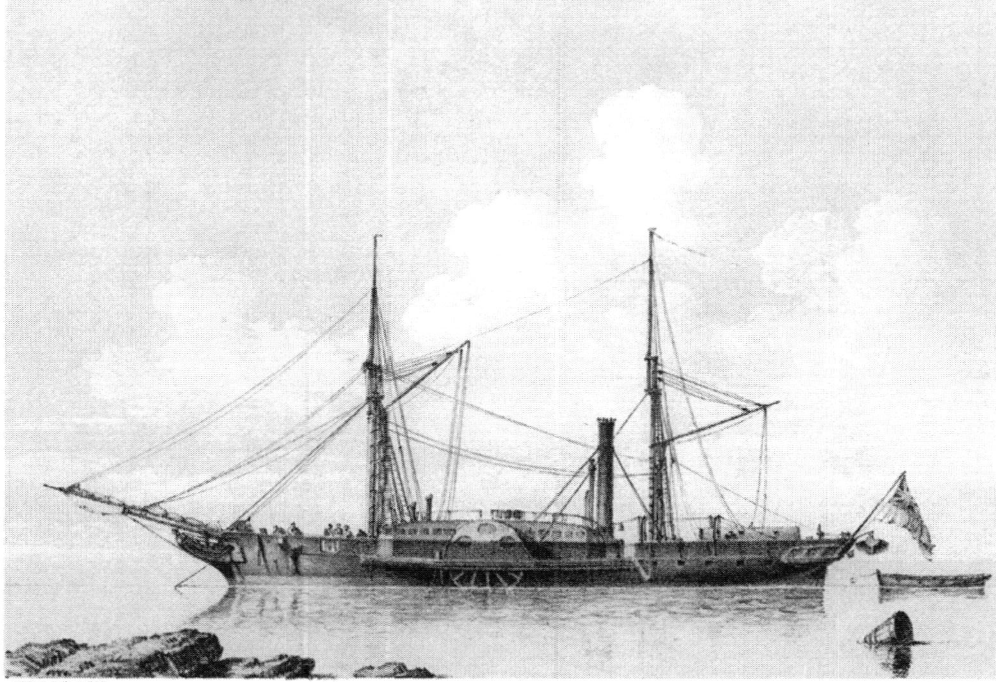

J. Ward, Del. et Lith.

THE STEAM VESSEL

At anchor – Larboard broadside view – Calm.

The Steam Vessel

At anchor---Starboard broadside view ---Calm.

(*Eds:* The paddle steamer *Alban.*)

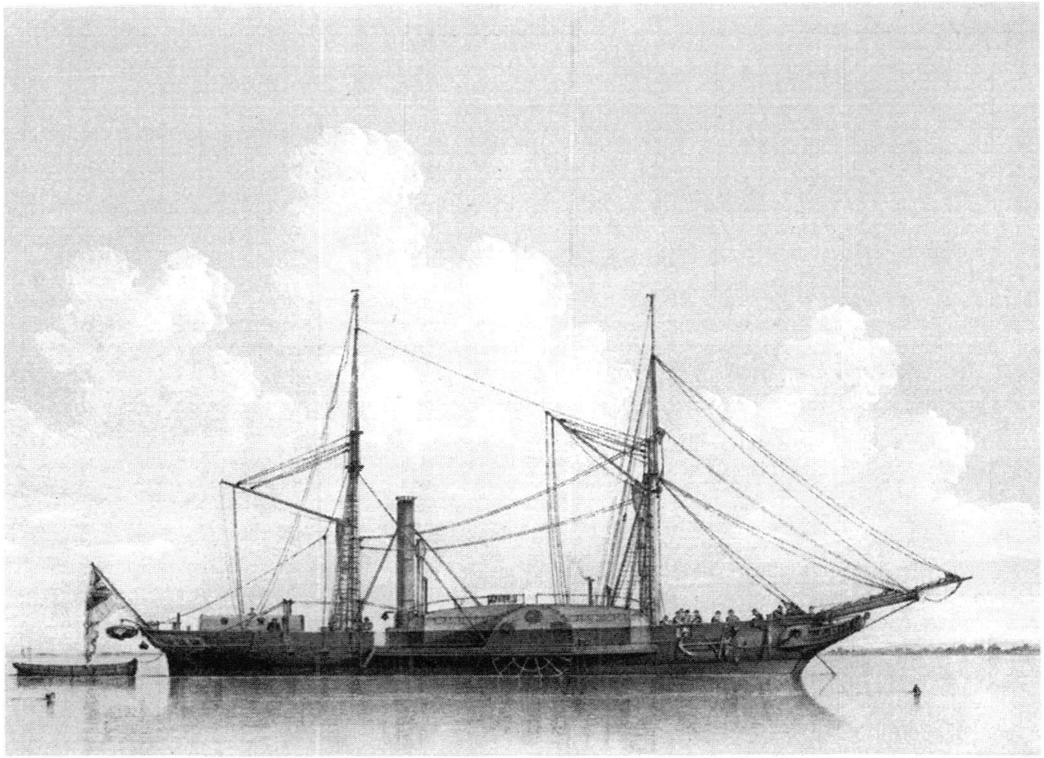

THE STEAM VESSEL

At Anchor — Starboard broadside view — Calm.

Untitled (Armed Schooner)

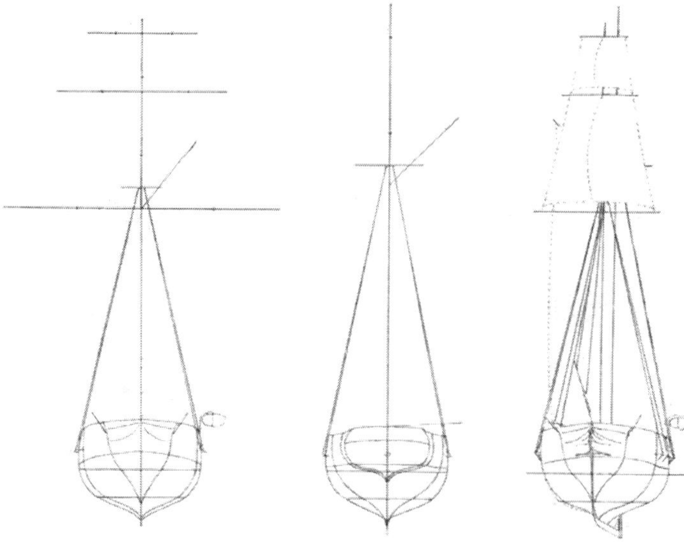

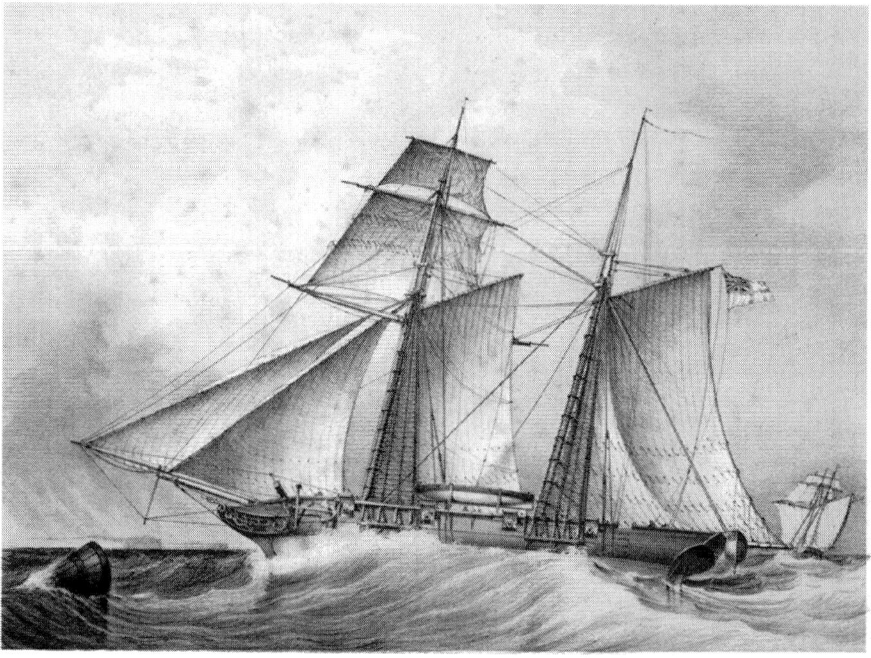

Untitled (Gun Brig)

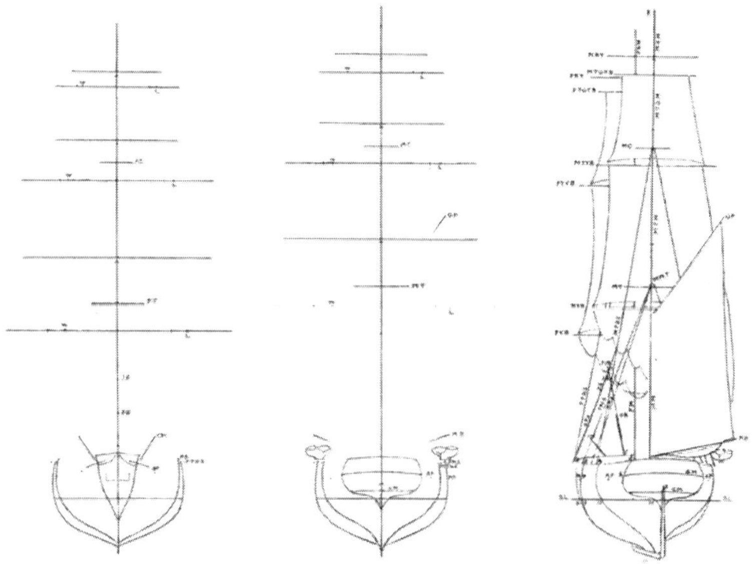

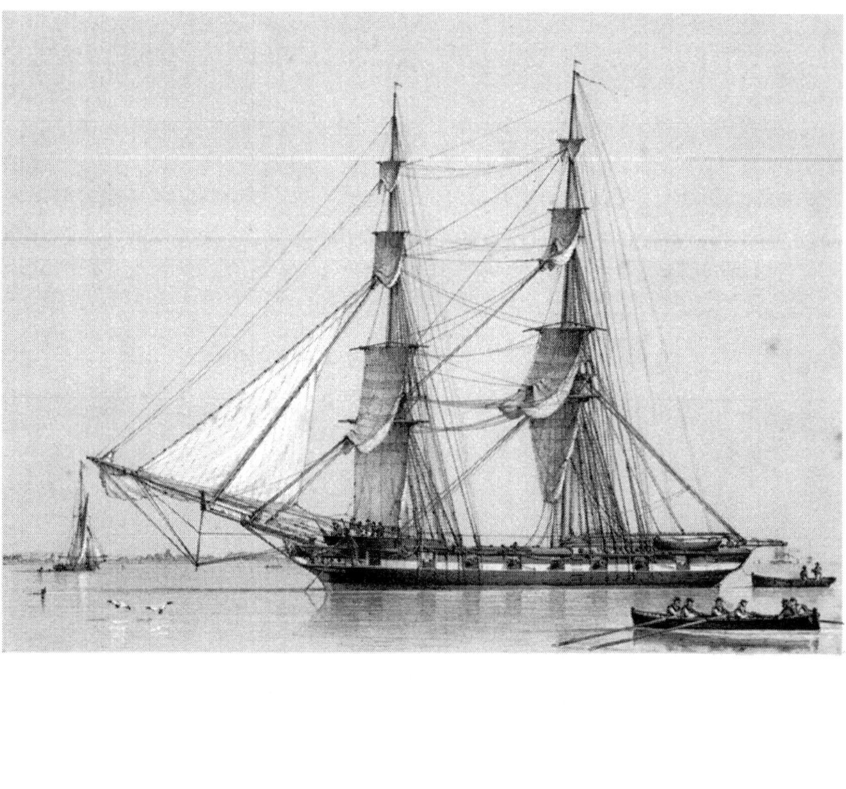

Untitled (6th Rate)

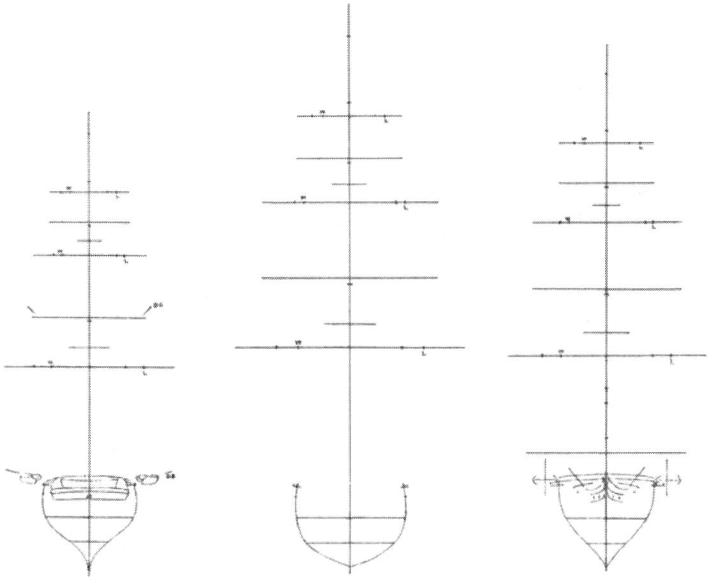

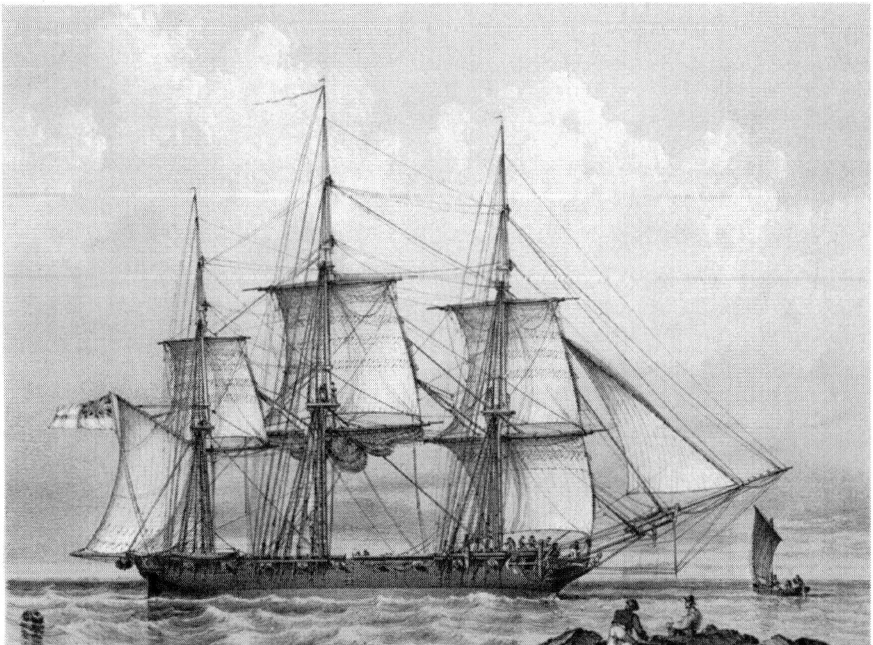

Untitled (4th Rate)

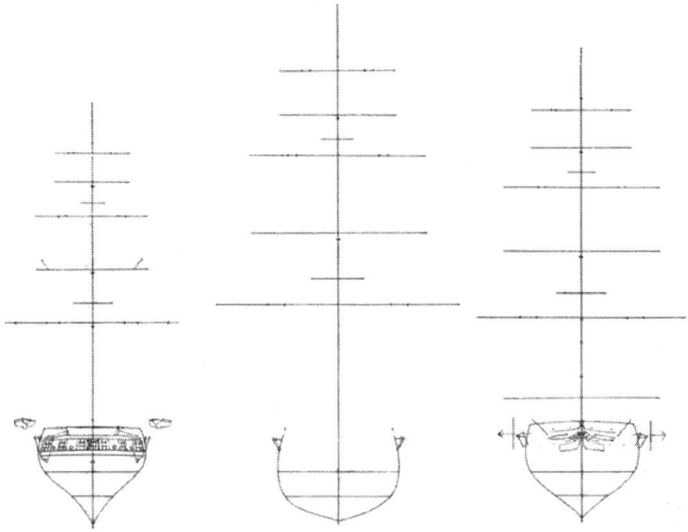

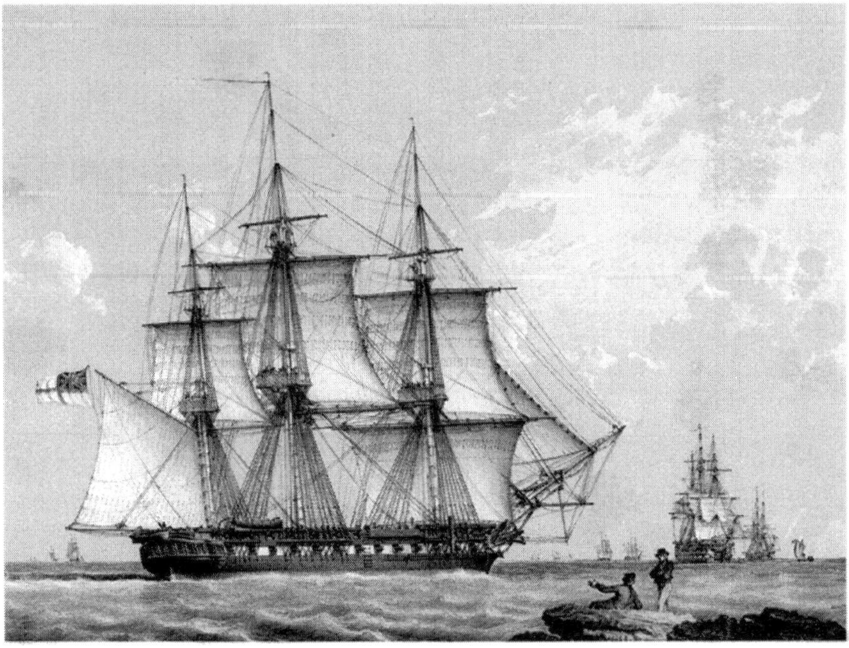

Untitled (3rd Rate)

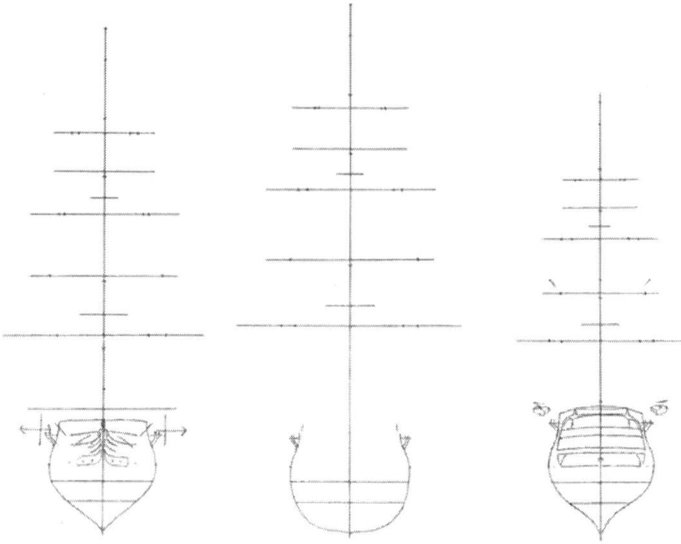

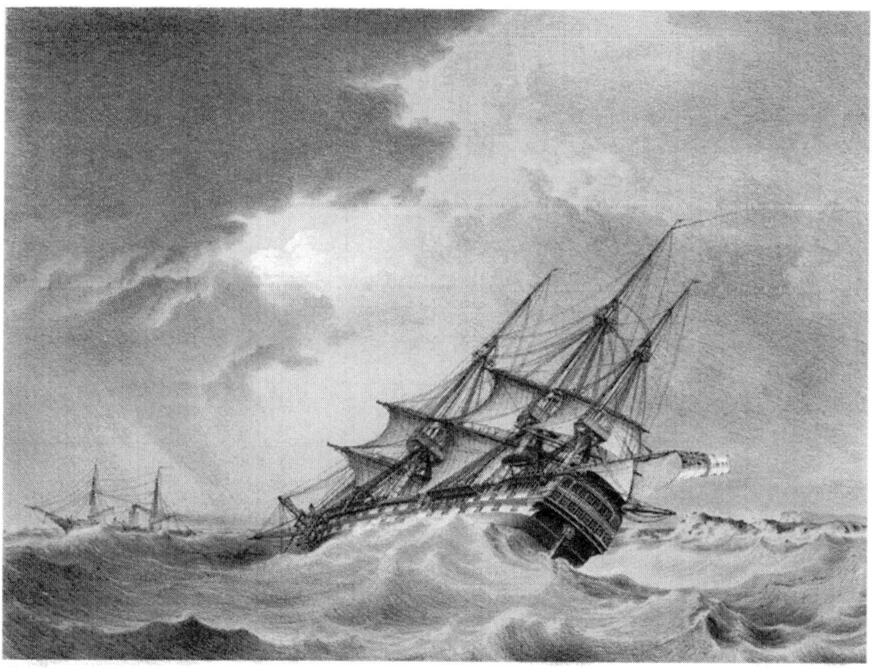

Untitled (2nd Rate)

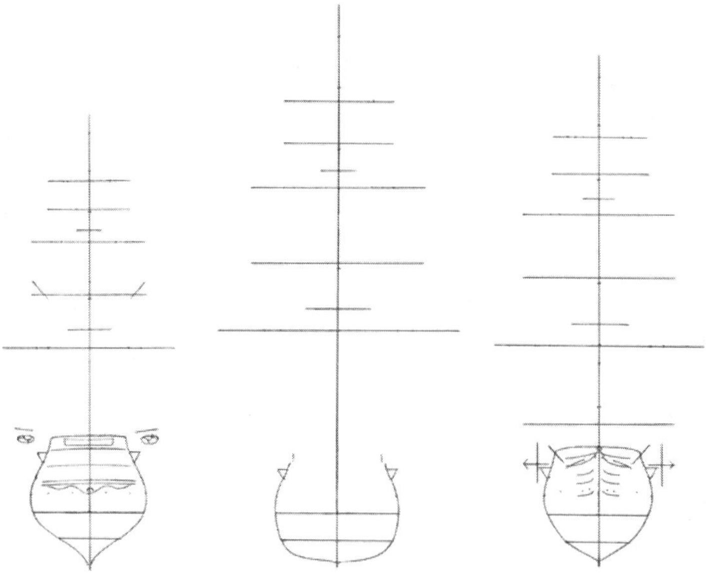

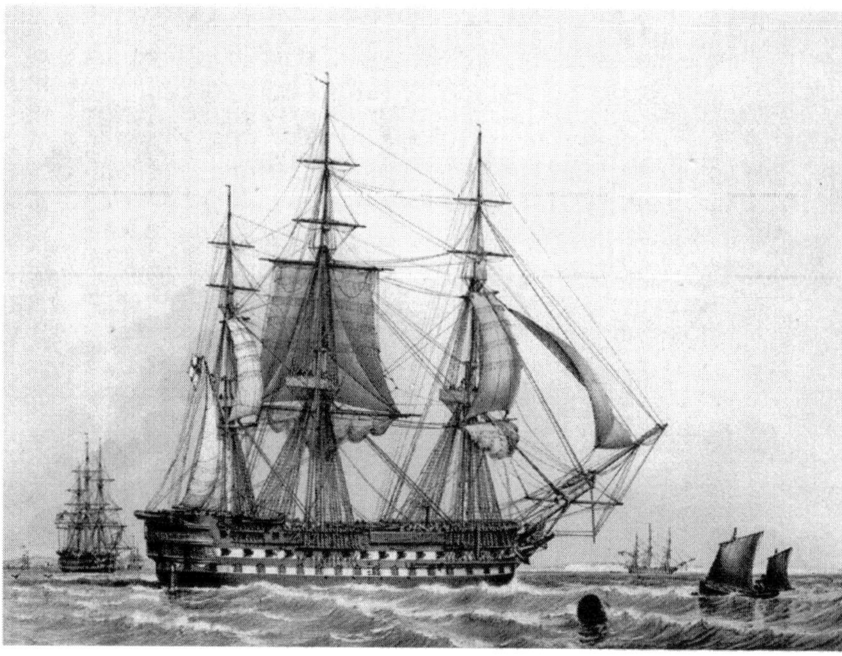

Untitled (1st Rate)

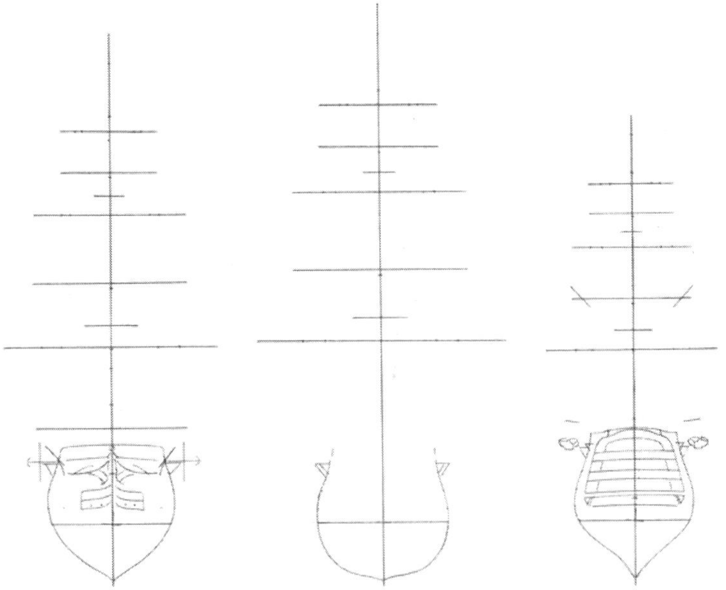

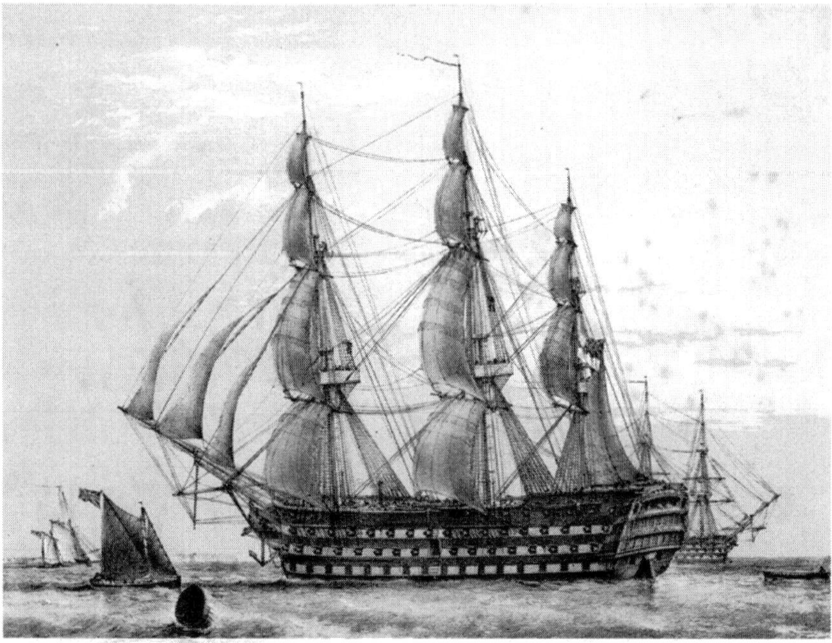

(*Eds*: HMS Britannia.[1] Bow view port side – at anchor)

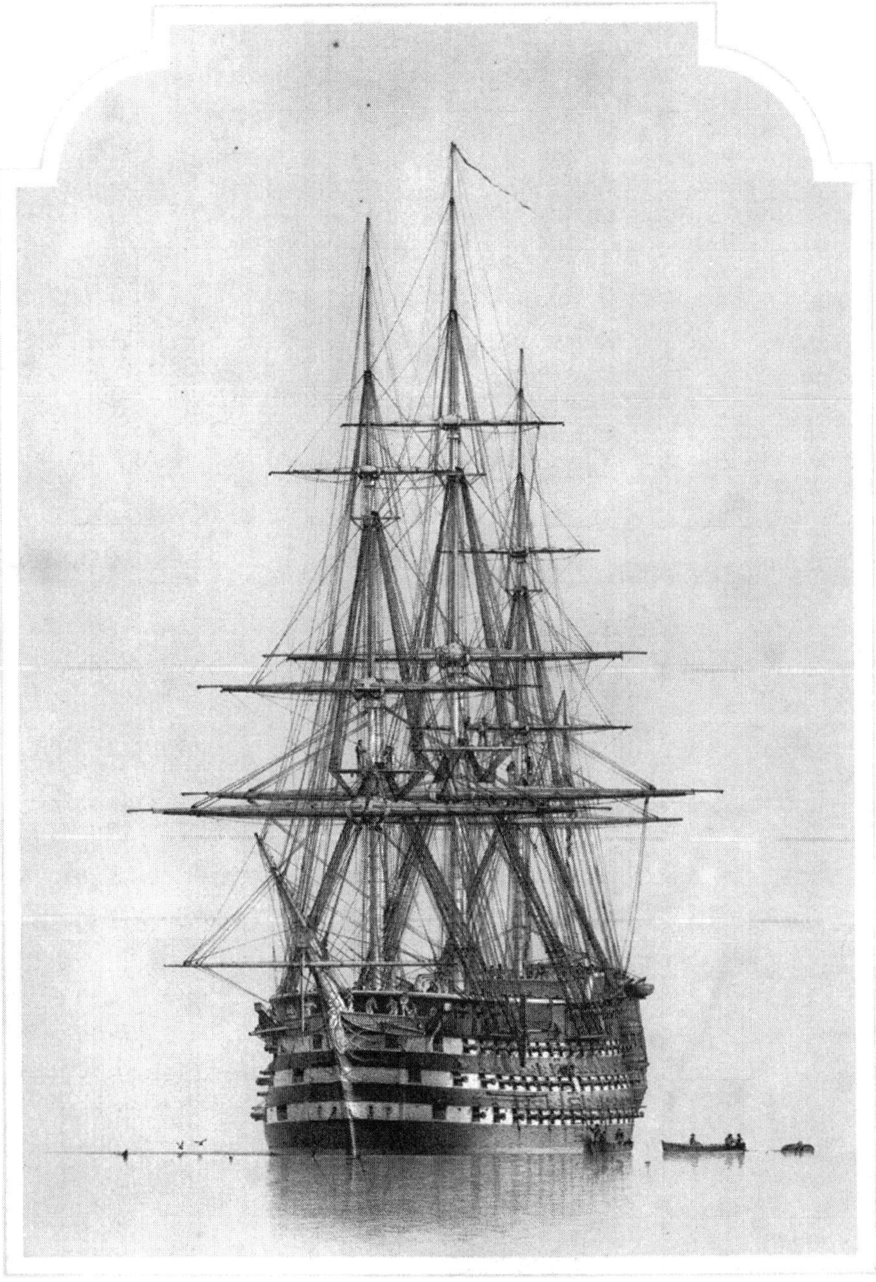

(*Eds*: HMS Britannia. Bow view port side – under-weigh)

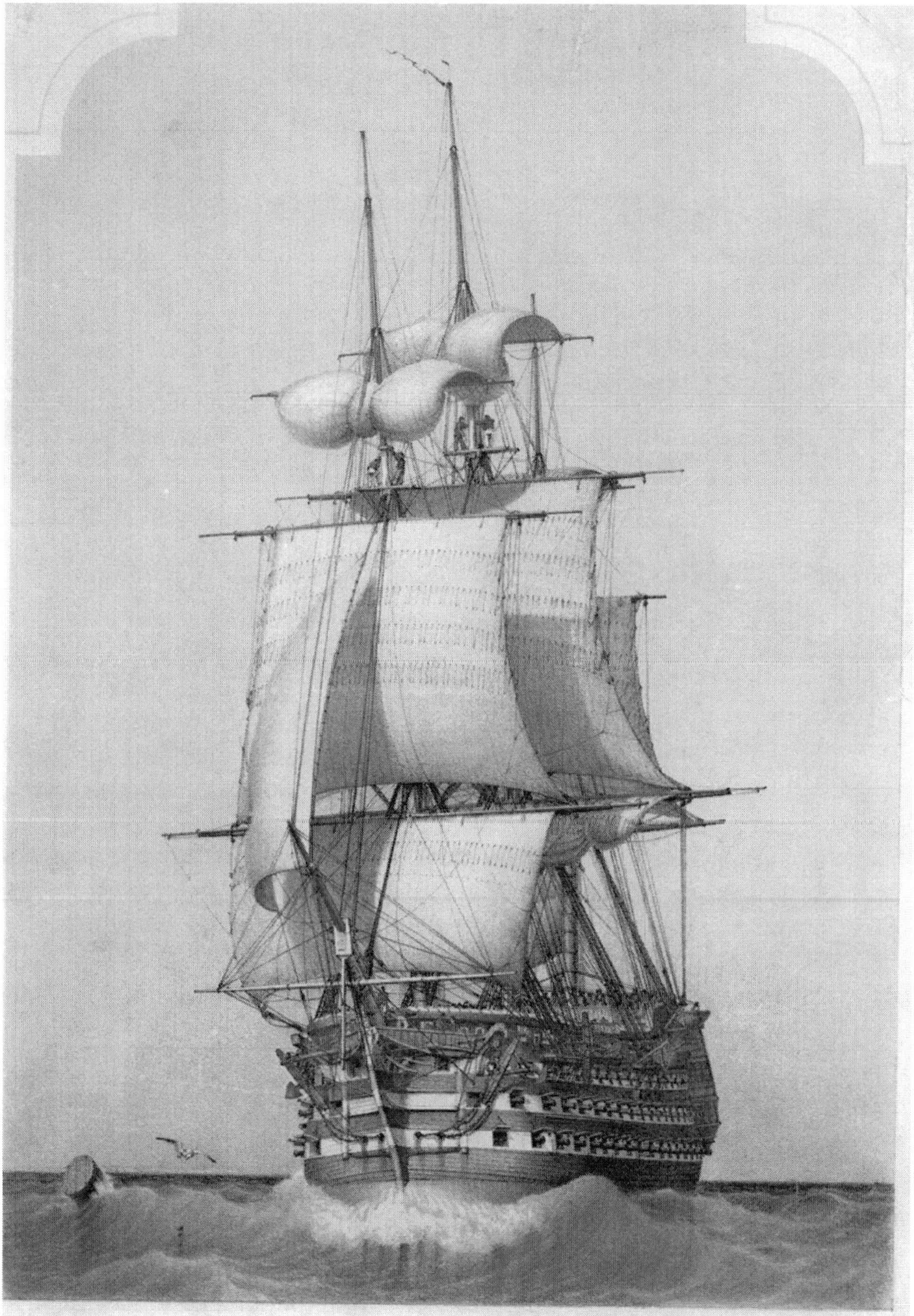

(*Eds*: HMS Britannia. Stern view port side – at anchor)

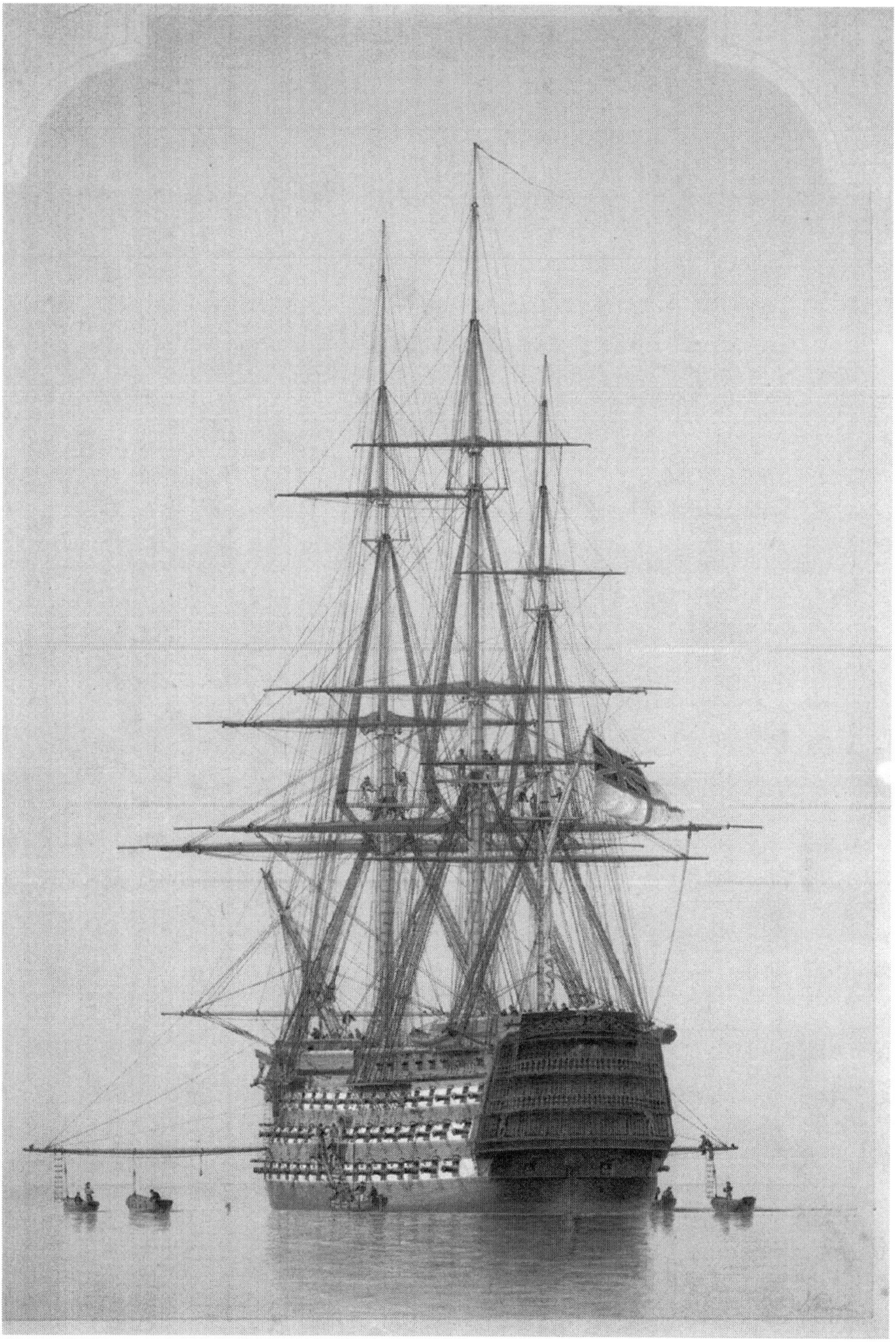

(*Eds*: HMS Britannia. Stern view starboard side, under-weigh)

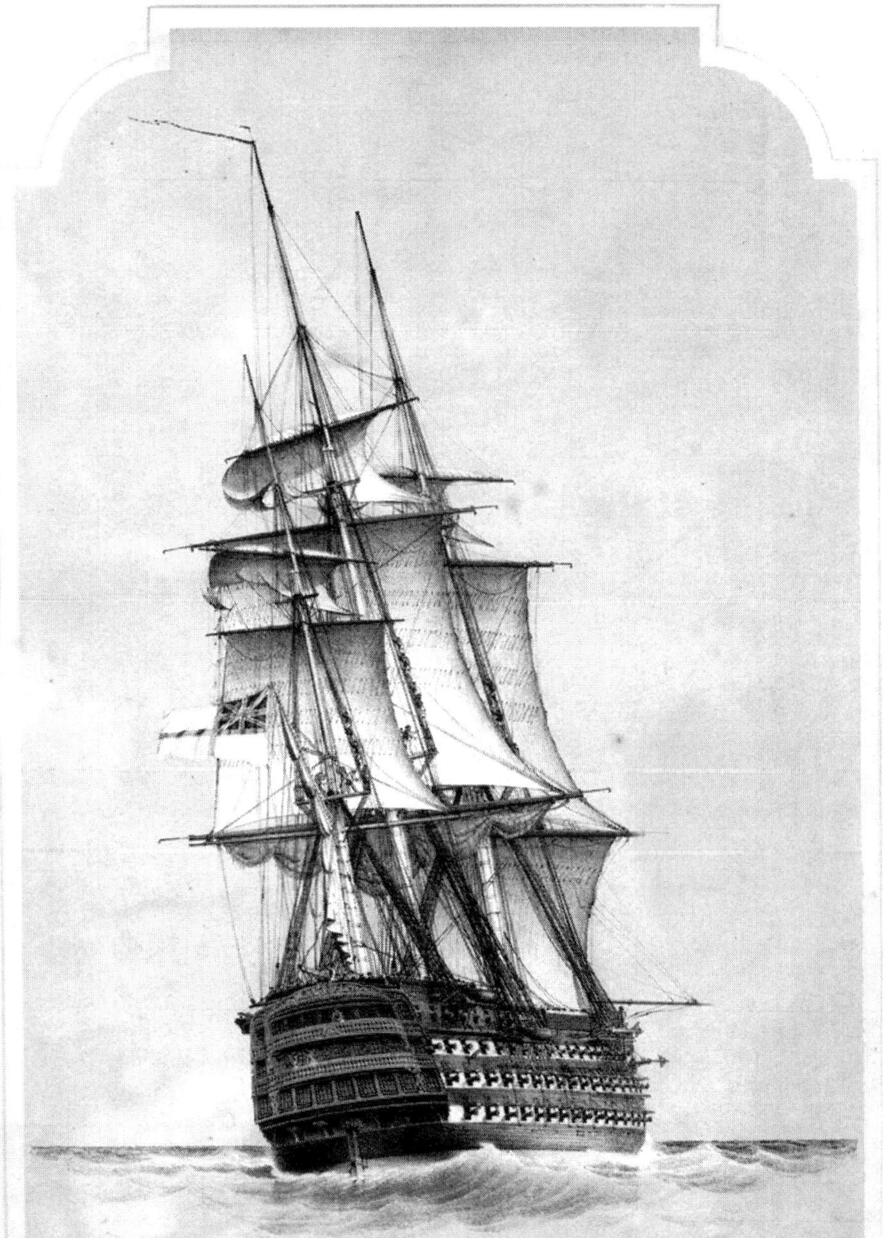

'Raymond' 1843

This print of the RAYMOND, Hugh McKay Commander/the first vessel direct from China to Hull is published commemorative of her arrival on the 14th October 1843

(W. Monkhouse of York)

(*Eds:* Built at Sunderland, Co. Durham, in 1840 by P. Austin & Son. She was jointly owned by Thomas, William and Isaac Ward, and her captain. The first vessel to bring a consignment of tea direct from China to Hull; the cargo totalled over 600,000 lb. The *Raymond* was purchased by Hart & Co. in 1846 and re-registerd in London; *Hull News* 13 and 20 October.)

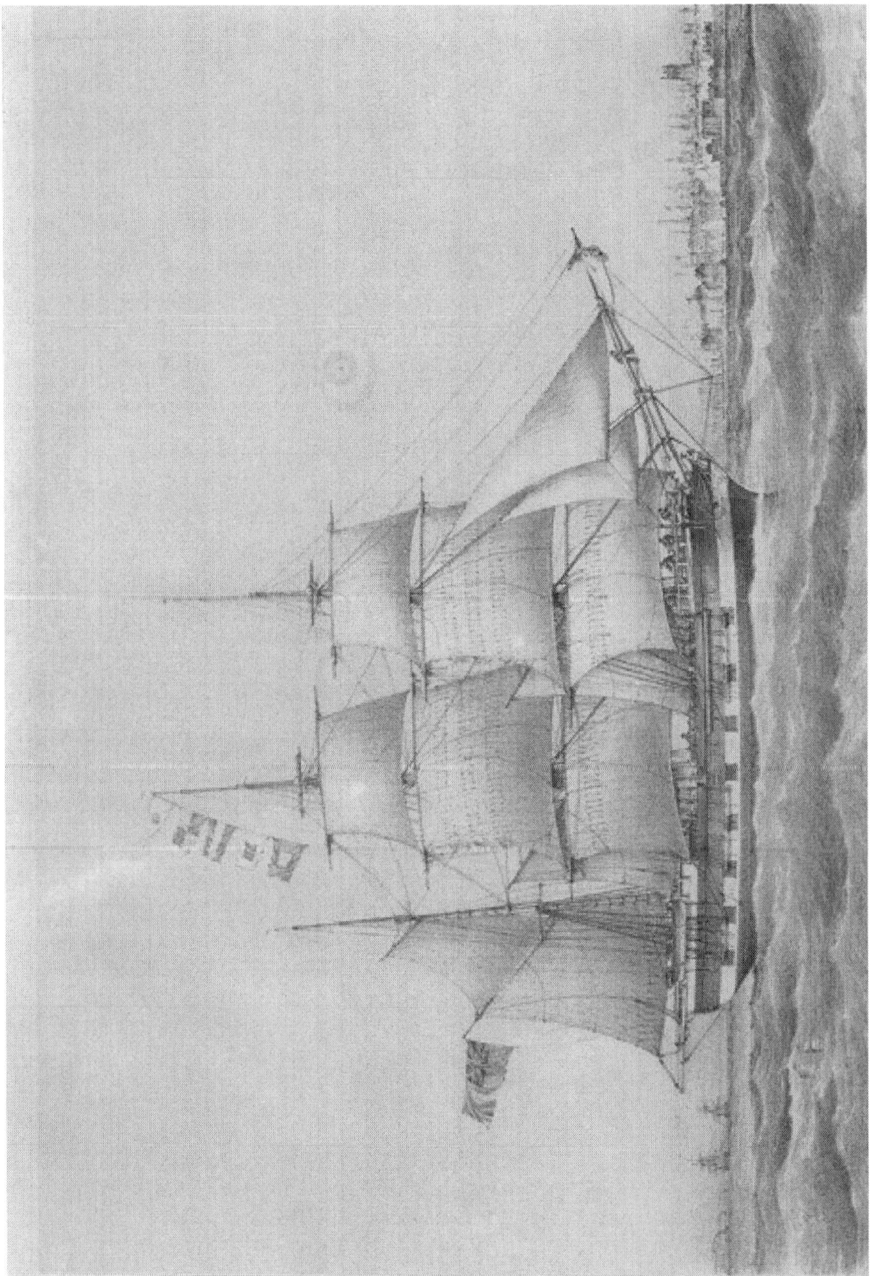

‘Wanderer’ 1845

Inscribed in ink on reverse:

Wanderer bound out to Hong Kong, China, 1845 Septr. With a full cargo of Manchester and other goods the first ship ever loaded a full cargo of goods to China from Hull and up to 1880 there has not been another part cargo delivered at Hong Kong port at Canton.

Followed by: ‘John Priest, master mariner, commander, returned home to London in 11 mos with 500 tons tea 40 feet to the ton at £7.10 per ton 360 tons register. Ship cost £3000 ready for sea [J.H £3.750]’

(*Eds:* This handwritten inscription beneath the image bears the initials J H for John Hall, to whom this print belonged, as did the English Alphabet pages in paper covers. Aged 22, Hall was admitted a younger brother of Hull Trinity House, 27 September 1797, at the same time he qualified to pilot vessels in the seas between the Humber and the Naze of Norway. He was Master Warden when the foundation stone of the Hospital in Carr Lane was laid 18 September 1833, and chairman of the building committee when the foundation stone of the Carr Lane Almshouses were laid 6 April 1837. He was still chairman when the foundation stone of the new Trinity House chapel was laid 25 October 1839. It is not known whether the lithographs were acquired direct from the artist or from the sale of the studio contents 1853.The *Wanderer* was built at Sunderland, Co. Durham, in 1844, and wholly owned by William Priest the elder, until 1852 when 30 shares were sold to Johann Heinrich Fredricks of Lancaster. Lost 18 February 1853.

Ward painted a canvas, c 1844-9, of the *Ruby*, *Wanderer,* and *Garnet*, three vessels belonging to Priest & Son. A port profile watercolour study of another Hull vessel of the same name, very similar in appearance, but ship rigged, built 1835 by Edward Gibson, was offered for sale (lot 771, 19 November 2009; Tennants, Leyburn) measuring approx 6 x 8 in, off Spurn, with a pilot cutter on the starboard side.

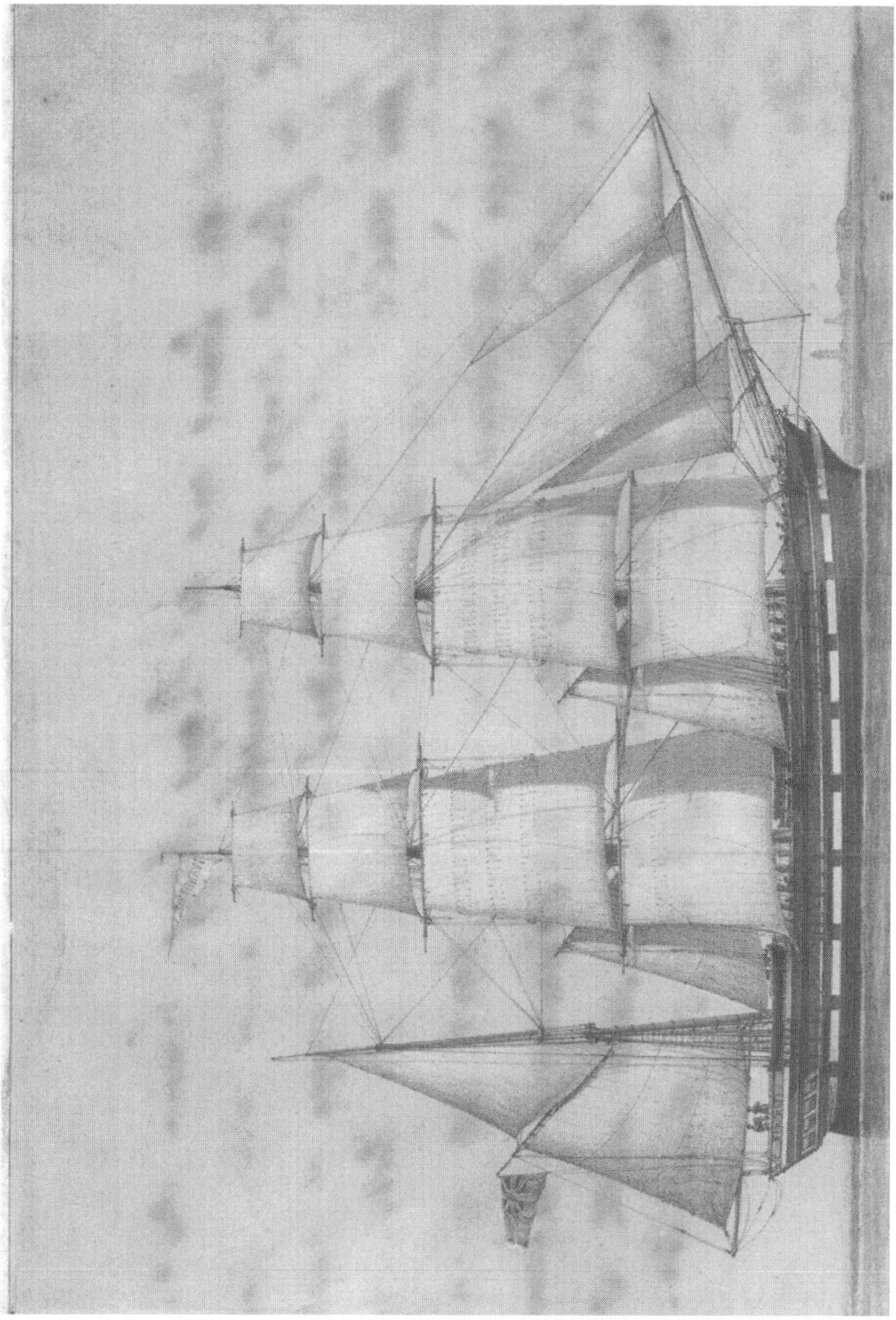

Regatta 1847

HULL GRAND REGATTA/ 28th September 1847/ The yacht *Hilda* Thomas Richards Esq. Owner, winning the Challenge Cup value £50, given by the Members of the Royal Yorkshire Yacht Club, to whom this print is respectfully dedicated

(W. Monkhouse of York)

(*Eds:* Beneath the image are the names of the principal vessels, *Hilda*, *Whim*, *Phebe* and *Sylph.* The *Whim* belonged to the Hull merchant and shipowner, Joseph Gee, for whom Ward produced a number of canvases of vessels Gee owned or had an interest in; notably the *William Lee* which in 1838 returned to Hull from Calcutta after re-establishing direct trade from Hull to India. Gee was Vice-Commodore of the RYYC 1847-51 and a member of the Royal Yacht Squadron.)

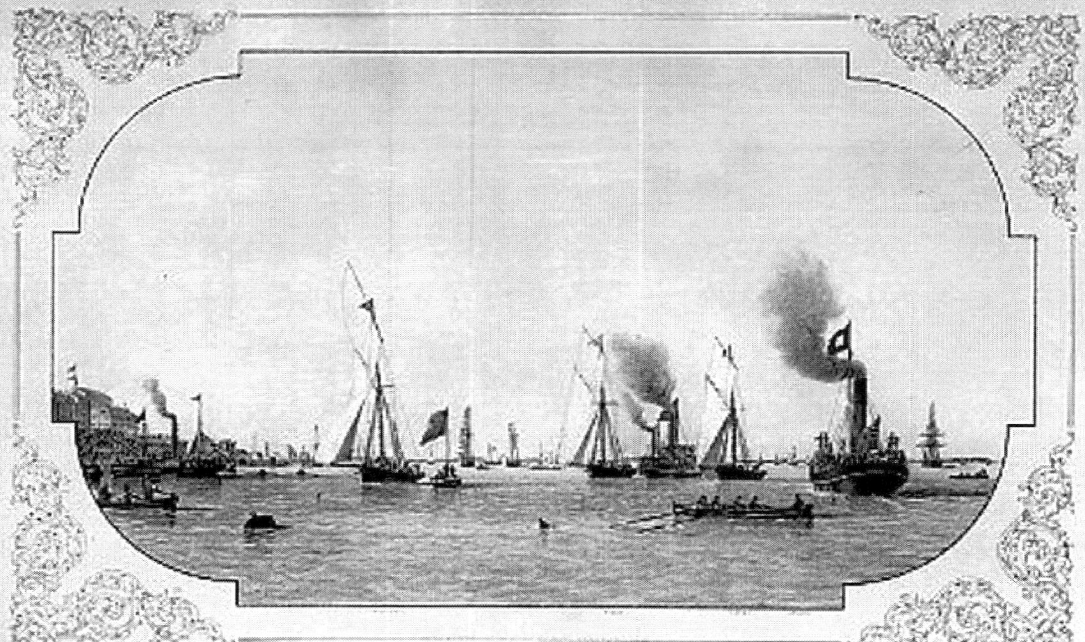

HULL GRAND REGATTA.

The Yacht HILDA, Thomas Richardson Esq. Owner, winning the Challenge Cup value [illegible] given by the Members of the Royal Yorkshire Yacht Club to whom this print is respectfully dedicated

by their very obedient servant
John Ward.

'Dandie Dinmont' 1848

To George Cammell Esqre. Of Hull/This print of the iron built clipper schooner DANDIE DINMONT is respectfully dedicated by his obdnt servant John Ward

(Goddard and Lancaster of Hull)

(*Eds:* Built at South Shields in 1848 by Thomas Marshall for George Cammell, this iron vessel was lost in the Baltic trade 18 March under the command of Capt. Newby. She was named after the character (who also gave his name to a breed of dog) in Walter Scott's 'Guy Mannering' and furnished with an appropriate male figurehead.)

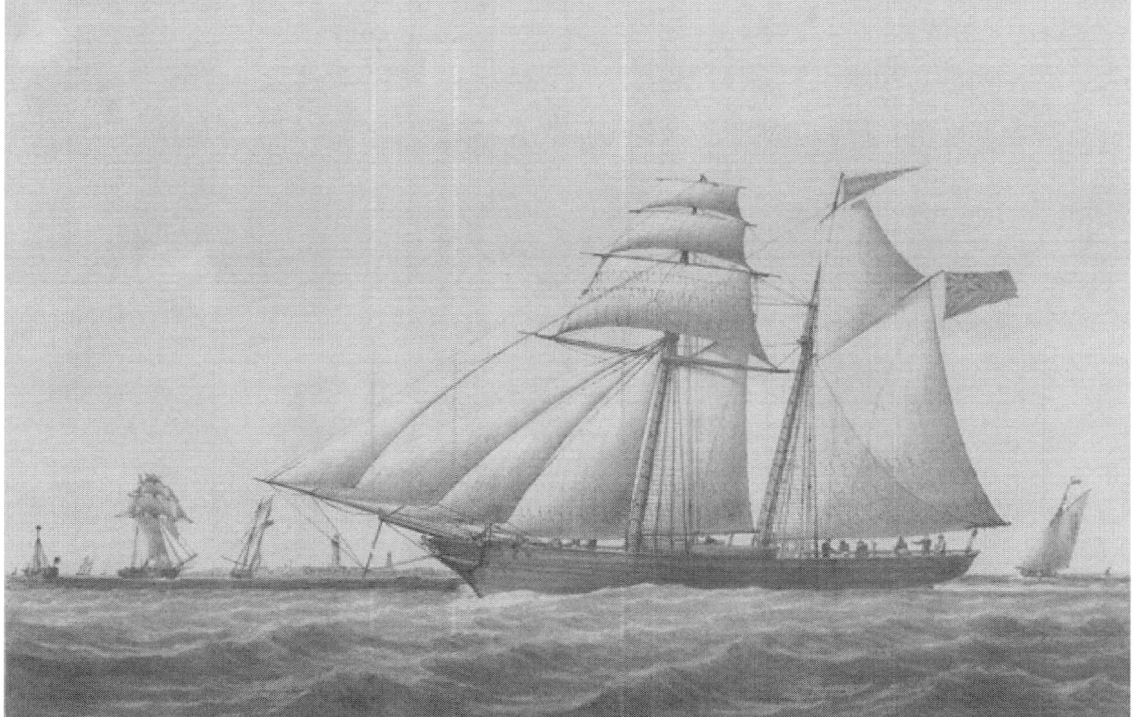

To Henry Cammell Esqr. of Hull

This print of the new Hull Clipper Schooner [illegible] is respectfully dedicated by his Obt. Servant John Ward

'Columbine'

This Plate of the iron steam packet COLUMBINE is respectfully dedicated to the Proprietors by their Obedient Servant William Lewis

(W. Monkhouse of York)

(*Eds:* This iron hulled vessel, 122 tons and 112ft long, 15ft. wide, built by H Smith & Sons at Gainsborough Lincolnshire and engined by Penn & Son, Greenwich, was launched in May 1843. The *Columbine* carried up to 500 passengers daily from Hull to the Trent, a distance of 52 miles in around two hours.)

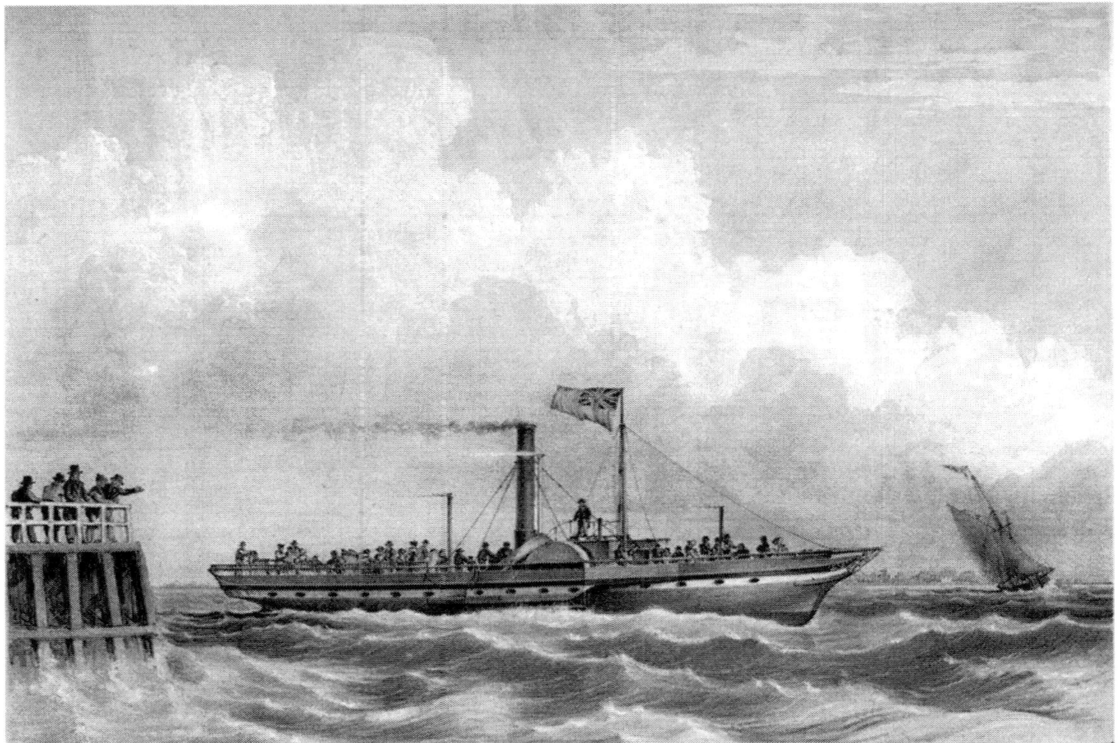

J. Ward. Del. et Lith.

Printed by W. Monkhouse York

THIS PLATE OF THE IRON STEAM PACKET

COLUMBINE

is respectfully dedicated to the Proprietors

by their Obedient Servant

William Lewis

1848. *Price,*

THE

ENGLISH ALPHABET,

ARRANGED FOR THE USE OF

HOUSE AND SIGN PAINTERS,

WRITERS, &c.,

BY J. WARD, 2, NORTH-STREET, HULL.

Entered at Stationers' Hall, London.

INTRODUCTION.

Upwards of thirty years' practise as a House and Sign Painter, has left an assurance that there is considerable room for a work of instruction in the Writing Department, and that such a work, pointing out the mechanical formation of the Letters, and the best method of setting them out in words, would be not only acceptable, but of great service to the profession, more especially the younger members, saving them much valuable time, now spent in blindly endeavouring to learn that which can be immediately acquired. The present series of Alphabets are therefore brought forward as a guide to the Art of Lettering, and a work suitable to the present time.

In selecting the Letters great care has been exercised to take them from Type of approved form, and which were considered correct specimens of the several characters, the proportions of each are shown by their division into parts, thus the A is five parts (which may be considered as inches or any suitable measure) in height, and in width six; the B also five parts in height, and but five in width; and the C four and a third part in width; these proportions and that of the other Letters will be seen on referring to the plates. The object in putting the Letters into parts or divisions is (as well as shewing the proportions,)to facilitate their arrangement in setting out on the signboard, &c.,examples of which are given, see Plate 6, Plate 7 being devoted to the shadows, and Plate 8, scales of proportions of letters from 3 to 10 inches.

In submitting the English Alphabet to the profession it is anticipated it will be found sufficiently explicit, and that it will meet with the support of those for whose instruction it has been arranged, and who would do well to impress on their memory the following table of proportions as highly desirable in practice, all Letters (whatever may be their size) to be considered as five parts in height.

Table showing the width of Roman Capital Letters in proportion to their height.

A, 6 parts	D, $5\frac{1}{2}$.	G, $5\frac{1}{3}$.	J, 4.	M, $6\frac{1}{3}$.	P, $4\frac{3}{5}$.	S, $3\frac{2}{3}$.	V, $5\frac{1}{3}$.	Y, 6.
B, 5.	E, $4\frac{3}{4}$.	H, 6.	K, 6.	N, $5\frac{3}{5}$.	Q, $5\frac{1}{3}$.	T, $4\frac{3}{5}$.	W, $7\frac{2}{3}$.	Z, $4\frac{1}{2}$.
C, $4\frac{1}{3}$.	F, $4\frac{3}{5}$.	I, 3.	L, $4\frac{3}{4}$.	O, 5.	R, $5\frac{1}{2}$.	U, $5\frac{1}{3}$.	X, 6.	&, 5.

The formation of the Letters being understood, it becomes necessary to point out their arrangement on the signboard, as a general rule for which, divide the length of the board by the required number of spaces and parts, the quotient showing their exact size, which, if multiplied by five, gives the correct height of the letter. As an example, suppose the name WARD is to be set out on a board thirty inches in length, figure one, plate six; in this name there are four letters, and on referring to plate one, Roman Capital Letters, they will be found to occupy twenty-four and two-third parts, to these are to be added the spaces between the letters and at each end of the word; in the present example there is no space between the W and A, (see figure 2,) in consequence of the W being an overhanging letter and the A a spreading one, had any space been allowed, the W would have appeared detached from the other letters, and awkwardly set out; it has also been necessary to allow only one and a half space from the end of the board to the W from the same cause, had two spaces been allowed the name then would have been too much to one end; the arrangement is therefore as follows, from the edge of the board to the W, one and a half space, W seven and two-third parts, A six parts, from A to R one space, R five and a half parts, from R to D one space, D five and a half parts, and from D to the end of the board two spaces, altogether thirty parts and spaces and a fraction, which fraction may be struck off as of no moment; now as the board is thirty inches in length, if divided by thirty the required amount of parts and spaces, it gives one as the quotient, that is one inch as the size of each part and space, this if multiplied by five, gives five inches as the height of the letters, as seen at figure three, same plate, the squares being considered as inches, this figure shows also the name set out in outline, and although, in this instance, the letters are set out in squares, in practice there is no occasion for such, beng adopted at present to show that the letters are exactly the same as those of plate one, figure four being considered as white letters on a black ground.

A further example of setting out is shewn at figure five, which represents a board six feet three and a half inches in length, the number of parts and spaces required being seventy-five and a half, in this reduce the length into inches and divide by seventy-five as in the former example, multiplying the quotient by five to know the height of the letters; from the seperating stop to the W and from the W to A there is no space between, and from P to A only half a space, in order that the words may appear properly set out; other letters in the Alphabet require allowances also to be made. As respects the raising of letters so as to make them appear to stand out from the board, and also as to the cast shadow, a careful examination of plate seven will point out, that a tracing of the letter will shew the proper outline, by lowering it and placing it to either side, answering to the true cast shadow as produced by the Sun's light at a certain elevation.

With reference to the plate of scales, it will be seen that each scale is divided into five parts for the height of the letter, having divisions also of thirds and fourths for the width; this plate may be cut up or others made by it, and in setting out letters take the scale to correspond with the length required, for instance, if J. WARD, PAINTER, is to be set out in ten inch letters, strike two lines at ten inches apart, one for the top and the other for the bottom of the letters, (see figure five, plate six), then set off from the end of the board two parts (by ten inch scale) and commence with four parts for the letter J, one part from J to the seperating stop, one part for stop, seven and two third parts for W, six parts for A, one part from A to R, five and a half parts for R, one part from R to D, five and a half parts for D and so on to the end, they will then be properly set out, and can be filled in with paint by any one at all capable of laying on color with a hair pencil or paint brush.

The formation of the Letters being understood it is now necessary to point out thier arrangement into words, as a general rule for which divide the length of the board by the required number of spaces and parts, the quotient shewing thier exact size, which if multiplied by 5 gives the correct height of the letter. As an example, suppose the name WARD is to be set out on a board 30 inches in length. (1, plate 6) In this name there are four letters and on refering to plate 1 they will be found to occupy 24⅔ parts, to these are to be added the spaces between the letters and at each end of the word; in the present example there is no space between the W and A (fig^e 2) in consequence of the W being an overhanging letter and the A a spreading one, had any space been allowed the W would have appeared detached from the other letters and awkwardly set out; it has also been necessary to allow only 1½ space from the end of the board to the W from the same cause, had 2 spaces been allowed the name then would have been too much to one end. The arrangement is therefore as follows, from the edge of the board to the W 1½ space, W 7⅔ parts, A 6 parts, from A to R 1 space, R 5½ parts, from R to D 1 space, D 5½ parts, from D to the end of the board 2 spaces, altogether 30 parts and spaces and a fraction, which fraction may be struck off as of no moment; now as the board is 30 inches in length if divided by 30 the required amount of parts and spaces it gives 1 as the quotient; that is 1 inch as the size of each part and space, this if multiplied by 5 gives 5 inches as the height of the letters, as seen at fig 3 the squares being considered as inches. this figure shows the name set out in outline, 4 being considered as white letters painted on a black ground.

A further example of setting out is shewn at figure 5 which represents a board 6 feet 3½ inches in length, the number of spaces and parts required being 75 and a half, in this case reduce the length into inches and divide by 75 as in the former example, multiplying the quotient by 5 to know the height of the letters; from the separating stop to the W and from the W to A there is no space, and from P to A only ½ a space. As respects the raising of letters and the cast shadow a careful examination of plate 7 will point out that a tracing of the letter will show the proper form by lowering it and placing it to either side.

ROMAN CAPITAL LETTERS. *Pl.1.*

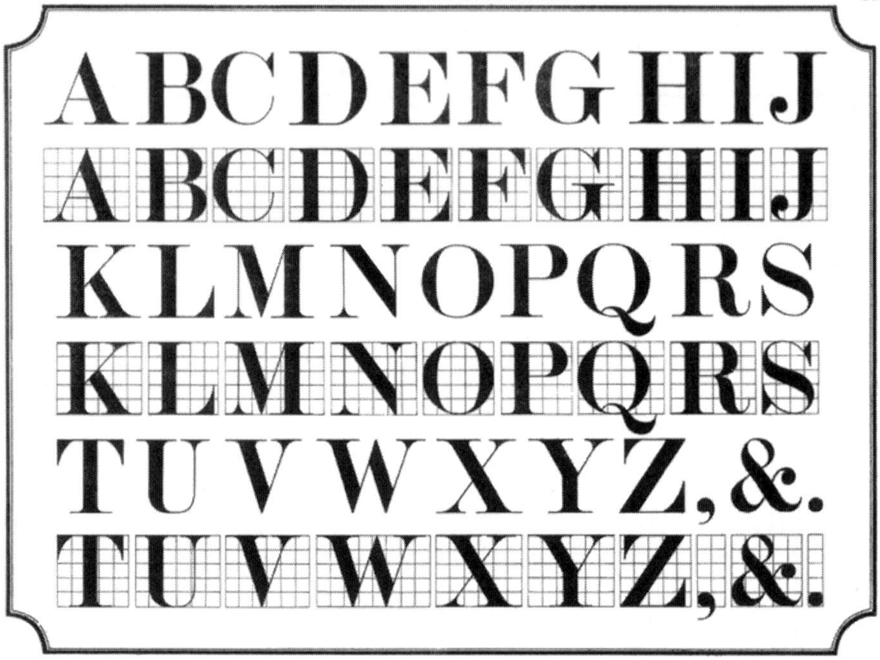

ROMAN LOWER CASE LETTERS, FIGURES, &c. *Pl.2.*

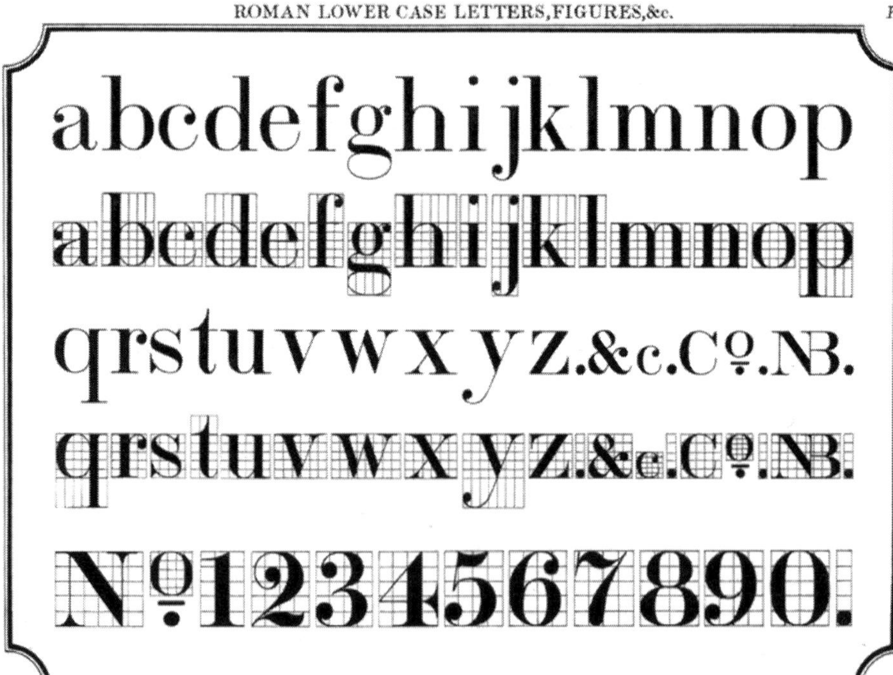

ITALIC CAPITAL LETTERS. *Pl.3.*

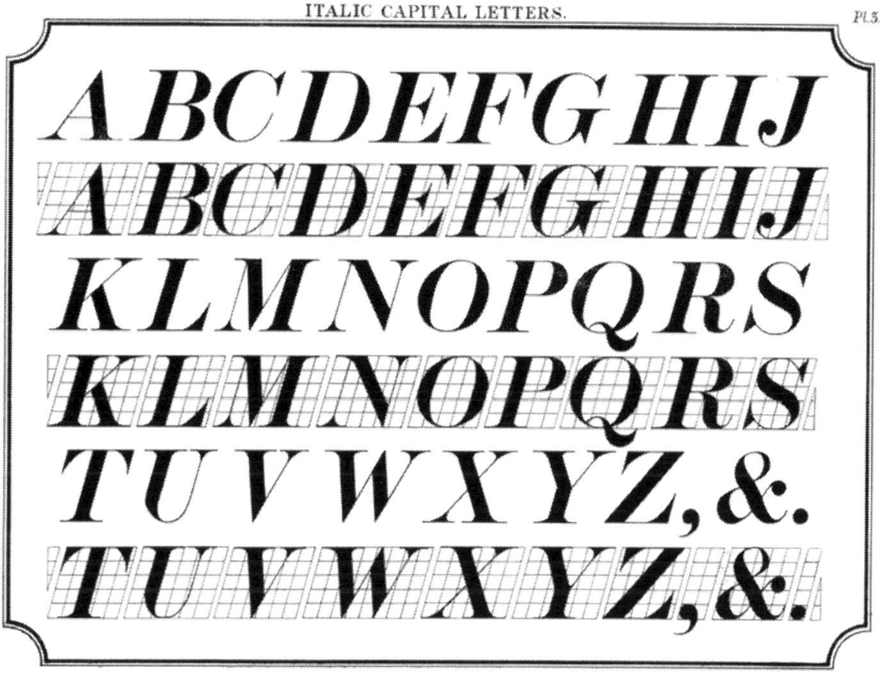

ITALIC LOWER CASE LETTERS, FIGURES, &c. *Pl.4.*

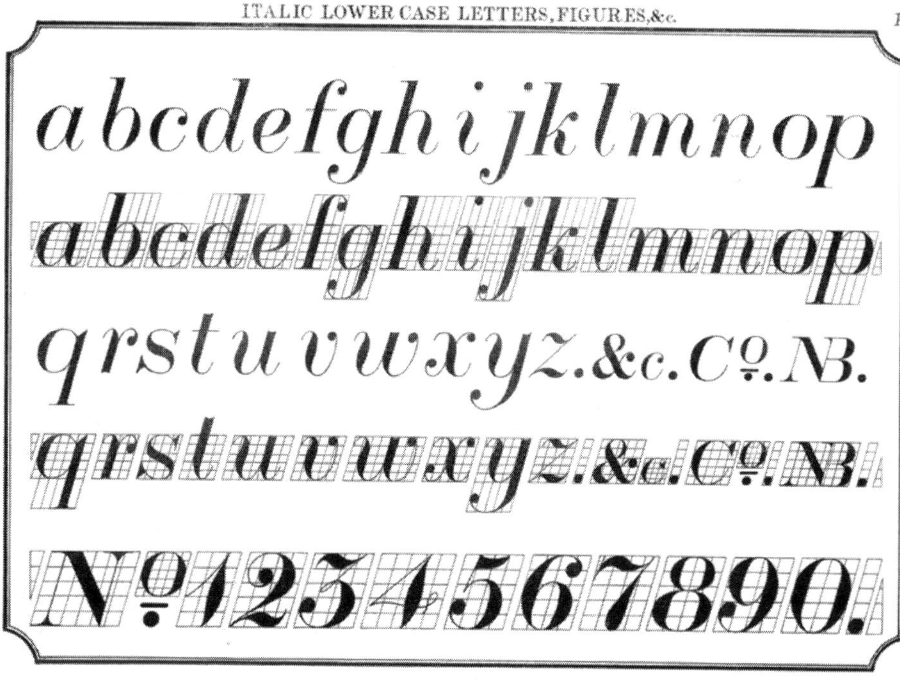

EGYPTIAN AND BLOCK LETTERS, FIGURES, &c. Pl. 5.

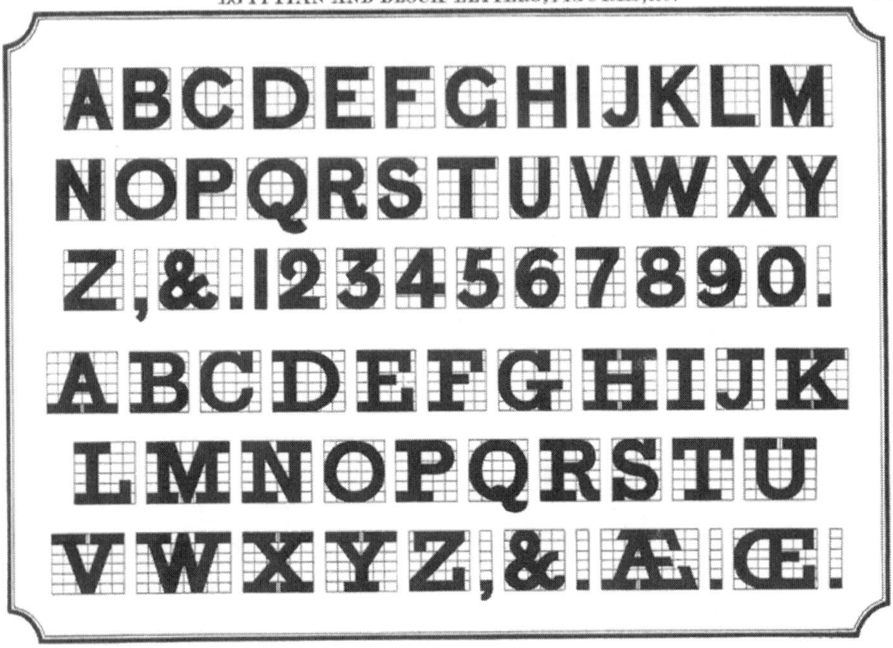

Pl. 6.

EXAMPLES.

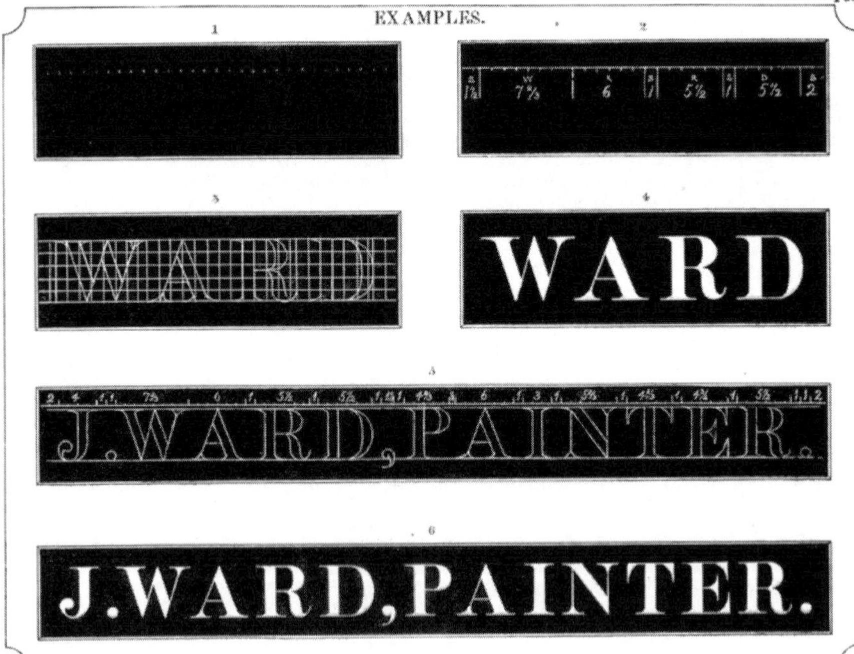

EXAMPLES.

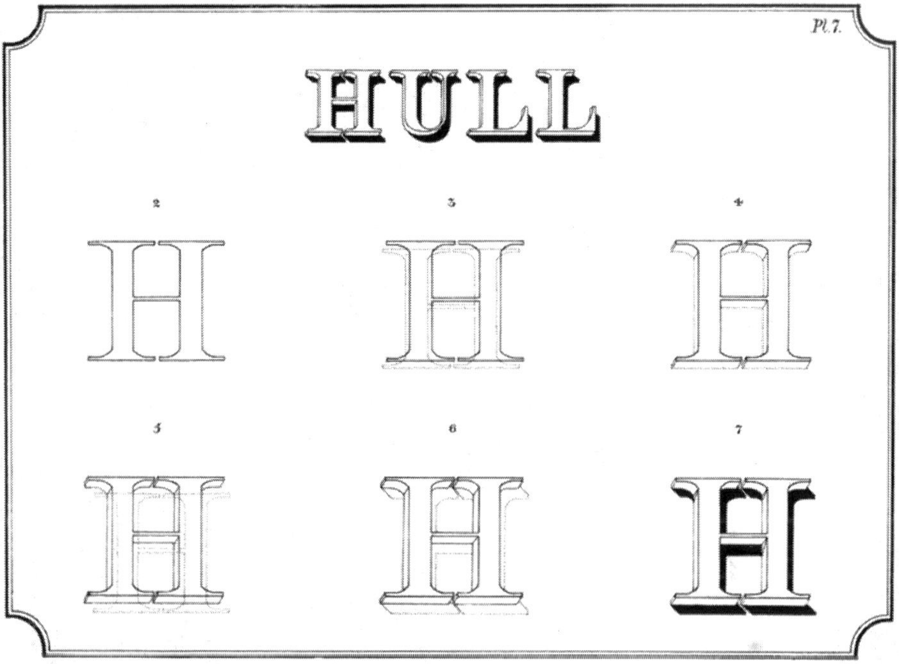

On reverse of the plates are images as follows:

1. Sloop or smack of 160 tons
2. Sloop or smack; dandy rigged
3. Schooner of 120 tons
4. Brigantine; hove to on the larboard tack
5. Brig of 223 tons
6. Ship of 650 tons
7. Ship of 375 tons

Plate missing. Maybe it had the proportions of letter on both sides, or the reverse was blank, so there was no incentive for it to be kept by the maritime enthusiast. Ward actually mentions the possibility of cutting up the plate for ease of sorting out the letters.

Chapter 4

Epilogue

At the zenith of his career, John Ward was taken with cholera during the great epidemic of 1849. He died at his new address at No. 2, North Street, on 29 September 1849 in the presence of his pupil and assistant W F Settle. Ward was buried the next day in the Castle Street cemetery, mourned by his family and his fellow Freemasons of the Humber Lodge No 57.

Ward, who joined the Humber Lodge in 1827, was elected Worshipful Master two years later. He presented a self-portrait to the Lodge where it hung until it was destroyed in 1941 when the Osborne Street premises were severely damaged in an air raid. Thankfully, a photograph has been preserved but two other self-portraits sold from his studio in 1854 cannot now be traced. Similarly, no example is known to survive of a lithographic portrait he had prepared and inscribed; 'John Ward, Mr. Painter 1848'.[1]

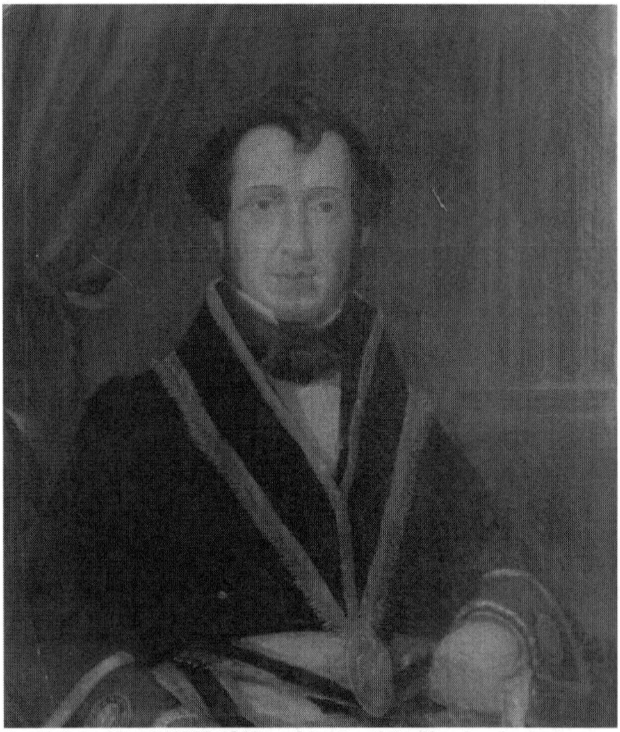

Fig. 61 John Ward (1798-1849) as Master of the Humber Lodge. Photograph of self portrait, the latter was destroyed.

Although we know much about Ward as an artist, we know relatively little about him as a husband, father, and citizen of Hull, although what has survived indicates an exemplary character. For example, at the age of thirty-eight he bravely dived into the Hull docks to rescue a small boy;

> On Friday afternoon, a boy about nine or ten years of age, leaning over the Lock Pit, and fishing in the Junction Dock [i.e. Princes Dock] Basin, overreached himself, and fell into the water, at the imminent danger of his life, as there was no boat or vessel over the spot. In this critical state Mr John Ward, master painter, of High Street who happened to be near, and was alarmed by the cries of a boy being in the Dock, ran thither, and instantly plunged into the Dock, with his shoes and clothes on, expecting the body to rise to the surface, but as it did not, grappling hooks were procured, and in a few minutes it was raised taken to Mr Hudson's, druggist, and attended to by seven respectable medical gentlemen who eventually succeeded in restoring animation. A pecuniary reward was offered to the painter, for his intrepid conduct but he very handsomely declined it, alleging that he had only performed what he considered to be his duty and what he should at any time under the same circumstances.
>
> *Hull Advertiser*. 12 February 1836

No personal documents have survived that may shed further light on his character and personality but an impression may be gleaned from his desire to become a Freemason. This facet of his life is a distinctive personal commitment that deserves much closer study than the following brief sketch of his Masonic career allows.

Freemasonry in England emerged in its organised form through the creation of a Grand Lodge in 1717 and its first *Book of Constitutions* six years later. There followed an extensive period of dispute as to the legitimacy of these constitutions and it was not until 1813 that a United Grand Lodge of England was formed. Its work was to standardise principles and procedure, define regalia, record membership, authorise the founding and closure of lodges, and establish a disciplinary code. When Ward entered his apprenticeship as an artisan painter, there were some 647 lodges in existence. Over the remaining decades of the century, that number was set to triple.

In Hull, four (briefly five) Masonic lodges appear in the record from c.1759 that flourished for varying lengths of time. Two in particular attracted Ward's attention; Minerva Lodge formed in 1783 and Humber Lodge in 1809. Why, at the age of twenty-seven did Ward become interested in Freemasonry? A summary of some of its main features, generally understood as a 'system of morality, veiled in allegory and illustrated by symbols', may offer some clues.

'To Live Respected and Die Regretted'

These words, taken from the ceremony required of a master of a lodge at his installation, offer a digest of the aspirations of fellow Freemasons. The exact words unaltered and still in use today, provide a reminder; 'that rising to eminence by merit you may live respected and die regretted'. This implies that membership alone would not suffice and that Masonic 'merit' was required. What did this imply? Ward would have been made aware that he was entering into a society that required a belief in a Supreme Being but was not a religion or a substitute for a religion. This would have had practical relevance in relation to the contested rights of Roman Catholics at the time and growing dissent from the Established Church. The fervour of evangelical reform arising from the ministry of John

Wesley (1703-1791) was finding a sympathetic response, especially in the north of England with all the associated controversies that this implied.

Ward was also born at a time of disquieting political unrest with rebellion in Ireland, revolution in France, naval mutinies, and the threat of invasion during the Napoleonic wars. With the prospect of seditious activities spreading throughout the country, the Unlawful Societies Act of 1799 was designed to ban all organised meetings behind closed doors. In response, the United Grand Lodge not only demanded strict conformity with its provisions but also required masters of lodges to 'cheerfully conform to the laws of the country in which you reside' and 'not to be concerned in plots or Conspiracies against Government, but patiently to submit to the decisions of the Supreme Legislature'.

Lodge meetings were, as a consequence, avowedly multi-faith and discussion of religion and politics were expressly forbidden. Membership was to be clearly non-denominational and open to men regardless of race or colour. At the core of the various ceremonies that Ward would have encountered were three main principles; "Brotherly Love, Relief and Truth". In modern parlance; reciprocal respect, charity, and education. Binding these principles together was the notion of fraternity, implying a shared purpose in a bond of friendship and common endeavour; e.g. 'to judge with candour, admonish with friendship, and reprehend with mercy'. These principles were further explained in terms of "Five Points of Fellowship" namely, brotherly regard, mutual support, awareness of personal needs, respect for confidences, and active loyalty. When John Ward passed through the final stages of his raising to the rank of Master Mason, these principles would have been demonstrated to him.

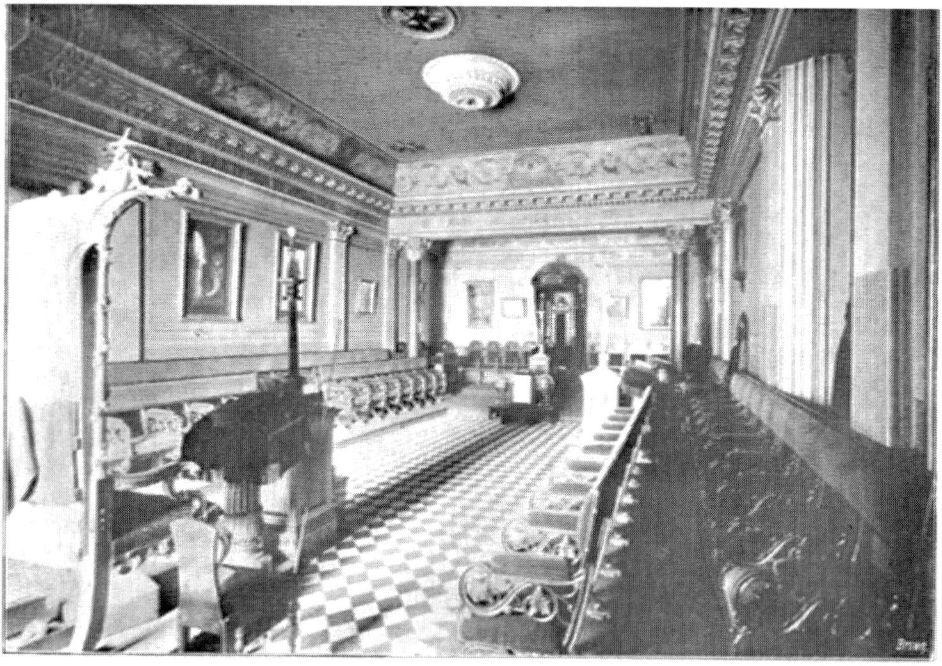

Fig. 62 Humber Lodge No 57 c.1910. Note the celestial and terrestrial globes at the far end, presented by William Crow R.N.

At a time of barely developed welfare provision, scant educational opportunities, and limited access to medical assistance, such fraternal organisations had a direct relevance with charitable acts featuring as the hallmark of a practising Freemason.[2]

If these were the main features of Freemasonry in general, what might John Ward have experienced more concretely? Existing documents are few and prone to misinterpretation. There are, for example, several 'John Ward's' in the Masonic records. What follows must therefore be considered to be provisional and open to further inquiry.[3]

It would appear that Ward originally became a member of the Hull Minerva Lodge. However, he joined the Humber Lodge in 1827 with several other brethren led by William Crow, (1770-1834) a former Lieutenant in the Navy who had recently been installed as Worshipful Master. Relatively wealthy, Crow made a significant contribution to Freemasonry in Hull and strongly influenced Ward's career; certainly masonically and quite possibly artistically through access to Crow's network of naval contacts.[4]

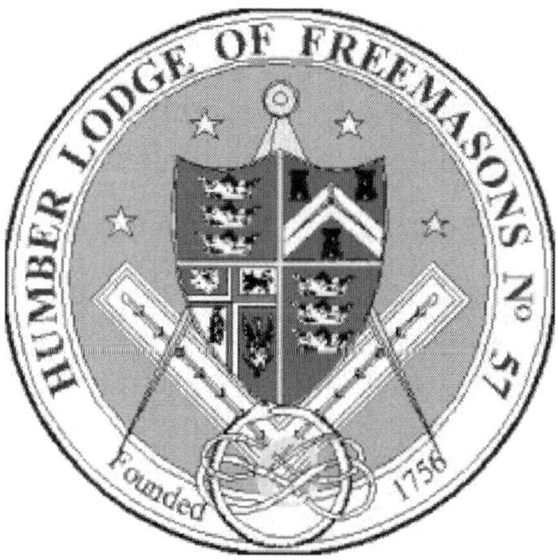

The reasons for the mass migration from Minerva were probably due to its financial difficulties and a desire by Crow and others to make a fresh start that included ambitious plans for the Humber Lodge to build its own Masonic Hall. In common with many other lodges, meetings were held in rooms rented in local inns. In the search for greater respectability and with an emphasis on improving ceremonial and Masonic procedure, a general trend developed towards securing purpose-built premises. Crow donated one hundred guineas towards the cost of the new Humber Lodge building, land was acquired, and the hall opened in October 1827.

John Ward and John Leonard, probably his brother in law, had joined during May and June of that year with thirteen other members from Minerva Lodge. They came from a variety of occupations; butcher, watchmaker, tobacconist, victualler, schoolmaster, master mariner, farmer, ship builder, shopkeeper, plumber and glazier, cooper, builder – a typical cross section of the membership of provincial Masonic lodges at this time.[5]

It is probable that amongst other reasons, Ward would have been influenced in his decision to join the Humber Lodge by William Crow. It seems highly likely that Crow would have offered strong support as a senior member of the Lodge to Ward's election as Master. This election arose within two years of him becoming a joining member, the shortest possible time to reach the chair of the lodge if normal procedures were followed. Moreover, in accepting this position, Ward would have known that it would also have been his duty to install his successor. This was to be once again, William Crow who served a second term in 1830-1831. Undertaking these duties and responsibilities was the most significant and important role to fulfil in the cycle of the Masonic ceremonial year.

Indeed, the Masonic ceremonies he experienced would have mirrored Ward's own life history as they involved an allegorical journey from apprenticeship through to the achievement of mastery of a craft. Through this experience, he would have encountered symbolic working tools that would allegorically assist him in sustaining that mastery; e.g. the Square teaches morality, the Compasses, impartial justice etc. For Ward and other craft based members, these ceremonies had an educative potential that was largely unavailable by other means before the advent of compulsory schooling.

John Ward took full advantage of these opportunities, pursuing his Masonic career with sustained commitment and vigour. This is evidenced by his senior membership of a related branch of Masonry ("Royal Arch, Chapter"), and rising to receive honours in the Provincial Grand Lodge. This commitment would have involved a careful study of procedures and principles and regular attendance at meetings throughout the twenty-two years of his membership.

But if there was a single factor that drew Ward to become a Freemason, it was perhaps the fact that he was not just joining a fraternal organisation in a general sense, he was joining a society of people with whom he had close contact. Further research is needed to verify details from the surviving records, but there is some evidence to suggest that his father-in-law was a Freemason together with other significant individuals including Thomas Fletcher, painter of *Molly and Friends* - one of the earliest marine paintings at Hull and of the Fletcher family of painters to whom J C Ibbetson was apprenticed; John Willoughby, a pupil of Ibbetson, listed as a 'drawing master' and advertising himself as 'artist and painter in general'; Thomas Meggitt of the family of painters to whom Ward was apprenticed; Thomas Griffin, father of William Griffin a fellow apprentice with Ward; William Binks of the family of painters and marine artists, and Bethel Jacobs, master of the Humber Lodge in 1840, active in the Hull Mechanics Institute and chairman of the executive committee of the Hull School of Art, the latter championed by him and founded in 1861.

Membership of the Freemasons undoubtedly brought Ward into contact with a wider circle of potential clients. For example, a small canvas, painted in 1842 of the *Dwina and Ellen Crawford*, passed down in the family of Robert Morley Sawyer, a shareholder in the *Dwina* who was also a member of the Humber Lodge. Michael Wrangles Clarke of Winterton Hall, an active member of the Humber Lodge in the period after Ward's death, built up a choice collection of the former Worshipful Master's paintings. These works included the *William Lee*, probably acquired from the estate of Joseph Gee, the schooner *Juno*, the *Bee* Revenue Cutter, and the ship, *Raymond* which were all sold in 1887 when the contents of Clarke's house were dispersed.

John Ward was clearly well known and well regarded, exceptionally so when it is considered that he was surrounded by many of the leading citizens of the day including Dr J Pearson Bell, the Provincial Grand Master and Worshipful Master of Humber Lodge between 1842 and 1843 who delivered a funeral oration on the 30th September 1849;

> No man enjoyed the confidence of the members more than Bro. John Ward. His character was marked by honesty of purpose and strict integrity of principle. He was strongly attached to the Order, kind hearted and noble-minded, and exhibited an energy and enthusiasm which never deserted him under any discouragement, ever supporting principle against prejudice, and maintaining the excellence of Freemasonry by the strictest observance of its precepts.....The good he has done is present in our mind, and that good is free from the speck of alloy.[6]

Ward does not appear to have left a Will, perhaps unsurprising considering his sudden demise "after an illness of only seven hours and a half". The contents of his studio were not dispersed until four years after his death when Messrs. Oates and Capes 'received instructions from the Administratix'. Since the artist's wife had predeceased him, the four beneficiaries would have been his eldest daughter, Esther Leonard Ward, one of three still living in Hull and Mary Ellen and Emma being the other two. The remaining daughter, Sarah Elizabeth born in 1829, had married Leonard Clark and emigrated to South Africa in the year following her father's death.

Ward's studio sale catalogue lists paintings, drawings, lithographs, plates (for engraving), litho stones, and two lithographic printing presses. There were ninety-nine lots of lithographs amounting to several hundred prints and each lot of up to forty items sold for between 12s and 19s 6d.- the highest being paid for coloured examples. Only three of his drawings and watercolours were offered for sale and the rest of his studies and sketches were probably acquired by his business partner William Settle. Oil paintings for sale included the three marine studies by William Anderson that had been in Ward's premises since at least 1827, and works by Peeters, Ovenden, and Whitcombe. (see Chapter 1).

As well as a self-portrait, there were three other works outside Ward's usual range, a painting of a dog, a cattle piece, and a crucifixion. The highest price for a single lot was the £21 paid for *The Return of the William Lee*. Since the original was presumably still in the hands of her owners, this is clearly another rendition of this subject.

Ward's Legacy

A fitting tribute to Ward's artistic achievements may perhaps best be heard in the voice of the auctioneers, Oates and Capes, who presented the contents of his workshop and studio for sale on 3rd February 1853;

> The Auctioneers respectfully intimate to connoisseurs of fine paintings, aspirants to true naval architecture, and captains, that the late John Ward spent a fortune in visiting the principal shipbuilding establishments of Her Majesty. Close study, labour and untiring energy were devoted for a period of seventeen years, to place him in the high position of one of the first marine painters in the land; and in order to support this assertion, it is only needful to draw attention to the fact that upwards of one hundred of his paintings have been engraved and published showing every description of vessel, from boat to the largest ship in the Royal Navy, and the various positions in which they are seen upon the sea, from the calm to the storm. And further to observe, that his productions have been duly appreciated and admired by some of the highest officers in the navy and judges of high standing.

Notes

Part One: References

Chapter 1

1. Chapters 1 and 2 have been abridged from the following sources;

- Credland, A. G. *John Ward of Hull, Marine Painter 1798-1849.* Hull, City of Kingston upon Hull Museums and Art Galleries, 1981.
- Credland, A.G. *Marine Painting in Hull through Three Centuries.* City Museums and Art Galleries, Beverley, Hutton Press Ltd, 1993.
- A. G. Credland, "The Carters and the Hull Art Scene in the Nineteenth Century" in Bell, G. H. et al., *H B Carter & Sons: Victorian Watercolour Drawing and the Art of Illustration.* Pickering, Blackthorn Press, 2006.
- A. G. Credland, "John Ward of Hull, Marine Painter, 1798-1849" in Bell, G. H. et al., *Northern Seascapes and Landscapes*. Pickering, Blackthorn Press, 2008.

2. Cobbett, W. *Rural Rides.* London, A Cobbett, 1853.
3. Greig, J., ed. *The Farington Diary*, 8 vols., London, Hutchinson, 1922-1928.
4. See: Fawcett, T. *The Rise of Provincial Art; Artists, Patrons, and Institutions outside London 1800-1830*. Oxford, Clarendon Press, 1974.
5. Elwin, H., ed. *The Autobiography and Journals of Benjamin Robert Haydon.* Macdonald: London, 1950 (1st edition 1853).
6. Bermingham, A. *Learning to Draw: Studies in the Cultural History of a Polite and Useful Art.* New Haven and London, Yale University Press, 2000.
7. His signature 'John Ward, painter' appears in the book of Rules and Orders, and list of members of the Hull Mechanics Institute, preserved in the Hull archives. On the same page are the names of a joiner, cabinet maker, smith, hat manufacturer, clockmaker, and law stationer.
8. See: Comment, B. *The Panorama.* London, Reaktion Books Ltd, 1999, and Oettermann, S. *The Panorama: History of a Mass Medium.* New York, Zone Books, 1997.
9. *Mogg's New Picture of London and Visitors Guide to its Sights*. London, E Mogg, 1846.
10. Elmes, J. *Metropolitan Improvements: London in the Nineteenth Century.* London, Jones & Co, 1827-1831.
11. *Theatrical Observer*. 17th January, 1824.
12. Russett, A. *George Chambers 1803-1840: His Life and Work.* Woodbridge, Antique Collectors Club, 1996.
13. Haydon, B.R., ed. Frederick Wordsworth Haydon. *Correspondence and Table Talk.* (2 vols.) London, Chatto and Windus, 1876.
14. Credland, A. G. "William Coates of Hull – a Marine Artist Rediscovered." *East Yorkshire Historian,* Vol.10, 2009, pp.75-80.

Chapter 2

1. See Harbron, D. "John Ward Painter (1798-1849)" *Burlington Magazine* 1941.
2. A letter to his father dated 18th August 1798 is illustrated with vignettes of actions with the French Navy, four Mediterranean coastal outlines, and a profile view of "HMS Bellona"

(*National Maritime Museum: PAF5593*). The 'Bellona' (1760-1814) was one of the most illustrious vessels of the British Navy and one of the first to be copper sheathed, greatly aiding speed, manoeuvrability, and longevity.

3. Redgrave, S. A. *Dictionary of Artists of the English School.* (2nd ed. 1878) Bath, Kingsmead Reprints, 1970. See also: Briefel, A. *The Deceivers: Art Forgery and Identity in the Nineteenth Century*. Ithaca and London, Cornell University Press, 2006.

4. 'Harpies' derived from Greek and Latin - "snatchers" - winged creatures, perpetually hungry, capable of carrying people off to the underworld or inflicting terrible punishment and torment, sometimes depicted as robbing food from the blinded King Phineus because he prophesised too truly and revealed too much truth to humans.

5. See: Keay, J. *The Honourable Company: A History of the English East India Company. London*. Harper Collins, 1991.

6. Anon. *An Account of the Rise and Progress of the Subscription Library at Kingston-Upon -Hull established 6th December 1775.* Hull, W. Rawson, 1810.

7. Cuthbert Brodrick (1822-1902) was articled in 1837 to the Hull architect H F Lockwood (1811-1878. Brodrick set up his own practice in the town in 1845 and later opened offices in Leeds and London. In November 1852, he was appointed architect for the Hull Royal Institution, opened by Queen Victoria and Prince Albert in 1854. Further commissions followed including Leeds Town Hall (1858) and the Grand Hotel, Scarborough (1862-7), the latter being his last major work.

8. Another example now in the Hull Maritime Museum is a view of the Indiaman, "Wellington" in dock at Blackwall, from Moses' *Sketches of Shipping*, printed by Chatfield and Coleman (1824). Stamped "Hull Mechanics Institute" with printed label on reverse; "Hull Mechanics Institute, Established June 1st 1825". Inscriptions in ink; 'for copying First Year, 10 days, Afterwards - - - days. Fine for keeping beyond time stated per day 2d.' *Hull Maritime Museum* [M1.1580].

9. *The Literary Gazette* Vol 10. London , James Moy 1826.

10. "To the Public: The Hull and East-Riding Institution for the Promotion of the Fine Arts, July 20th 1827".

11. "Bellerophon" – great hero of Greek mythology, slayer of monsters and rider of Pegasus, the winged horse. See also: Campbell, C. *The Intolerable Hulks: British Shipboard Confinement* 1776-1857. Tuscon, Arizona, Fenestra Books, 2001.

12. Diana Villar, author of *John Wilson Carmichael:1799-1868*. Portsmouth, Carmichael and Sweet Ltd, 1995, suggests that "John Ward from the Hull School" contributed to the Newcastle exhibitions. The dates and subjects are not cited and whilst surviving catalogues (1822 - 1831 and 1835 -1836 inclusive; Newcastle City Library) refer to John Ward of London (a different artist by the same name) further clarification is needed.

13. See: Usherwood, P. *Art for Newcastle: Thomas Miles Richardson and the Newcastle Exhibitions 1822-1843.* Newcastle, Tyne and Wear County Council Museums, 1984.

14. See: Smith, G. *The Emergence of the Professional Watercolourist: Contentions and Alliances in the Artistic Domain, 1760-1824.* Aldershot, Ashgate Publishing Ltd, 2003, and Clarke, M. *The Tempting Prospect: A Social History of English Watercolours.* London, British Museum Publications Ltd, 1981.

15. Quoted in Hardie, M. *Watercolour Painting in Britain, Vol II, The Romantic Period.* London, Batsford, 1967.

16. It may be noted that Frederick, younger brother of Phineas Lowther was also a drawing master in Hull and in an advertisement of 1811 claimed to be a pupil of John Varley of London.

17. An exact copy in watercolour by Carmichael of Ward's *Dandie Dinmont* print is in the collection of the Laing Art Gallery, Newcastle-upon-Tyne. The vessel was built at South Shields on Tyneside.
18. For a comprehensive overview see; Abbey, J. R. *Life in England in Aquatint and Lithography* 1770-1860. San Francisco, Alan Wofsy Fine Arts, 1991, and Bicknell, P., and Munro, J. Gilpin to Ruskin: *Drawing Masters and Their Manuals,* 1800-1860. Cambridge, Fitzwilliam Museum, 1987.
19. The tradition goes back to the seventeenth century: images by N.I. Visscher after Jan Porcellus, *Icones variorum navium Hollandicarum*, 1627; then Reinier Noom, *Verscheyde schepen en gesichten van Amstel redam; A van der Laan*, ('Delightful Sea, Land and River Prospects'), c.1720 with titles in Dutch, French and English. In France, J. J. Baugean (1764-1819) *Recueil de petites marines*, Paris 1817 and *Collection de toutes les espèces de bâtiments de guerre et de bâtiments de marchands*, Paris 1852. The latter had seventy- two plates.
20. See Munday, J. *Edward William Cooke 1811-1880.* Woodbridge, Antique Collectors Club, 1996.
21. See: Twyman, M. *Lithography 1800-1850.* London, Oxford University Press, 1970.
22. Hullmandel printed (amongst many other works) Samuel Prout's *Microcosm*; see Fig.48.
23. See: Bell, G.H., Credland, A.G., and Richardson, R. *H B Carter & Sons:Victorian Watercolour Drawing and the Art of Illustration.* Pickering, Blackthorn Press, 2006, and Bell, G.H, (ed). *Theakston's Guide to Scarborough.* Pickering, Blackthorn Press, 2002.
24. From notes supplied by a descendant.
25. See M.V. and D. Brewington. *The Marine Paintings and Drawings in the Peabody Essex Museum* Salem, Mass, 1968, inv. 1727.
26. His exhibited works in London during the 1840's were predominantly naval and from 1842 to the last appearance in 1847 were almost exclusively so; Royal Academy 1831, 1840, 1841, 1842, 1843 and 1847; British Institution 1843, 1844, 1845 and 1847; Royal Society of British Artists 1841, 1844 and 1845.
27. A member of the family of lithographers, Francis J. Monkhouse married at the Centenary Chapel, York, Sarah, daughter of C. Appleton, architect, of Anlaby near Hull (*Hull Advertiser,* 27 May 1854).

Chapter 3

1. HMS *Britannia*, designed by Sir William Rule in 1812, was laid down on no.1 slip, Plymouth dockyard in December 1813 and finally launched 20 October 1820, a first rate of 120 guns, 2,602 tons, builders measure, length 205 ft with a 53½ ft beam. Commissioned 19 January 1823, she did alternate spells of duty as flagship in Portsmouth and then with the Mediterranean fleet based in Malta before returning to be Guardship of the Ordinary at Portsmouth in August 1850. In 1854, she sailed to the Crimea where her rocket boats were in immediate action at Odessa on 22 April. Flying the flag of Vice Admiral Dundas, she led the attack by the Anglo-French fleet bombarding Sebastopol on 17 October 1854. She returned to Portsmouth and was laid up for several years before being recommissioned on 1 January 1859 to become the first training ship exclusively for the education of Royal Naval cadets. Moored originally in Haslar Creek she was moved to Portland and finally to Dartmouth in September 1863. By 1865 the *Hindostan* had joined her to cope with the rising numbers of cadets. She was replaced by another vessel and finally by college buildings ashore all of which took her name.

Portrayals of HMS *Britannia* were a prominent feature of John Ward's later career. His largest and last work, *HMS Britannia and Units of the Fleet off Spithead*, signed and dated J. Ward 1847, oil on canvas, 67 in x 97 in (see Fig. 55) was offered for sale at auction, lot 572 'Maritime Sale' Christies, South Kensington, 2 November 1995. It was not sold, but purchased later from the owner with grants from the Heritage Lottery Fund and the Science Museum Prism Fund.

Painted as Ward's Academy piece of 1847 (item 357, address given as 23 North Street, Hull) it was originally acquired by Edward Bates, the Liverpool merchant and ship owner. He subsequently became a director of Cunard, receiving a baronetcy in 1880 and died in 1896. Ward's painting passed by descent including Sir Percy Bates, 4th Bt. (1879-1946) and then out of the family in 1950 variously to Arthur Holiday Esq., private collector and art dealer; Parker Gallery London 1960; Jule Stein, New York, ophthalmologist and philanthropist and founder and president of the Music Corporation of America in 1924, and to the Parker Gallery in 1973 who sold it to the final owner before being purchased by Hull Maritime Museum.

It was exhibited at the major retrospective of John Ward's contribution to marine painting held at the Ferens Art Gallery, Hull in 1981; *John Ward of Hull Marine Painter 1798-1849*.

Chapter 4

1. The legend on the lost lithographic portrait of Ward refers to him as 'Mr Painter' which in the past has been interpreted as 'marine painter'. This should probably now be read as 'master painter' as described in the 12th February 1836, *Hull Advertiser* press report (op cit).
2. A "Humber Lodge Fund of Benevolence" was formed in January 1830 and by the end of 1908 had resources amounting to £10,318.4d. See; Shaw, G.A. *History of the Humber Lodge No 57.* London, A. Brown & Sons Ltd., n.d., c.1910.
3. The authors are grateful for the assistance of the Secretary of the Humber Lodge and Dr B Hovell in tracing the Masonic career of John Ward. See also; www.yorkshirehistory.com/The Masonic Heritage of Kingston Upon Hull.
4. For a comprehensive biography of William Crow's career, see Hovell B, www.yorkshirehistory.com
5. See Harrison, D. "Freemasonry, industry and charity: the local community and the working man". *Voluntary Action*: Vol 5 Number 1, Winter 2002, pp 33-46.
6. John Ward's decaying headstone from his resting place in the Castle Street cemetery was removed in 1966 and erected in the west porch of Hull Trinity House chapel.

Part Two: Catalogue of the Lithographs and Associated Studies in the Hull Maritime Museum

Section A: MERCHANT VESSELS

A selection of studies of merchant vessels, each 13 ½ in x 19 in, stitched along the left margin and with fold over, beige, paper cover lightly glued at fold. Back cover blank, front cover with printed title, each line a different typeface, enclosed within a broad decorative frame:

1.

Price

Marine Studies
OF
BRITISH MERCHANT VESSELS,
DESIGNED AND LITHOGRAPHED
BY
John Ward
HULL

M.C.PECK, PRINTER, LOWGATE, HULL

The initials J.H. applied in pencil, top right.

2. Introductory page, within a single line decorative frame:

MARINE STUDIES
OF
BRITISH MERCHANT VESSELS

In submitting the present Series of Views of British Merchant Vessels to public notice, it is respectfully intimated that they are chiefly intended for the use and instruction of those desirous of obtaining correct information in Marine Drawing.

Although it must be admitted that the acknowledged want of such information presents a favourable opportunity for bringing forward So desirable a Work; yet to render it still more serviceable, in this instance, the proportions of the Vessels, their detail, arrangement, and incidents have received the most minute attention. And in order to form a useful and general work of reference to the Student and Artist, with the broadside representation is given a Scale of Feet to assist in determining their respective proportions.

At the same time it is presumed the series will not be unacceptable to those connected with the Mercantile Shipping interests of this country, to whom this Work is particularly and respectfully dedicated by their

Obedient Humble Servant
JOHN WARD

HULL, 23, North-Street

****

A loose introductory sheet, MARINE STUDIES OF BRITISH MERCHANT VESSELS, is marked in pencil '16 Lithos, Sailing vessels, 17/6', evidently from the top of a job lot sold at auction.

Note that all images described as tinted, have a cream/'eau de nil' background to sky and sea; more often than not areas are left in reserve to create cloud effects which enhance the image. Each of these tinted images has a defined picture area. For the prints featuring a single defined image the picture area is approximately 7½ in by 11½ in. References to 'open lettering' means that each letter has a double outline with a void between:

3. First lithograph, two subjects, placed one above the other, sideways to the viewer after turning the previous page, no tinting and no framing to the images, open lettering.
a. Upper SLOOP or SMACK, of 160 tons/Preparing to sail-Anchor hove short-Calm –Scale of Feet [0-20]
b. Lower SCHOONER, of 120 Tons / J. Ward del. et lith. Hull Printed by W. Monkhouse, York / At anchor –Sails loose-Light air of wind-Scale of Feet [0-20]
4. Second lithograph, two subjects, one above the other, sideways on to the viewer after turning the previous page, no tinting and no framing to the images, open lettering.
a. Upper BRIG, of 223 Tons/ Under way-Before the Wind-Yards squared-Scale of Feet [0-20]
b. Lower SHIP of 650 tons/ J. Ward del. et lith. Printed by W. Monkhouse, York/Riding at anchor-Sails furled.-Wind ahead-Scale of Feet [0-20]
5. Third lithograph. Single subject, cream tinted sky with clouds, a defined picture area 7¾ in x 11½ in, open lettering used for name of ship type.
Title above image MARINE STUDIES, and immediately beneath image are key numbers 1 and 2 / J. Ward del. et lith Printed by W. Monkhouse, York. / SLOOP/ 1. Before the wind – Larboard bow view 2. Stern view- At anchor. Strong Breeze.
6. Fourth lithograph. Cream tinted, open lettering.
MARINE STUDIES, key numbers 1 and 2/John Ward. del et lith. Printed by W. Monkhouse, York. / SCHOONER/1. Before the Wind-Studding sails set. 2. Close hauled on Starboard tack. Light Breeze
7. Fifth lithograph. Cream tinted, open lettering.
MARINE STUDIES, key numbers 1 and 2/John Ward del. et lith. Printed by W. Monkhouse, York./BRIG /1. At anchor-Bow view 2. Underway-yards braced sharp up. Calm.
8. Sixth lithograph. Cream tinted, open lettering.
MARINE STUDIES/key numbers 1 and 2/John Ward del et lith. Printed by W. Monkhouse, York / SHIP /1. At anchor -stern view. 2. Starboard bow view-Wind on the quarter. A breeze springing up.
9. Seventh lithograph. Cream tinted, open lettering.
MARINE STUDIES /key numbers 2, 4, 1 and 3/John Ward del et lith. Printed by W. Monkhouse York. / MERCHANT VESSELS/1.Ship moored to the Buoy- preparing to Sail 2. Brig at Anchor. 3. Schooner. 4. Sloop. Calm.
078,032

****

A loose page, 11 in by 15 in with the printed title THE BRITISH MERCHANT SERVICE was probably intended as a 'half title' for a set in paper wrappers, though one would have expected this to be British Merchant Vessels so perhaps it was a discarded alternative.

****

Loose prints

Note that the small lithographs that are cream tinted have a defined picture area varying from 5½ in to 6 in by 8in to 8½ in. In the larger kind the picture area is approximately 7½ in by 11½ in.

****

10. No title or signature, cream tinted sheet 8½ in x 11¼ in, image area 6 in x 8 in. Buoy yacht [*Ariel*], starboard broadside view, flying flag of Hull Trinity House.

Ward painted an oil on canvas of the Hull Trinity House, 'Buoy yacht *Zephyr* off the Hull waterfront, c. 1835.

11. Cream tinted with cloud effects, on an untrimmed sheet of 13 in x 17½ in overall, picture area 7½ in x 11½ in, port bow view of vessel and numerous smaller views.

Headed MARINE STUDIES /key numbers 1 and 2 immediately below image/ John Ward del. et lith. Printed by W. Monkhouse, York. /SLOOP/1.Before the Wind- Larboard bow view 2 Stern view- at Anchor. Strong Breeze.

Also hand coloured; blue pennant with yellow cross, at top of mast, and red ensign on boom. Same as 5.

12. Not cream tinted, undefined picture area, open lettering.

J. Ward del et lith. Hull Printed by W. Monkhouse, York/SLOOP / At anchor and under-weigh on the Starboard tack- weather view.

13. Not cream tinted, no defined picture area, open lettering.

SLOOP or SMACK, of 160 Tons /Preparing to Sail.-Anchor hove short-Calm. Scale of Feet [0-20]

Same as 3a

14. Tinted, black lettering; sheet 9 in x 11 in overall, image 5¾ in x 8½ in/J.Ward Del et Lith. Hull Printed by W. Monkhouse, York./SLOOP or SMACK/Dandy rigged, –going free, off FLAMBOR'O HEAD

15. Not tinted, no defined picture area (this, the only example, is coloured), the initials JW on pennant at masthead.

SLOOP OR SCOTCH SMACK/ Getting under-weigh-heaving the anchor-on the HUMBER.

No legend.

16. Undefined picture area, black lettering.

SCHOONER/J. Ward del et lith. Hull. Printed by W. Monkhouse, York/Sailing by the wind-on the Larboard tack-Lee view-light breeze.

17. Cream tinted, open lettering.

MARINE STUDIES, key numbers, 1 and 2, below image/John Ward del et lith. W. Monkhouse, lith^{r} York./SCHOONER/1. Before the wind-Studding sails set 2. Close hauled-Starboard tack. Light Breeze.

Hand coloured and uncoloured examples.

See no.6.

18. Not tinted, no defined picture area, open lettering.

SCHOONER of 120 Tons/J. Ward del. et lith. Hull Printed by W. Monkhouse, York/At anchor- Sails loose-Light air of wind.-Scale of Feet [0-20]

Same as 3b.

19. Tinted, with cloud effects, plain black lettering.

J. Ward del et lith. Hull Printed by W. Monkhouse, York/BRIGANTINE/Hove to- on the larboard tack-off the S. Foreland.

012; and 027, not tinted

20. Ditto but not tinted, no defined picture area.
21. Headed MARINE STUDIES/ key numbers 1 and 2 immediately below image/J. Ward Del.et Lith. Hull. Printed by W. Monkhouse, York /SCHOONER/1.Before the wind – Studding sails set 2. Close hauled- Starboard tack Light breeze.
See 17
22. Tinted port view, open lettering
Headed MARINE STUDIES/ key numbers 1 and 2 immediately beneath image /John Ward del.et lith. Printed by W. Monkhouse, York. / BRIG/ 1. At anchor –Bow view 2. Underway – yards braced sharp up. Calm.
Same as 7.

23. Port view, no defined picture area, black lettering.
BRIG/J. Ward Del et Lith. Hull /Close-hauled on the Larboard tack- calm-entering the HUMBER/Printed by W. Monkhouse, York.
24. Port side view, not tinted, no defined picture area, open lettering.
BRIG of 223 Tons/ Under way-Before the wind-Yards squared- Scale of Feet [0-20]
Same as 4a.
25. Tinted with cloud effects, open lettering but of freer form than other similar lettering.
J. Ward del et lith. Hull /BARQUE, of 295 Tons/Printed by W. Monkhouse, York/ Larboard broadside view.-Showing signals.-Scale of Feet [0-20].
Vessel displays a swallowtail pennant with a plain cross, a name pennant with lettering in reversed order, GARDI etc. at the main, and a five pennant code hoist on the mizen.
25a On the reverse is part of a proof pull of the text from the 'English Alphabet', not in its finished form but executed on the stone by hand in a neat cursive script, probably executed by Ward in his own studio as a trial: 'The formation----to either side'.
26. No defined picture area, black lettering.
SHIP /J. Ward Del. et Lith. Hull Printed by W. Monkhouse, York/Lee Broadside view-blowing a fresh gale-off the HUMBER.
27. Cream tinted, stern and starboard bow views.
Headed MARINE STUDIES/ key numbers 1 and 2 immediately beneath image/ John Ward del. et lith. Printed by W. Monkhouse / SHIP/ 1. At anchor-Stern view 2. Starboard bow view-Wind on the quarter. A breeze springing up.
Coloured and uncoloured examples.
Same as 8.
28. Cream tinted, open lettering.
J. Ward del et lith. Hull/ SHIP, of 375 Tons/Printed by W. Monkhouse. York./In full sail.-Studding sails low and aloft.-Wind right aft.-A steady breeze.
29. Not tinted, no defined picture area, open lettering.
SHIP, of 650 Tons/ J. Ward del. et lith. Hull Printed by W. Monkhouse, York./Riding at anchor.-Sails furled.-Wind ahead -Scale of Feet, [0-20]
Same as 4b.
30. Cream tinted, a steamer.
Headed MARINE STUDIES/ John Ward del.et lith. Hull Printed by W.R. Goddard. Hull/Published by I. Ward 23 North St. Hull 7 April 1845.
No other titles but the paddle steamer, in starboard and port views, is identifiable as the *Vivid* from the name pennant at the main, flying flag of General Steam Navigation Co. At the fore and a three pennant code hoist at the mizen.
Compare with item 37.

The *Vivid*, and her sister ship the *Waterwitch* figure strongly in Ward's output. An oil of the two vessels was painted by him and engraved in 1839 by W. G. Reeve. There is also a small panel painting of the *Waterwitch*, the squared up drawing for which is at the Peabody Essex Museum, Salem, Mass.
The two Hull – London steamers built in 1836 for the Humber Union Steam Packet Co. were sold to the General Steam Navigation Co, London, in 1841.
31. Cream tinted, open lettering. This is the same print as seventh and final lithograph in set bound in paper cover.
Headed MARINE STUDIES / key numbers immediately below image 2, 4, 1, 3 / John Ward del et lith. Printed by W. Monkhouse, York/MERCHANT VESSELS/ 1. Ship moored to the Buoy-preparing to sail 2. Brig at anchor 3. Schooner 4. Sloop. Calm'
Also a non tinted version, minus title.
It is either derived from the oil painting on panel, 10 in by 14 in, entitled *The Maese, Amazon, and Dandie Dinmont* or the painting was derived from the print or a study for it.
Same as 9.

****

Large sheets with diagrammatic views, sail plans etc in conjunction with a finished image. Untrimmed they measure 15 in by 11 in. Name of the variety of vessel is in plain black type face:

32. Fig. 1, starboard side, fig2. Plan view, components of vessel numbered 1-28, fig.3 transverse section, divided vertically to show bow and stern, scale 0-20.
Main image, starboard stern view and starboard broadside
SLOOP/J. Ward del et lith. Hull Printed by W. Monkhouse. York/At anchor and under-weigh on the starboard tack-weather view.
Lightly coloured; pennant at main with initials J.W.
Same main image as 12.
33. Another sloop but untitled. Figs 1-9, schematic, views at all angles, plan view etc.; figs. 10 and 11 stippled images, scale 0-20.
34. Figs. 1-3 starboard side, plan view and transverse section with bow and stern, components numbered 1-58 ,scale 0-25.
SCHOONER / J. Ward del et lith Hull Printed by W. Monkhouse, York/ Sailing by the wind.- on the Larboard tack.-lee view.- light breeze.
Same main image as 16.
35. Figs.1-3 port side and plan views, transverse section with bow and stern view, components numbered1-69, scale 0-30.
BRIG/J. Ward del et lith Printed by W. Monkhouse, York / Close- hauled on the Larboard tack-calm-entering the HUMBER.
Port broadside view, Spurn lighthouses visible
36. Figs. 1-3 starboard and plan views, and transverse section showing bow and stern, components numbered 1-99, scale 0-30. SHIP/ J. Ward del. et lith .Hull Printed by W. Monkhouse York/ Lee broadside view-blowing a fresh gale –off the HUMBER.
Four pennant code hoist. Some hand coloured examples.
37. Nine figures; figs 8, 6 and 9, mirroring the stippled images below, components numbered 1-61, scale 0-40.
Bow, port broadside and stern views, name pennant *Vivid,* a three pennant code hoist.
STEAM VESSEL/J. Ward del et lith. Hull Printed by W. Monkhouse, York./ At anchor—signal for sailing, Blue Peter flag at the Fore.-In HULL ROADS.

Compare with item 30.
Coloured example and a number of cut down, uncoloured versions.
38. A pull of a print of the port starboard view of a dismasted vessel off a rocky coast, water colour and crayon, within a decorative outline.

****

Two pencil drawings of a schooner are evidently preparatory studies but perhaps for oil paintings rather than prints cf. Squared up drawing of the Waterwitch, starboard stern view, signed John Ward, bottom right (5½ in by 6¾ in and starboard broad side view, squared up on an inch grid (5½ in by 7 in).

****

A pen and wash of a sloop also shows part of a schematic drawing of the stern most of it lost through trimming.

Section B: NAVAL VESSELS

The present writer has not seen a collection of the ten views of naval vessels, from Revenue cutter to steamer, in paper covers but has seen a cloth bound version with calf spine and corners with a leather label glued to the front cover with the title in gilt letters Ward's British Navy (10¼ in x 14 5/16 in). From an East Yorkshire source this was sold at Sothebys, May 1980. As well as the two introductory sheets and ten naval prints, all on cream tinted background, there is the lithograph of the ship Raymond, published in 1843 (see below). The subjects were assembled in random order and not according to rates. A set was recorded by William Senior, of the Admiralty library, in 1922, entitled 'Draughts, Plans and Illustrations of the Different Rates and Classes of Vessels in the British Naval Service. Drawn and Executed by John Ward, 2 North Street, Hull, 1848' (*Mariners Mirror*, 1922, p.53). The inclusion of the address suggests this was either a set with a paper cover and printed title on the front, or, since he refers to 'two published books of studies of the period by John Ward', perhaps the original paper cover was bound in with the prints in hard cover. The other book was entitled 'Marine Studies of British Merchant Vessels'. He says that 'the latter contained ten plates, and there were two or three editions of it, the dates of which I have not been able to ascertain'. A response to this note by Tom Sheppard, curator, says that the Hull museum had 'a copy of the book he published containing the alphabet in various designs for the use of signwriters, and on the back of each of these sheets is one of his lithographs of shipping' (*Mariners Mirror,* vol.8, 1922, p.125). A cover and several sheets are from the prewar collection but the most complete sequence, though one sheet is missing, was purchased in 1983 from a descendant of John Hall, a brother of Hull Trinity House, and a contemporary of Ward's.
After Ward's first showing at a London exhibition, 'Seapiece' at the Royal Academy in 1831, it was not until 1840 that his work appeared again 'The Northern Whale Fishery' and 'Shipping piece' the following year. Thereafter he exhibited at the R.A, British Institution and Royal Society of British Artists, 1842-47, the overwhelming majority of the contributions featured naval vessels.

Note that the names of the vessel types are rendered in open lettering. Though many are trimmed the full size of each sheet is 11 in by 15 in, and picture area approximately 6 in by 8 in:
39. *First introductory page:*
'A series of Ten Views illustrative of the several rates and classes of Vessels in Her Majesty's Navy, Lithographed in the tinted manner from Drawings taken at the different

Naval Establishments, by J. WARD and expressly executed as a work of information and instruction.
The series contains the Revenue Cutter; Schooner; Gun-brig; Corvette of 18 Guns; Frigate of 36 Guns; Frigate of 50 Guns; 74 Gun-ship; 84 Gun-ship; First Rate of 120 Guns; and the Steam Vessel.
To such as have not had the opportunity of seeing those bulwarks of the Nation, the Wooden Walls of Old England the present series will contain a clear and picturesque delineation of some of the most approved vessels at present afloat; and to those desirous of studying Marine Drawing, an opportunity is afforded of obtaining that which as a work of reference will be highly desirable, every care having been taken with the proportions and detail of each, with their positions, spars, rigging, canvas, &c.'
40. *Second introductory page.*
'It is necessary to state that in the accompanying Views the Revenue Cutter is represented from the dimensions of the Greyhound; the Schooner from the Wanderer; Gun-brig from the Nautilus; Corvette from the Vesta; the 36 Gun Frigate from the Pique; 50 Gun Frigate from the Vindictive; 74 Gun ship from the Bellerophon; 84 Gun ship from the Asia; the First Rate from the Britannia; and the Steam Vessel from the Alban.
These views were originally intended to illustrate a work containing Draughts, Plans and Sections of vessels with their dimensions, displacement and tonnage; forming a Guide to Drawing for the purposes of Painting, and the Marine Profession generally.
That the work has not been published arises not from a doubt of its success or utility but from circumstances which for a time preclude the possibility of bringing so difficult yet desirable a work before the public- whose patronage with that of the Commanders, Builders and Artists generally, J. Ward is anxious to obtain.'
41. Port side view, cream tinted, open lettering.
J. Ward Del et Lith. Printed by W. Monkhouse, York/ THE REVENUE CUTTER /Getting under way –Jib and mainsail hoisted- Broadside view-Light air of wind.
The *Greyhound* appears in the navy lists from 1793-1844.
Ward exhibited *HMS Pique, Nautilus and Greyhound* at the Royal Academy in 1843.
42. Port side view, cream tinted, legend (Ward and Monkhouse etc.) omitted.
THE ARMED SCHOONER/Larboard tack-Broadside view-blowing fresh.
The *Wanderer,* built by Betts of Mistleythorn.
43. Lightly tinted, but no cloud effects.
THE GUN BRIG/J. Ward Del. et Lith. Printed by W. Monkhouse York/At anchor-Sails Loosed-Light air of Wind.
Also versions with legend beneath image, or between title and description of sailing aspect, or no legend at all.
The *Nautilus*, built in 1807 by Betts of Mistleythorn.
In 1843, Ward exhibited *HMS Pique, Nautilus and Greyhound* at the Royal Academy, and *HM Brig Nautilus and Revenue cutter Bee in Hull Roads.*
44. Starboard view, cream tinted, open lettering.
A SIXTH RATE-18 GUN CORVETTE/ Close hauled-Starboard tack- Weather broadside view.
Legend omitted.
The *Vesta*, built at Bermuda in 1806.
An oil on panel, 6 in by 9 in, in a private collection is related to this; pasted on the back is an old hand-written label,' Corvette 28 guns' (sic). Starboard view, cream tinted, open lettering.

45. J. Ward Del. et Lith Printed by W. Monkhouse, York/ A FIFTH RATE -36 GUN FRIGATE/Hove to- Larboard tack-Lee bow view-Light breeze.
Also example without legend.
The *Pique*, 1633 tons, built at Plymouth in 1834 and named after a French prize. Notorious for her 'smartness' she was laid up at Portsmouth between1846-1851 and after many years service was sent to the breakers yard. There are two watercolour studies, 5 ½ in by 8 in, for this print, see below.
In 1843 Ward exhibited *HMS Britannia and Pique*, *HMS Pique, Nautilus and Greyhound* at Royal Academy, and in 1843 *HM ship Britannia and Pique* at the British Institution and also at the British Institution in 1844 *Pique, Nautilus and Raven* [probably an error for *Greyhound*].
46. Starboard view, cream tinted, open lettering.
J. Ward Del. et Lith Printed by W. Monkhouse, York./ A FOURTH RATE-50 GUN FRIGATE /Close hauled-Starboard tack- Weather quarter view.
Also examples without legend.
The *Vindictive* built as a third rate at Portsmouth in 1813 and reduced to fifty guns in 1832. Wrecked in 1871. A watercolour, 7 in by 9 in, is evidently a study for another view of this vessel; port side view with cutter and various naval vessels. On the left a seaman is beaching a rowing boat, while another stoops down near the bow.
HMS Vindictive at anchor, calm was exhibited at the Royal Society of British Artists in 1844, and *A 50 gun frigate at anchor* at the RSBA in 1845.
47. Cream tinted but with dark lowering clouds, vessel heeled over in storm conditions, port, three quarter stern view
A THIRD RATE-74 GUNS /Close reefed topsails-Larboard quarter view-A gale-Lee shore.
No legend.
Bellerophon formerly the *Waterloo*, built at Portsmouth in 1818, renamed in 1824 and employed for harbour service in 1848.
See 58.
48. Starboard view, cream tinted with sea and cloud effects, defined image area, open lettering.
J. Ward Del. et Lith. Printed by W. Monkhouse, York/ A SECOND RATE-84 GUNS /Hove to –Main topsail aback-Courses hauled up-Jib sheet eased off.
Legend sometimes missing.
The *Asia*, built at Bombay in 1824, she was Codrington's flag ship at the battle of Navarino in 1827; broken up in 1908.
Ward exhibited 'A ninety gun ship' at the Royal Academy in 1842
49. Cream tinted, port view, three gun decks, open lettering.
A FIRST RATE-120 GUNS/ Going free-wind abeam-Lee Larboard quarter view-moderate breeze.
Legend omitted.
Britannia, built at Plymouth in 1820 and commissioned three years later. Flagship at Portsmouth between 1836 and 1851. In 1859 she was commissioned as a cadet training ship and broken up ten years later.
Ward exhibited *Stern view of HM Britannia, 120 guns*, *Bow view of HMS Britannia, 120 guns* at the Royal Academy in 1842, and at the British Institution in 1843, *Britannia and Pique* and at the British Institution in 1844, *HM ship Britannia and Pique.*
50. Port view, cream tinted, open lettering.
J. Ward Del et Lith Printed by W. Monkhouse, York /THE STEAM VESSEL/ At anchor-Larboard broadside view-Calm.

Also untinted version, trimmed to the image.
51. Starboard view, cream tinted, open lettering; this is a separate drawing, not merely a reversal of the port view.
THE STEAM VESSEL /At anchor-Starboard broadside view-Calm.
Legend omitted.

****

A pencil study of *Alban*, signed 'J.W.Sep.5 1841' is in the Peabody Essex Museum, USA. This is the only clear evidence of a date when Ward was active making drawings of naval vessels in preparation for his lithograph series.

Other naval items:
52. THE CUTTER/Sailing by the wind- starboard tack-Lee bow view-Strong breeze.
No legend. This vessel is flying the naval white ensign.

****

Watercolour; port broadside and stern views of HMS *Britannia*, with booms out (cf. litho), lounging sailor on rocks in foreground. Dimensions 9 in by 13½ in mounted on board 11½ in by 16 in; trial brush work on card around drawing. Clearly a study for a lithograph which is now lost or perhaps never executed (see Fig.*19*).

****

A watercolour of HMS *Howe*, 120 guns, 7¾ in by 7 in., is a starboard broadside view with bow turned slightly toward the viewer. No surviving print is known. The vessel was launched in 1815, laid up at Sheerness for 25 years and returned therein 1844 after being flagship in the Mediterranean.

****

There are two watercolours of the starboard broadside view of the Fifth Rate (Pique), with slight differences in detail (sails and features on horizon). They are the same size as the lithographed image, 5½ in by 8 in, and were clearly executed as studies for it. The print also differs slightly in detail from both of these.

****

Also a watercolour drawing of a single decker, displaying 13 guns, 10 in by 14 ½ in. The sea is flat and featureless and there are no background details.

****

A watercolour of the starboard view of a paddle steamer flying the white ensign at stern.

****

In a totally different manner, drawn freely in pen and pencil with coloured washes added are three other naval subjects. A sloop, port stern view, laid down on card, an additional strip of paper has been added to accommodate top of mast (15 in by 12 in overall); a port bow view of a man of war, in full sail, ensign flying (19¼ in by 12½ in) and port stern view of a man of war, three masted, single decker, all sails furled (16½ in by 11¼ in.) See figs. 20, 21 above.

****

Large sheets with schematic drawings; 15 in x 11 in. when uncut. Cream tinted, generally with cloud effects. The main images approximately 6 in by 8 in.

Eight sheets; all the subjects except Revenue Cutter and steamer *Alban*.

53. Figs 1-3 three vertical sections above main image, bow, stern, and bow turned slightly to starboard, topsails raised. The armed schooner [title omitted], cream tinted, port view.
No legend.
54. Gun brig
55. Sixth rate
56. Fifth rate
57. Fourth rate
58. Third rate
59. Second rate
60. First rate
Similar sheets for First to Sixth rates. All tinted but untitled. The gun brig and the 6th rate have key letters on the masts and yards.

H.M.S. BRITANNIA
A set of four sheets (all untitled) showing two bow and two stern views. Each untrimmed sheet 13¼ in x 9½ in; the image 9 in x 13 in decorative inset upper corners to frame. No titles or legend.
The *Britannia* features prominently in Ward's later work and is the main subject of his academy piece for 1847, a huge canvas, 67 in by 97 in, depicting *HMS Britannia and units of the fleet off Spithead.* The *Vessels of the British Navy* at the British Institution, also in 1847, may be the same canvas. A rather smaller oil, 12 in by 20 in *HMS Britannia at anchor with the fleet* is in a private collection.
Ward exhibited *A stern view of HMS Britannia* and *A bow view etc.*, at the Royal Academy in 1842, also *HMS Britannia and Pique* at the Royal Academy in 1843; at the British Institution in 1843, *Britannia and Pique* and *H M Ship Britannia and Pique* at the British Institution in 1844.
61. Bow view, port side, at anchor sails furled. Tinted overall. Not signed.
62. Bow view, port side, under-weigh. On both these the figurehead of Britannia carrying a shield is clearly visible.
Also a coloured version, not signed.
63. Stern view, port side, at anchor, sails furled. Tinted overall.
Hand coloured version; signed J. Ward, bottom right of the image.
63a. A proof, the boat booms extending from the sides of the vessel which appear in the finished print are absent. On reverse is the text from the second naval introductory sheet 'It is necessary to state that in the accompanying Views— J. Ward is anxious to obtain etc.' Upon turning the page of the letter press is seen sideways on.
64. Stern view, starboard side, under-weigh; not signed
Hand-coloured version; signed J. Ward bottom right of the image.
There are two further prints of a first rate (three decker), neither with a title or legend:
65. Starboard view full sail, loungers on rocks to the right, slight tinting, 6 in by 8 in picture area. The image frame has been defined by an inked line, no lettering.
66. Port, bow view, full sail, tinted, no lettering, 4¼ in by 7¾ in. picture area. The figurehead identifies it as the *Britannia.*
No other examples of these views are known.

Section C: A Guide for Sign Writers
Fold over, beige paper cover, stitched adjacent to fold (stitches broken and plates now loose), back plain, front cover has printed title, each line in a different type face. A complete

set except for plate 8, each 8½ in by 11 in; purchased from a descendant of John Hall, brother of Hull Trinity House.

67. Front cover:

1848 Price

THE
ENGLISH ALPHABET
ARRANGED FOR THE USE OF
HOUSE AND SIGN PAINTERS
WRITERS, &c
BY J. WARD , 2 NORTH STREET,HULL
Entered at Stationers' Hall, London

68. Recto:

INTRODUCTION

'Upwards of thirty years practise as a House and Sign Painter, has left an assurance that there is considerable room for a work of instruction in the Writing Department, and that such a work, pointing out the mechanical formation of the Letters, and the best method of setting them in words, would be not only acceptable, but of great service to the profession, more especially to the younger members, saving them much valuable time, now spent in blindly endeavouring to learn that which can be immediately acquired. The present series of Alphabets are therefore brought forward as a guide to the Art of Lettering, and a work suitable to the present time.

In selecting the Letters great care has been exercised to take them from type of approved form, and which were considered correct specimens of the several characters, the proportions of each are shown by their divisions into six parts, then the A is five parts (which may be considered as inches or any suitable measure) in height, and in width six; the B also five parts in height, and but five in width; and the C four and a third part in width; these proportions and that of the other Letters will be seen on referring to the plates. The object in putting the Letters into parts or divisions in (as well as shewing the proportions) to facilitate their arrangement in setting out on the signboard, &c, examples of which are given, see Plate 6, Plate 7 being devoted to the shadows, and Plate 8, scales of proportions of letters from 3 to 10 inches.

In submitting the English Alphabet to the profession it is anticipated it will be found sufficiently explicit, and that it will meet with the support of those for whose instruction it has been arranged, and would do well to impress on their memory the following table of proportions as highly desirable in practice, all Letters (whatever may be their size) to be considered as five parts in height.

Table showing the width of Roman Capital Letters in proportion to their Length.

A, 6 parts D, 5 ½. G, 5 ½. J, 4. M, 6 1/3. P, 4 2/3. S, 3 2/3. V, 5 1/3. Y,6.
B, 5. E,4 ¾. H,6. K, 6 N, 5 2/3. Q, 5 1/3 T, 4 2/3 W, 7 2/3. Z, 41/2
C, 4 1/3 F, 4 2/3 I, 3 L, 4 ¾ O, 5 R, 5 ½ U, 5 1/3 X, 6. &, 5.

69. Verso

'The formation of Letters being understood, it becomes necessary to point out their arrangement on the signboard, as a general rule for which, divide the length of the board by the required number of spaces and parts, the quotient shewing their exact size, which, if multiplied by five, gives the correct height of the letter. As an example, suppose the name WARD is to be set out on a board thirty inches in length, figure one, plate six; in this name there are four letters, and on referring to plate one, Roman Capital Letters, they will be found to occupy twenty-four and two-third parts, to these are to be added the spaces between the letters, and at each end of the word; in the present example there is no space between the W and A, (see figure 2), in consequence of the W being an overhanging letter and the A is a spreading one, had any space been allowed, the W would have appeared detached from the other letters, and awkwardly set out; it has also been necessary to allow only one and a half space from the end of the board to the W from the same cause, had two spaces been allowed the name would then have been too much to one end; the arrangement is therefore as follows; from the edge of the board to the W, one and a half space, W seven and two-third parts, A six parts, from A to R one space, R five and a half parts, from R to D one space, D five and a half parts, and from D to the end of the board two spaces, altogether thirty parts and spaces and a fraction, which fraction may be struck of as of no moment; now as the board is thirty inches in length, if divided by thirty the required amount of parts and spaces, it gives one as the quotient, that is one inch as the size of each part and space, this if multiplied by five, gives five inches as the height of the letters, as seen at figure three, same plate, the squares being considered as inches, this figure shows also the name set in outline, and although in this instance, the letters are set out in squares, in practice there is no occasion for such, be [i, omitted]ng adapted at present to show that Letters are exactly the same as these of plate one, figure four being considered as white letters on a black background.

A further example of setting out is shewn at figure five, which represents a board six feet three and a half inches in length, the number of parts and spaces required being seventy-five and a half, in this reduce the length into inches and divide by seventy-five as in the former example, multiplying the quotient by five to know the height of the letters; from the seperating [sic] stop to the W and from the W to A there is no space between , and from P to A only half a space, in order that the words may appear properly set out; other letters in the Alphabet require allowance also to be made. As respects the raising of letters so as to make them appear to stand out from the board, and also as to cast the shadow, a careful examination of plate seven will point out, that a tracing of the letter will shew the proper outline, by lowering it and placing it to either side, answering to the true cast shadow as produced by the Sun's light at a certain elevation.

With reference to the plate of scales, it will be seen that each scale is divided into five parts for the height of the letter, having divisions also of thirds and fourths for the width; this plate may be cut up or others made by it, and in setting out letters take the scale to correspond with the length required, for instance, if J.WARD, PAINTER, is to be set out in ten inch letters, take two lines at ten inches apart, one for the top and the other for the bottom of the letters, (see figure five, plate six), then set off from the end of the board two parts (by ten inch scale) and commence with four parts for the letter J, one part from J to the separating [sic] stop, one part for stop, seven and two third parts for W, six parts for A, one part from A to R, five and a half parts for R, one part from R to D, five and a half parts for D and so on to the end, they will then be properly set out, and can be filled in with paint by any one at all capable of laying on color[sic] with a hair pencil or paint brush.

70. Recto

Pl.1 ROMAN CAPITAL LETTERS

Alphabet within decorative frame.

71. Verso; a merchant vessel, picture area not defined, open lettering.

SLOOP OR SMACK of 160 tons/ Preparing to sail-Anchor hove short-Calm-Scale of Feet [0-20]

No legend. Upper part of double sheet; see 3a.

72. Recto

Pl.2 ROMAN LOWER CASE LETTERS, FIGURES, &c

Alphabet within decorative frame.

73. Verso; a merchant vessel, cream tinted, solid lettering.

J. Ward del et lith Hull Printed by W. Monkhouse, York /SLOOP OR SMACK/Dandy rigged,-going free,-off FLAMBOR'O HEAD

See 13.

74. Recto

Pl.3 ITALIC CAPITAL LETTERS

Alphabet within decorative frame.

75. Verso; open lettering, no defined picture area

J. Ward del.et lith. Hull Printed by W. Monkhouse, York./SCHOONER, of 120 tons/At anchor.-Sails loose- Light air of wind-Scale of Feet [0-20]

See 3b.

76. Recto

Pl.4 ITALIC LOWER CASE LETTERS, &c

Alphabet within decorative frame.

77. Verso, cream tinted, plain black lettering.

J. Ward del.et lith. Hull Printed by W. Monkhouse, York. /BRIGANTINE/ Hove to,- on the larboard tack- off the S.FORELAND.

See 19.

78. Recto

Pl.5 EGYPTIAN AND BLOCK LETTERS, FIGURES, &c

79. Verso, no defined picture area, open letters, no legend.

BRIG of 223 tons/Under way-Before the Wind-Yards squared-Scale of Feet [0-20)

See 4a.

80. Recto

Pl. 6 EXAMPLES

J.WARD, PAINTER, used as example

81. Verso; open lettering, no defined picture area.

J. Ward del.et lith. Hull Printed by W. Monkhouse, York/SHIP, of 650 Tons/ Riding at anchor-Sails furled.-Wind ahead.-Scale of Feet, [0-20]

See 4b.

82. Recto

Pl.7 EXAMPLES

HULL used as example

83. Verso; cream tinted, open lettering. J. Ward del et lith. Hull Printed by W. Monkhouse, York/ SHIP, of 375 Tons /In full sail.-Studding sails low and aloft.-Wind right aft.-A steady breeze

See 28.

* Recto /Verso, pl.8.

This last page is missing and no example is known, maybe it had the proportions of letters on both sides (or the reverse was blank) and so there was no incentive for the maritime enthusiast to keep this page. Also Ward actually mentions the possibility of the reader cutting up the plate for ease of setting out his letters.

The stitching of this book has been cut and the pages of the booklet are loose, most have at some time been mounted and framed.

The Marine Studies, the English Alphabet series and many of the naval and mercantile sheets with sections and plans, in the Hull Maritime Museum collections, were originally the property of John Hall, who aged 22, was admitted a younger brother of Hull Trinity House, 27 September 1797, at the same time as he qualified to pilot vessels in the seas between the Humber and the Naze of Norway. He was master Warden when the foundation stone of the Hospital in Carr lane was laid 18 September 1833, and chairman of the building committee when the foundation stone of the Carr lane Almshouses was laid there 6 April 1837. He was still chairman on 25 October 1839 when the foundation stone of the chapel was laid 25 October 1839. Amongst his papers there is an invitation from the Hull Dock Company to attend the ceremonial laying of the foundation stone of the Junction Dock in 1827. Opened in 1829 it was later named Princes Dock, after Albert, the Prince Consort of Queen Victoria. It is not known whether the prints were acquired by Hall directly from the artist in the 1840s or from the sale of his studio contents in 1853. See also the Wanderer, below.

Section D: Commemorative Prints

During the time Ward was preparing his prints for the proposed manual for marine painters he also produced a handful of lithographs marking the launch of a particular vessel or some especial event in its career. Perhaps the most accomplished and attractive print is that celebrating the first grand regatta of the Royal Yorkshire Yacht Club in 1847.

84. Tinted, but no sky detail, vessel flies a five pennant code hoist; 7¾ in by 11½ in).

J. Ward Del. et Lith Printed by W. Monkhouse, York

This Print of the RAYMOND Hugh McKay Commander/The First Vessel direct from China to Hull, is published commemorative of her arrival on the 14th October 1843.

Built at Sunderland, Co. Durham, in 1840, by P. Austin and Son. She was jointly owned by Thomas, William and Isaac Ward, and her Captain, Hugh McKay. In 1843 this vessel was the first to bring a consignment of tea drect from China to Hull; the cargo totalled over 600,000 lb. The *Raymond* was purchased by Hart and Co. in 1846 and reregistered in London (Hull News,13 October, and 20 October,1843 for contemporary account).

85. Starboard broadside view, defined by a border scribed in ink. Signed in ink John Ward 1845,bottom right. Some watercolour and crayon treatment and written on the reverse, in ink :

'Wanderer bound out to Hong Kong China 1845 Septr with a full cargo of Manchester and other goods the first ship ever loaded a full cargo of goods to China from Hull and up to 1880 there has not been another part cargo delivered at Hong Kong part at Canton

John Priest Master mariner Commander returned home to London in 11 mos with 500 tons tea 40 feet to the ton at £7.10 per ton 360 tons register

Ship cost £3000 ready for sea. [J.H £3.75O]

****

The initials are those of John Hall to whom this print belonged, along with the merchant vessel set and 'English Alphabet' in paper covers.

The *Wanderer* was built at Sunderland, Co. Durham, in 1844 and wholly owned by William Priest the Elder, until 1852 when thirty shares were purchased by Johann Heinrich Fredricks of Lancaster. She was lost on the 18 February 1853. Ward painted a canvas, c.1844-9, depicting three vessels owned by the firm of Priest and Son, *Ruby, Wanderer and Garnet.*

86. Depicted within a decorative frame, 8 in by 13¼ in, the image size is 7 in by 12¼ in. Beneath the image, identifying the principal vessels, are the names HILDA, WHIM, PHEBE and SYLPH.
I.Ward del.et Lith. Hull. Printed by W. Monkhouse. York.

HULL GRAND REGATTA

28th September 1847

The yacht HILDA Thomas Richards Esq. Owner, winning the Challenge Cup value £50, given by the Members of the Royal Yorkshire Yacht Club, to whom this print is respectfully dedicated

by their very obedient servant

John Ward

Also hand coloured prints.
The *Whim* belonged to the Hull merchant and shipowner, Joseph Gee, for whom Ward produced a number of canvases of vessels that he owned or had an interest in, notably the *William Lee* which in 1839 returned to Hull from Calcutta after re-establishing direct trade from Hull to India. Gee was Vice Commodore of the RYYC from 1847 to 1851 and a member of the Royal Yacht Squadron. A similar composition was lithographed by Dutton after a drawing by William Frederick Settle, pupil of Ward, of the 1851 Regatta.
87. Also in Hull collection is a proof of a small image of a cutter yacht, starboard bow view, flying a swallow tailed pennant, with indeterminate motifs, is probably a commodore's pennant.
Port broadside view off Spurn, tinted but no sky effects, hand coloured. Sheet 16 in by 21½ in, image size 12 in by 17½ in.

88. Tinted, with cloud effects.

John Ward del et lith. Printed by Goddard and Lancaster. Hull

To George Cammell Esqre of Hull

This print of the Iron built Clipper Schooner DANDIE DINMONT is respectfully dedicated by his Obd^nt^ Servant

John Ward

****

Built at South Shields in 1848 by Thomas Marshall for George Cammell, this iron vessel was lost in the Baltic trade 18 March 1854 under the command of Capt. Newby. She was named after the character in Walter Scott's 'Guy Mannering' and furnished with an appropriate male figurehead. An oil painting with an almost identical composition is in the Hull connections and a watercolour drawing by John Carmichael, another notable marine painter, exactly reproduces the print in size and content (Laing Art Gallery, Newcastle).
A painting (12 in by 18 in) with a composition almost identical to the print is either a preparatory study executed in oils rather than watercolour or maybe copied from the print. Another oil which was possibly painted by Ward with the intention of producing a lithograph is port broadside view of the schooner Fannie Voase, off Spurn. The vessel was built in 1819 and lost in 1838 and the canvas was probably painted as a commemorative piece in the latter year, or even later.

89.

J. Ward Del. et Lith. Printed by W .Monkhouse, York

THIS PLATE OF THE IRON STEAM PACKET

COLUMBINE
is respectfully dedicated to the Proprietors
By their Obedient Servant
William Lewis

Built by H. Smith Gainsbro'   Engined by Penn & Son, Greenwich
[Further text lost by trimming of margin.]

****

There are also three aquatints after major oil paintings by Ward, all of them ship portraits of Hull paddle steamers: the P.S *Victoria*, engraved by R. G. Reeve, a vessel built in 1837 for the Hull Steam Packet Co and two others for their rivals in the Hull-London trade, the P.S. *Wilberforce*, engraved by R. G. Reeve, 1838, and the PSS *Vivid and Waterwitch*, engraved by R.G and A.W. Reeve, 1839.

INDEX